Shakespeare Films

Shakespeare Films

*A Re-evaluation
of 100 Years of Adaptations*

Peter E.S. Babiak

McFarland & Company, Inc., Publishers
Jefferson, North Carolina

LIBRARY OF CONGRESS CATALOGUING-IN-PUBLICATION DATA

Names: Babiak, Peter E. S. author.
Title: Shakespeare films : a re-evaluation of 100 years of adaptations / Peter E.S. Babiak.
Description: Jefferson, North Carolina : McFarland & Company, Inc., Publishers, 2016. | Includes bibliographical references and index.
Identifiers: LCCN 2016014916 | ISBN 9781476662541 (softcover : acid free paper) ∞
Subjects: LCSH: Shakespeare, William, 1564–1616—Film adaptations. | English drama—Film adaptations. | Film adaptations—History and criticism.
Classification: LCC PR3093 .B25 2016 | DDC 791.43/75—dc23
LC record available at https://lccn.loc.gov/2016014916

BRITISH LIBRARY CATALOGUING DATA ARE AVAILABLE

ISBN (print) 978-1-4766-6254-1
ISBN (ebook) 978-1-4766-2352-8

© 2016 Peter E.S. Babiak. All rights reserved

No part of this book may be reproduced or transmitted in any form or by any means, electronic or mechanical, including photocopying or recording, or by any information storage and retrieval system, without permission in writing from the publisher.

Front cover: Elizabeth Taylor and Richard Burton in *The Taming of the Shrew*, 1967 (Columbia Pictures/Photofest)

Printed in the United States of America

McFarland & Company, Inc., Publishers
 Box 611, Jefferson, North Carolina 28640
 www.mcfarlandpub.com

Table of Contents

Preface   1

Introduction   5

1. Silent Shakespeare   25
2. The Classical Hollywood Period to World War II   39
3. Olivier and Welles   56
4. Kurosawa   69
5. Kozintsev   84
6. Zeffirelli   99
7. Kott, Brook, Richardson and Polanski   114
8. The 1970s and 1980s   124
9. Branagh   136
10. Millennial Shakespeare   151

Conclusion   166

Chapter Notes   181

Works Cited   186

Index   198

Preface

Prior to the turn of the last century, much of the critical literature that deals with the adaptation of Shakespeare's plays in mainstream film has been limited in its usefulness for two reasons. Firstly, there has been a tendency to emphasize the importance of the director as the auteur (or sole creator) of a filmed adaptation of a play, which generally means that films have been analyzed almost exclusively in terms of the director's vision and techniques. This has led to a tendency to ignore patterns of similarity that exist between works produced by different filmmakers working in the same socio-historical period. Secondly, some established paradigms for the classification of filmed adaptations of canonized literary works have not adequately addressed the complexities of cinematic adaptations of Shakespeare where the language is contemporary, the settings modern or alternative, and the play reduced to subtext. As a result, some critics dealing with Shakespeare on film have assumed that the period from 1971 to 1989 represents an "18-year gap" during which no filmed adaptations of Shakespeare were attempted in mainstream cinema. Prior to the turn of the century, critical studies of Shakespeare in the cinema have tended to avoid discussion of films that cannot be adequately evaluated under established critical paradigms.

Over the last decade, material that had not previously been addressed in studies of Shakespeare in the cinema has begun to attract scholarly attention, both in conference presentations and in peer-reviewed articles. Simultaneously, theorists have noticeably begun to move away from the insistence on the text itself mandated by formalist criticism, and have begun to develop new paradigms for examining the relationship between a seminal play-text and a resultant film adaptation. This study attempts to take the next logical steps by filling in the gaps between these recent theorists and these recent practitioners in adaptation studies, and the gaps between recent adaptation theory and practice and 20th-century adaptation theory and practice.

This study undertakes a critical reexamination and fundamental repositioning of the standard canon of films based on Shakespeare's plays. It has two main arguments. Firstly, it is proposed that the crucial element distinguishing one film from another is the impact of social, cultural and historical contexts. Secondly, it argues for the inclusion of films that up to now have not been considered part of the canon of Shakespeare in the cinema. Again, the influence of contemporary cultural and sociological contexts is the central element in this analysis. This approach has led to a largely historical format for the study. Some chapters are devoted to specific periods of time, as the clearest way to take account of the contextual influences; other chapters reevaluate the work of established auteurs of Shakespeare in the cinema by contextualizing their work within the sociohistorical period of its production. This approach preserves the established canon of Shakespeare in the cinema, while providing a more inclusive paradigm for inclusion of works into the canon than had previously been available.

This study would not have come into existence without the work of Kenneth Branagh, for it was Branagh's film of *Henry V* that instigated my fascination with Shakespearean film adaptations. Although my chapter on his work presents my analysis of three of his adaptations of Shakespeare, what I have neglected to communicate in my scholarly discussion is my enjoyment of them and enthusiasm for them. When researching a paper on *Henry V* for the 2005 annual conference of the PCA/ACA, although I had viewed the film at least nine times prior to preparing the paper, I was still shocked to realize how good the film is. I also remember anxiously anticipating the 1994 release of *Much Ado About Nothing* on home video, and just as anxiously anticipating the 1997 release of *Hamlet* on home video, as I was dying to see both films again, and to share them with friends and relatives. Although I had already seen several of the other works discussed in this study, it was *Henry V* that led to my fascination with this subject, and it is my hope that this study will instill this fascination in others.

This study would not have been possible without the loving support of my family, including my parents, partner and children, or the editorial support of the members of my supervisory and examination committees. My supervisory committee was comprised of Christopher Innes, the Canada Research Chair in Performance and Culture; Marie Rickard, the Master of Winters College at York University; and Derek Cohen, of the Graduate Program in English at York University. The examination committee included

Richard Vela, PCA/ACA Area Chair for Shakespeare on Film and Television; Fran Beer, of the Graduate Program in English at York University; and Livy Visano, of the Department of Social Science at York University. I am pleased and honored to note that my association with all of these people has also extended beyond the parameters of this project, and I am deeply grateful for their ongoing support in a variety of capacities and efforts.

A portion of Chapter 3 appeared in *Cineaction* 41 in "Maintaining the Dual Perspective: Orson Welles and Chimes at Midnight" (1996), and portions of chapters 4 and 7 appeared in "Or Image of that Horror: The Apocalyptic Visions of Peter Brook and Akira Kurosawa" in *The Silk Road of Adaptation: Transformations Across Disciplines and Cultures* (ed. Laurence Raw; Cambridge Scholars, 2013). I am grateful to the presses for granting permission to republish that work.

I would like to mention the names of a few people who did not see the completion of this study, but should be remembered here. David Porter provided much badly-needed guidance during my early life, and his influence is greatly missed. Brendan Gabis was a great friend during a period of transition in my life, and left us far too early. Don Fine greatly influenced my decision to pursue graduate studies and become a teacher myself; the memory of his classroom informs the practice of mine. As one of the last duties of his professional career, and in the last few months of his life, Robert White recommended me for acceptance into doctoral-level studies.

Finally, neither my paternal nor my maternal grandparents saw the completion of this study; however, their memory and example enabled it to be completed.

Introduction

A Brief Look at Adaptation Studies

Prior to the turn of the last century, the usefulness of studies dealing with filmed adaptations of canonized literary texts has been limited by the tendency of critics to view a seminal literary text as a discrete entirety, and to evaluate the effectiveness of a film adaptation in terms of the thoroughness with which it represents that entirety which is the seminal literary text. This has led to a preponderance of both overt and covert "fidelity criticism" in published adaptation studies throughout the history of the field. In *Adaptation Revisited*, Sarah Cardwell summarizes several critical issues that have influenced studies of the adaptation of canonized literary texts into contemporary visual media, throughout the history of the field:

> The study of adaptation arose in an environment that valued literature over the newer arts of film and television, and that steered its investigations in directions that would validate and valorise literary art over audio-visual arts. The growth of medium-specific theories (such as those extolled by Bluestone) worked to counter-balance the field, promoting film as a unique and valued art form in its own right; however, medium-specific beliefs proved extremely problematic for theorists eager to explore the possibilities for "equivalence" in adaptation.
> Responding to both the flaws of essentialist medium-specific approaches and lingering prejudices regarding the superiority of the literary medium over film and television, the comparative approach drew upon established theories of narrative and semiotics to offer a coherent understanding of the process of adaptation and the relation of an adaptation to its source. Developed from the 1970s onwards, the comparative approach was refined and polished, until McFarlane's work (in the 1990s) offered a more rational, theoretically sound and methodologically consistent model for comprehending adaptation than had ever been proposed before. Yet, as McFarlane himself admitted, the comparative approach is limited, especially in terms of considering the influence of factors other than the source novel upon adaptations. Notably, the comparative approach, because of its preoccupation with the source novel/adaptation relationship, neglects issues of social and institutional contexts, intertextuality and genre [72–73].

Elsewhere, Cardwell describes how the pluralist approach to adaptation studies was developed to address the limitations of the medium-specific and comparative approaches: "The pluralist Film Studies of the 1980s and 1990s ... placed film within the broader context of culture, playing down its specificities as a medium ... 'culturalist' approaches to film aimed to isolate the filmic text as an object of study, challenge simplistic evaluative aesthetic criticism, and recognise film's locus within a wider cultural context" (84). Cardwell attempts to resolve this dilemma by differentiating between "adaptation" as a cultural process, and "an adaptation" as a cultural artifact. She proposes that all adaptations of a given text represent a stage in the gradual development of an "ur-text" or "meta-text" that "stands outside and before each retelling of the story, and which contains the most fundamental parts of the tale without which an adaptation would lose its identity as that tale" (25–26). Cardwell's central ur-text or meta-text is entirely a conceptual proposition, relegating the seminal play and any adaptations to the status of physical artifacts of a larger cultural process. Cardwell's concept of the meta-text still reveals a tendency to view a literary text as related to a conceptualized entirety.

Writing in 2010, Deborah Cartmell and Imelda Whelehan echo this tendency to conceive of an adapted text as an entirety; however, they also seem to conceive of the relationship between a text and its adaptations as reciprocal rather than linear: "One of the seductions of adaptation criticism is that the literary text will not disappear, and its traces (often obscured or unacknowledged) come to the surface in numerous ways, just as an adaptation, particularly a successful one, inhabits and imprints itself upon the notional 'original'" (12).

Although Cardwell asserts the primacy of the conceptual meta-text, Jonathan Dollimore and Alan Sinfield, in *Political Shakespeare*, assert that Shakespeare is a contested social icon, and that representations of Shakespeare's plays are attempts on the part of adaptors to infuse their position with Shakespeare's cultural authority. Arguing from the perspective of Cultural Materialism/New Historicism, Sinfield writes:

> Almost like a religious relic, he [Shakespeare] constitutes a powerful cultural token. Shakespeare's plays are one site of cultural production in our society—they are one of the places where our understanding of ourselves is worked out and, indeed, fought out. A culture is a signifying system through which ... a social order is communicated, reproduced, and explored. This signifying system has continually to be produced—social orders and cultural orders must be seen as being actively made: actively and continuously, or they may quite quickly break down.... Shakespeare's plays constitute an influential medium through which certain ways of thinking about the world may be promoted and others impeded, they are a site of cultural struggle and change [154–155].

Introduction 7

Note that Dollimore and Sinfield also insist on referring to the plays as discrete entireties, and how they also fail to address cases in which a Shakespearean play is represented in the cinema with no claim being made to Shakespeare's cultural authority. Embedded, rather than overt, references to the play-texts of *The Tempest*, *Hamlet*, *Macbeth*, and *King Lear* are clearly evident in Wilcox's *Forbidden Planet* (1956), Mazursky's *Tempest* (1982), Disney's *The Lion King* (1994) and Kurosawa's *Kumonosu-djo* (1957), *Warui Yatsu Hodo Yoku Nemuru* (1960) and *Ran* (1985).[1] These films are also products of cultures which possess clearly established traditions in the adaptation of Shakespeare in film, and clearly appropriate thematic and narrative elements of the plays in their structure; however, no mention of their source is made in their credits, thereby complicating any argument that they are intended to assume any of the cultural authority we normally associate with Shakespeare. Although these films present elements of narrative and character that several members of their audience will associate with Shakespeare, the majority of the audience will perceive them as contemporary works with no relationship to the Shakespearean canon.

Dealing with the specific instance of representation of Shakespeare's works into contemporary visual media, Jack Jorgens has suggested that filmmakers are confronted with two basic choices when adapting the plays for the cinema: which mode of cinematic representation, and which strategy of orientation to the canonized text to utilize. Also conceptualizing Shakespeare's plays as discrete entireties, Jorgens identifies three basic modes of cinematic representation: the theatrical mode (8), the realistic mode (8), and the filmic mode (10). In "Two Dimensional Shakespeare: King Lear on Film," Peter Holland elaborates on Jorgens' definitions by stating that "the theatrical mode has as its model the camera's record of a theatrical performance, the camera as the eye of a theatre audience" (50), and that the realistic mode "create[s] a precisely imagined and powerful world in which the actors move"[2] (53). Holland further notes that "filmic films of Jorgens' third type accept the peculiar intensity of the visual over the aural, of sight over sound, that is fundamental to the cinema…. It finds analogies for the theatricality of Shakespeare's plays in the ways it draws attention to itself as film" (56–57). Of the strategies of orientation to the text that Jorgens identifies (22), Holland writes, "Jorgens also suggests … three ways of treating the text as a Shakespeare play, three degrees of distance from the original: presentation, interpretation, and adaptation…. There is one further category … to add to Jorgens three: a deconstruction of the text" (57).

As the theatrical mode of representation reduces the camera to the status of passive observer rather than active agent, cinema here is used purely as a recording device; therefore, uniquely cinematic methods of constructing meaning must be neutralized in order to maintain an exclusive relationship between the dramatization and the play. Similarly, when the orientation strategy of a presentation (a production that uses the complete play, and does not attempt to find visual alternatives to dialogue and stage directions) is utilized, "the artist attempts to convey the original with as little alteration and distortion as possible" (Jorgens 12). At its worst, according to Jorgens, this orientation strategy allows the filmmaker only "to prove that it is possible for actors to speak every word of a Shakespeare play before an audience and be completely untrue to its spirit" (ibid.). At its best, Jorgens argues, this strategy allows the filmmaker to "[attempt] to preserve the balances and tensions of the original while in an open, improvisatory, exploratory way [seek] to rediscover its fluid, chaotic, Elizabethan essence" (ibid). Conversely, the realistic/illusionist and the filmic modes of representation actively use properties that are unique to cinema to construct meaning in the dramatization.

Although Jorgens' schema (as modified by Holland) initially seems comprehensive, several filmed representations of Shakespeare's plays present dynamics that do not easily conform to the categories that Jorgens and Holland posit. Coppola's *Godfather* trilogy and Godard's *King Lear* certainly have their genesis in Shakespeare's plays. However, they make no real attempt to engage the narrative functions of their sources, rendering their classification as "interpretations" or "adaptations" problematic. Although Welles' *Macbeth*, *Othello*, and *Chimes at Midnight* present their Shakespearean plays in contrast with visual countertexts that query and comment upon them, Welles makes no real attempt to take apart their Shakespearean plays. This makes any attempt to describe these three films as "deconstructions" of Shakespeare's plays problematic. Jorgens' schema privileges cinematic techniques such as cinematography, editing, and the use of diagetic and non-diagetic sound in determining whether or not a film may be considered to be a "realistic/illusionist" representation or a "filmic" representation. Under Jorgens' schema, Alymereda's *Hamlet* would be considered a realistic/illusionist interpretation of Shakespeare's play, yet there is a consensus among critics that Alymereda's *Hamlet* is far more self-reflexive than Jorgens' schema would consider it to be. As Thomas Leitch notes, "Most categorical discussions of adaptation ... [privilege] ... a small number of intertextual relations as exemplary of all adaptation and [pass] over the others in silence" (95).

In 2006, Linda Costanzo Cahir proposed the following "Aesthetic Rubric" in *Literature into Film*:

1. The film must communicate definite ideas concerning the *integral* meaning and value of the literary text, as the filmmakers interpret it.
2. The film must exhibit a collaboration of filmmaking skills....
3. The film must demonstrate an audacity to create a work that stands as a world apart, that exploits the literature in such a way that a self-reliant, but related, aesthetic offspring is born.
4. The film cannot be so self-governing as to be completely independent of or antithetical to the source material [263].

The language used by Costanzo Cahir (specifically her insistence on "the integral meaning and value of the text" as a singular artifact, and her characterization of the relationship between a seminal text and its filmic representation as analogous to that of parent-child, where the filmic "offspring" is never "completely independent of its textual parent") suggests that the tendencies to view literary texts as discrete entireties, and to "validate and valorise literary art over audio-visual arts" (Cardwell 72), persist. Cartmell and Whelehan, writing in 2010, confirm the persistence of this tendency when they say that "literature is seen to have a higher moral calling than its younger, and some have argued, lesser sibling" (13), but later challenge it: "Fidelity is tiresome as a critical strategy not least because it is an inexact science deployed to compare often something as inchoate as the 'spirit' of the thing; but the desire for it or the dread of it haunts many a film spectator's imagination and the intent lurks behind many a screenwriter's claim to get to the heart of the source text" (20). Thomas Leitch exhibits a similar skepticism: "adaptation theorists have persisted in treating fidelity to the source material as a norm from which unfaithful adaptations depart at their peril. Yet it should be clear by now that fidelity itself, even as a goal, is the exception to the norm of variously unfaithful adaptations" (127).

Finally breaking with the tendency to conceptualize Shakespeare's plays as discrete entireties, in 2006's *Collaborations with the Past: Reshaping Shakespeare Across Time and Media*, Diana Henderson suggests that adaptation can be characterized as a process of "diachronic collaboration" (3). In this process, auteurs, as "bearers of Shakespeare" (1), are engaged in a process of "cutting his glassy essence to bits in order to create newly evocative patterns" (ibid.) and "to remake him in our own image" (ibid.). Henderson's assertions are problematic: she never clarifies whether auteurs "collaborate" with the historical Shakespeare, or with the contemporarily canonized version of Shakespeare. However, her suggestion that the auteur cuts the essence of Shakespeare into bits and remakes him in our own image resolves many of the difficulties inherent in the critical approaches utilized by Cardwell, Dollimore, Sinfield, and Jorgens. Interestingly, Henderson devotes a chapter of her book to a study of *Ten Things I Hate About*

You as an adaptation of *The Taming of the Shrew*. Although Henderson may not be completely investing a teen film dramatized in contemporary English with the cultural authority of Shakespeare, her work displays a new tendency to consider even extreme modernizations of Shakespeare as objects worthy of study.

Where Cardwell's, Dollimore and Sinfield's, Jorgens and Holland's, and Costanzo Cahir's approaches have revealed the mutual tendency to conceptualize "Shakespeare" and his "plays" as discrete entireties, Henderson suggests that "Shakespeare" can be reduced to component parts and reshaped in a contemporary image. Michael Anderegg similarly notes that "Shakespearean films tend to include traces of of more traditional film genres" (2) and that "a Shakespeare film is most alive, most compelling, when the filmmaker finds in the text a 'grounding,' a tonal architecture, that the film can ride on" (12). Anderegg goes on to state that "the most exciting Shakespeare films ... are not necessarily the ones that retain the most of Shakespeare's text, but rather the ones that find ways to translate the energies of Shakespeare's language into an audio-video language of their own" (ibid.). Thomas Leitch also notes that adaptations are frequently "shoehorned" (103) into popular genres, and credits Zefirrelli's *Romeo and Juliet* as helping to establish the "teenpic" (ibid.) as a popular genre.

Publishing in 2006, Linda Hutcheon, in *A Theory of Adaptation*, expands on Cardwell's distinction between adaptation as a process and an adaptation as an artifact, by positing a tripartite definition of adaptation:

- An acknowledged transposition of another work or works
- A creative *and* an interpretive act of appropriation/salvaging
- An extended intertextual engagement with the adapted work [8].

In Hutcheon's view, adaptation is a practice that is not limited to the arts; adaptation permeates contemporary culture and media. Hutcheon cites the *Pirates of the Caribbean* film franchise as an example of a series of films adapted not from a novel or stage play, but rather from a theme park ride (138). Hutcheon characterizes adaptation as a much broader cultural practice, and posits a much broader series of parameters within which the processes and artifacts of adaptation may be discussed. The first of these parameters is identified by Hutcheon as "How?" (9), referring to the elements of a seminal work or works that are to be utilized in an adaptation. Kamilla Elliott notes that "adaptation commits the heresy of showing that form (expression) can be separated from content (ideas)—something both mainstream aesthetic and semiotic theories have resisted or denied" (133). In her discussion of "How?" elements of a seminal work are to be adapted,

Hutcheon lists "story" (10) or narrative, "themes" (10), "characters" (11), and "[t]he separate units of the story (or the *fabula*)" (11). The other parameters of adaptation that Hutcheon posits are "What?" (33), which refers to the medium of the proposed adaptation (33), "Who/Why?" (79), which refers to the direct influence that the adapters have on the adaptation (79), and "Where/When" (141), which refer to the socio-cultural or socio-historical context in which the adaptation is realized.

Hutcheon's Parameters as a New Basis for Study

Who/Why?—The Critical Norm

Studies of Shakespeare's plays in mainstream cinema tend to follow cinematic production practices when determining which of Hutcheon's parameters to use when evaluating a film, responding to Hutcheon's "What?" with "mainstream cinema," and to Hutcheon's "Who/Why?" with "the auteur(s) responsible for the film." Most studies of Shakespeare on film have tended to focus on these parameters. The auteur paradigm is still the predominant perspective in critical literature, as filmed versions of Shakespeare's plays are almost invariably credited as the work of the individual auteur—usually the director of the film. Jorgens' typology of adaptation reinforces this emphasis on the auteur by proposing a schema that emphasizes strategies that an individual artist uses to approach Shakespeare's plays.

Less often addressed is Hutcheon's "Where/When?" parameter. John Collick's *Shakespeare, Cinema and Society* does attempt to evaluate the influence of socio-cultural or socio-historical contexts on films of Shakespeare's plays. However, Collick's approach is anecdotal, moving from discussions of "Victorian bardolatry" (12–32) and British silent cinema (33–59) to specific problems encountered when discussing the works of Kozintsev (128–149) and Kurosawa (166–195). A systematic and comprehensive examination of the impact of socio-cultural or socio-historical contexts on films of Shakespeare's plays—which addresses Hutcheon's "Where/When?" parameter—can provide a broader understanding of the position of Shakespeare and his plays in contemporary culture.

How?—A Brief Case Study

Equally significant to this new approach is Hutcheon's "How?" parameter. In addition to supporting Henderson's implied assertion that the process of adaptation is one of reshaping a play's component parts rather than approaching a play as a discrete entirety, Hutcheon's broadened parameters offer scholars a wider understanding of the influence of Shakespeare on popular culture and contemporary cinema. This influence is not merely confined to direct adaptations of Shakespeare. It is pervasive in mainstream cinema and popular culture. John Ford's classic western films feature important characters who recite famous speeches from Shakespeare: in *My Darling Clementine*, Doc Holliday silences a rowdy saloon crowd that is preventing a travelling Shakespeare troupe from completing the fourth soliloquy in a performance of *Hamlet,* and completes the soliloquy himself when the lead actor in the troupe proves too intimidated by the crowd; in *The Man Who Shot Liberty Valance*, Dutton Peabody—the owner of "The Shinbone Star"—drunkenly recites the St. Crispin's Day speech from *Henry V* as he prepares a newspaper expose on the practices of the cattle barons, only to have his printing press trashed by a gang of thugs led by Valance. At first glance, a John Ford western might appear to be the antithesis of the cultural values we associate with Shakespeare in the cinema. Yet in "Shakespeare and National Identity," Nick Redfern points out that allusions to Shakespeare—and the cultural identity his works evoke—are integral to Ford's vision of the American frontier, into which the introduction of Shakespeare signifies the imminence of "the transformation of the wilderness into civilisation, for America it is the becoming of a nation."

Although the films of Charlie Chaplin, with their emphasis on visual slapstick comedy, again might seem antithetical to the cultural values associated with Shakespeare, Chaplin himself provides a reading of Hamlet's fourth soliloquy in *A King in New York*[3]: a film intended to gently satirize American cultural practices and the anti-communist paranoia of the late 1950s. The success of Vincent Price's graphic 1970s horror film franchise, Dr. Phibes, precipitated 1973's *Theatre of Blood*, a graphic horror film in which Price (in the role of an incompetent Shakespearean actor named Edward Lionheart) revenges himself on London's most prominent theatre critics (themselves played by notable Shakespearean performers) by murdering them according to Shakespearean motifs: a critic played by Michael Hordern is stabbed to death by several vagrants during the Ides of March, a critic played by Robert Morley has his beloved poodles fed to him in a meat dish, and, at the conclusion of the film, a critic played by Ian Hendry faces having his eyes put out. At each of these occasions, Price's character gleefully delivers the pertinent dialogue from the appropriate play. In all of these cases we are afforded a broader understanding of the position and function of Shakespeare, and his plays, in contemporary popular culture.

This is achieved by asking the questions prompted by Hutcheon's "How?" parameter, and looking at how elements of plays are incorporated into a film, even if the film—in its entirety—is not intended as a dramatization of Shakespeare.

"Where/When?"—A Brief Case Study

An application of Hutcheon's "Where/When?" parameter to a specific subgenre of mainstream cinema, referred to by Roger Ebert, in his *Chicago Sun-Times* review of *The Dresser*, as the "backstage movie," is equally productive. The "backstage movie" is a subgenre of mainstream cinema that has, as a narrative or thematic focus, the issue of cultural production itself. A brief study of mainstream "backstage movies," confined to those concerned with the cultural production of Shakespeare's plays, and structured around Hutcheon's "Where/When?" parameter might produce the following brief chronology[4]:

To Be or Not to Be, Lubitsch, 1942
Kiss Me, Kate, Sidney, 1953
The Dresser, Yates, 1982
Rosencrantz and Guildenstern Are Dead, Stoppard, 1990
Prospero's Books, Greenaway, 1991
Looking for Richard, Pacino, 1996
A Midwinter's Tale, Branagh, 1996
Shakespeare in Love, Madden, 1998
Hamlet 2, Fleming, 2008
A Bunch of Amateurs, Cadiff, 2008

Released in 1941, and starring Jack Benny and Carole Lombard, Lubitsch's *To Be or Not to Be* concerns the experience of a Polish theatre troupe at the advent of the Nazi occupation of Poland. Although the company stages a satirical production ridiculing Hitler, the company actor/manager, Tura, frequently plays Hamlet, and his colleague, Greenberg, secretly dreams of playing Shylock. This is unfortunate because their lack of talent is both lamentable and well-publicized.[5] Yet it is due to the effectiveness of an impersonation of Hitler performed by one of the company members, and a compelling recitation of Shylock's famous speech from Act III, scene i of *The Merchant of Venice*[6] that the troupe manages to escape to Scotland in a stolen military aircraft.

Sidney's *Kiss Me, Kate* was released in 1952, and concerns the performance of a musical version of *The Taming of the Shrew* which features a divorced couple in the roles of Katharine and Petruchio. In "Shakespeare Improved! Cole Porter Teaches the Old Bard New Tricks in *Kiss Me Kate*," Alan Vanneman notes that the couple, who re-establish their relationship through the performance of the musical, is obviously modeled on Alfred Lunt and Lynn Fontanne. Both films were released during the classical Hollywood period, and both conform to clearly established genres of the period: a time in which film production was entirely in the control of the major studios. Both films use recognizable genre stars in their lead roles: Jack Benny and Carole Lombard had established their reputations in "screwball" comedy films, and Howard Keel and Kathryn Grayson were solidly established as musical actors. Lubitsch was a renowned director of screwball comedies, and Sidney was a renowned director of musicals. In both films, the "background" of the Shakespearean performance advances a necessary motif. In Lubitsch's film, the allusions to *Hamlet* and *The Merchant of Venice* position theatre at the nexus of the centripetal pull of monologic discourse and the centrifugal pull of dialogic discourse. Earhardt's dismissal of Tura's Hamlet demonstrates the aesthetic philosophy of the monologic center of discourse, which imposes a unilateral, "proper" approach to enacting Shakespeare. Greenberg's performance as Shylock, which enables the troupe to outwit the Nazis and escape Poland, demonstrates the emergent voice of the heteroglossia appropriating Shakespeare in a carnivalesque fashion. In Sidney's film, the similarity of Fred and Lilli's relationship to the real life relationship of Lunt and Fontanne, and their re-establishment of their relationship through their performances as Petruchio and Katharine, posits a direct connection between art and life. The dramatic relationship of Katharine and Petruchio, with its implied therapeutic effect on the real life relationship of Lunt and Fontanne, shows that an Elizabethan play can have topical relevance in the New York of the 1950s.

Conversely, Peter Yates' *The Dresser*, released in 1982, frames Shakespearean stage performance in nostalgia. The film is set in the 1940s, and chronicles the final evening in the relationship between an actor/manager and his dresser, Norman, who refers to him solely as "Sir." Sir is portrayed as feeble and at the end of his life and career; it is only with the assistance of Norman that Sir is able to give his final performance. Based on Ronald Harwood's personal experience as the dresser to Sir Donald Wolfit, the Shakespearean performance in the film, like Sir himself, is presented as anachronistic, with many of Sir's performance techniques and flourishes seeming grotesquely exaggerated. Yates had established his reputation as a director of action films such as *Bullit* and *Murphy's War*, and as the director of the teen drama *Breaking Away*. Yates' background was therefore completely in popular cinema, with no clear connection to a tradition of theatrical or Shakespearean performance. This is significant because *The Dresser* was released at the mid-point of the "18-year gap," a time period in which no direct adaptations of Shakespeare's plays were attempted in mainstream cinema. Yates' film presents a Shakespearean actor/manager as an anachronism in a time period which saw Shakespeare's plays as an anachronism.

Released seven years after *The Dresser*, Stoppard's *Rosencrantz and Guildenstern Are Dead* undermines a contemporary tendency to canonize Shakespeare. Released only a year later than Branagh's *Henry V*, and within three months of Zeffirelli's *Hamlet*, Stoppard's film becomes a direct response by appropriating *Hamlet* (the most celebrated drama in the English canon), reducing it to its most insignificant characters, and inflating their importance within its diegesis. In the sense that it requires that its audience be able to differentiate between Stoppard's play-text and Shakespeare's play-text, and draw contrasts between them, it can be considered a "backstage drama." For example, *Hamlet* gives the chain of events that leads to the murder of Polonius as Gertrude's call for help, which is responded to by Polonius' call for help in response, which is further responded to by Hamlet's stabbing of Polonius through the arras. However, Stoppard's film gives this chain of events as Rosencrantz and Guildenstern inadvertently meandering behind the arras, surprising Polonius who calls for help, prompting Hamlet to stab Polonius through the arras. As a dying Polonius falls through the curtain, Rosencrantz and Guildenstern hide in the wings, staring guiltily. The effect of this reduction of the importance of Hamlet and Gertrude, coupled with this inflation of the importance of Rosencrantz and Guildenstern, is to turn one of the most complicated dramatic scenes in the canon of English theatre into an equally complicated comic scene.

When first staged in 1966, Stoppard's play showed that Shakespeare was indeed our contemporary (taking the central example from Jan Kott's book, published just one year before) by setting *Hamlet* in the frame of Pirandello and Beckett. And since satire always tends to confirm the importance of its target, Stoppard's apparent parody of Shakespeare's most iconic play also has the effect of reinscribing its significance. However, the film differentiates itself from the play by establishing a specifically 1990s context through which the action is seen. This is most obviously achieved through Stoppard's depiction of Rosencrantz and Guildenstern as embodiments of a current intellectual conflict. In the film, Tim Roth's Guildenstern[7] attempts to understand his predicament intellectually, through the use of logic and deduction, whereas Gary Oldman's Rosencrantz attempts to decipher his world experientially through the observation and manipulation of physical phenomena.[8] Tim Roth's Guildenstern initially uses logical deduction to satisfy himself that there is nothing at all surprising in the coin coming up "heads" 75 times in a row, whereas Gary Oldman's Rosencrantz only achieves a rudimentary understanding of the physical laws he observes.[9] This split corresponds with the two dominant intellectual traditions in Western thought: logical and intellectual analysis, versus observation and data analysis. Stoppard's film was released in a period in which portrayals of the possibilities of science and technology were shifting from a positive to a negative perspective. (The top 15 highest grossing films of the 1980s included *ET: The Extra-Terrestrial, Star Wars: Episodes V and VI, Batman, Back to the Future* and *Top Gun.* The top 15 highest grossing films of the 1990s included *Titanic, Jurassic Park 1* and *2, Terminator 2: Judgment Day* and *The Matrix.*) This shift in perspective highlights the difference between the two pedagogical traditions. Stoppard's film is clearly a response to this shift that demonstrates the equal inadequacy of both. But since Rosencrantz and Guildenstern are the observers, through whose eyes we see the action of *Hamlet*, in discrediting their viewpoints, Stoppard is also undermining the contemporary tendency to canonize Shakespeare, which can be seen as associated with the shift towards the humanistic intellectual approach.

While Stoppard employs a strategy of deflating a canonized play to the absurd in his approach to *Hamlet*, Peter Greenaway employs a strategy of expanding a canonized play outward to its furthest implications in his approach to *The Tempest*. Like *Rosencrantz and Guildenstern Are Dead, Prospero's Books* was released in a socio-historical context that was reclaiming "Shakespeare" as mainstream popular entertainment. Like Branagh, Greenaway is attempting to revitalize a canonized text. But unlike Branagh, Greenaway does not mold the play to conform to a popular audience's expectations of what a protagonist is and what a protagonist should do. Rather, Greenway deconstructs *The Tempest* in a celebratory manner, visually manifesting the traditions of renaissance art, architecture, and academic discourse that are presumed to have influenced its creation. *Prospero's Books*, then, can be considered a "backstage movie" in the sense that it is concerned with the socio-historical context that produced the text of *The Tempest*. The visual richness of Greenaway's presentation is later negated by Prospero's decision to drown his books, yet as Douglas Lanier notes in "Drowning the Book: Prospero's Books and the Textual Shakespeare," "The books are not lost: they are retrieved by the barbaric man-fish Caliban, here a wry surrogate for the enfant terrible director himself. In Greenaway's hands, Prospero's act of destroying his text only authorizes the film director's cinematic appropriation of it. 'Textual' transmission, thematised early in the film by a long traveling of an antique tome passed hand to hand between various creatures and ending with Greenaway's directorial credit, can now pass to the creature of the water, to a desecrater of books who nevertheless saves them from oblivion" (191).

Although Caliban has been depicted in the film as urinating, vomiting, and defecating on Prospero's books, he also saves them for posterity, which Lanier believes is a wry allusion on Greenaway's part towards directors who mold canonized texts to their own purposes, yet are responsible for maintaining the status of these texts as a dynamic force in our culture. In stating that Shakespeare "has become *the* quintessential text, the *Ur-book*, the model for English literary textuality, not a script but secular scripture" (175), Lanier presages the predicament that every film director who wishes to represent Shakespeare's work on film is faced with: the cultural capital of the canonized work immediately predisposes a belief that any attempt to dramatize a play will invariably be unworthy of it. On a certain level the filmmaker must then desecrate the play in the attempt to represent it in a manner that will engage the imagination of the filmmaker's contemporary audience. Judith Buchanan argues that the film's visual strategy of presenting words as text within visual frames indicates that "meaning has been largely wrested from the domain of the verbal" (*Shakespeare on Film* 177). Both Greenaway's and Stoppard's films suggest that the texts must be desecrated in being adapted, but also that they can also be explored to reveal possibilities that were not previously evident.

Released in 1996, Pacino's *Looking for Richard* explores esoteric concerns similar to those explored by Stoppard and Greenaway in its use of "man on the street" interviews, interviews with scholars, stagings of some scenes from *Richard III*, and comments from actors on the difficulties inherent in performing the play. However the driving force behind the film is Pacino's personal desire to both perform the part of Richard III, and to define the relevance and significance of *Richard III*, and by extension of Shakespeare, to his contemporary culture. Pacino appears both in the role of Richard III and addresses the camera directly as himself—the actor attempting to create a performance as Richard III. Branagh's *A Midwinter's Tale*, released the same year, is equally concerned with the efforts of an out-of-work actor named Joe, to establish the relevance of his production of *Hamlet* to a fading English town named "Hope." Joe hopes to revitalize both the town's increasingly stagnant community and his increasingly stagnant career through the production. The film begins with Joe directly addressing the camera concerning his current emotional and mental state of depression, and then chronicles his efforts to direct a company of eclectic performers through their production, despite a series of disastrous circumstances. Although *A Midwinter's Tale* is a highly amusing comedy, like Pacino's film it is concerned with the issue of an artist who is passionately connected to his art in a social context in which his art may be irrelevant. Two years later, Stoppard and Madden's *Shakespeare in Love* would again posit the notion that the Shakespearean play is directly connected to an individual personality. In Madden's film, young William Shakespeare is compelled to write *Romeo and Juliet* as an expression of the intensity of his proscribed love for a woman whose marriage to a lord has already been arranged, and in response to his failure to maintain his relationship with her. Throughout the course of the film, as the projected outcome of their relationship becomes increasingly hopeless, young William Shakespeare's play-text for *Romeo and Juliet* transforms from a comedy to a tragedy. The narrative arc of the film itself reflects the narrative arc of the play being composed and performed within it. *Romeo and Juliet* and *Twelfth Night* become vehicles through which the young William Shakespeare elevates his disastrous personal experience into the realm of art. In "*Out of Sight* and the Self-Reflexive Cinema of the 90's," Nooruddin Farooqi argues that "self-reflexivity" and "self consciousness" are significant characteristics of 1990s cinema. *Looking for Richard*, *A Midwinter's Tale*, and *Shakespeare in Love* were all released during the 1990s and are directly reflexive concerning the issue of artists as producers of art.

Hamlet 2, released in 2008, takes both a scatological and satiric perspective on the issue of cultural production. Like *A Midwinter's Tale*, *Hamlet 2* depicts an actor's last desperate attempt to validate his commitment to his profession by staging a production as a labor of love. Unlike the protagonist of *A Midwinter's Tale*, Dana (the protagonist of *Hamlet 2*) has little talent. The high point of his career is a herpes treatment advertisement he appeared in some 20 years previously. He is currently the drama teacher at a high school, and is told that the drama program is being cancelled. In desperation, Dana writes a sequel to *Hamlet* in which Hamlet and Laertes—having been transported into a time machine prior to their deaths—eventually manage to save Polonius, Ophelia and Gertrude. The production ends with Hamlet forgiving the ghost of his father, and with Christ forgiving God the Father for God the Father's sins: these dramatized absolutions confirm the degree to which Dana, in his act of artistic creation, has merely projected his personal neuroses[10] onto the text of *Hamlet*.[11]

Numerous references to American popular culture are made throughout the film, and, at its conclusion, the play turns out to be a huge success which is enjoying a run on Broadway—an ironic deflation of American popular culture, which in this film is portrayed as valuing kitsch over talent. Also released in 2008, *A Bunch of Amateurs* concerns the efforts of fading American action star Jefferson Steel[12] to reinvigorate his career by portraying King Lear in a stage production to be mounted in Stratford, England. Upon arriving, Steel is shocked to find that the production is being staged at an amateur theatre in Stratford St. John, rather than Stratford-upon-Avon. Like *Hamlet 2*'s Dana, Steel's pretensions (demands for a personal trailer, expensive food) are completely out of proportion to his talent; however, Steel eventually commits himself to the project and gives a compelling performance as Lear. The implication of this film is that the "amateurs," in their willingness to perform out of passionate commitment with no thought of any recompense, are more proficient in their approach to their craft than the "professionals" who are motivated largely out of narcissism and vanity. *A Bunch of Amateurs* also establishes an interesting "doppel" motif between Steel and Nigel Dewberry (represented in the film by the Shakespearean actor, Derek Jacobi), the acknowledged "star" of the company and winner of a plethora of regional Shakespeare competitions. Dewberry, ousted from his status by the arrival of Steel, becomes Steel's nemesis for much of the film, demonstrating that despite the disparity of their respective acting techniques and approaches[13] these men are equally adept in their respective roles as narcissistic prima donnas.

Just as the previous brief application of Hutcheon's "How?" parameter helps to broaden our understanding of the position and function of Shakespeare, and his plays, in contemporary popular culture, the application of her "Where/When?" parameter, provides us with an understanding of the impact of the contemporary socio-cultural or socio-historical contexts on adaptations of Shakespeare's plays in the cinema. Although the films discussed above belong to a subgenre that is concerned with the issue of cultural production, they differ greatly in tone and emphasis. *To Be or Not to Be* and *Kiss Me, Kate* give Shakespearean plays contemporary relevance which allows their protagonists to fulfill the generic expectations of the classical Hollywood period. Conversely, *The Dresser* portrays the performance of the Shakespearean production as anachronistic, and with a feeling of nostalgia—a tone consistent with the film's release at the mid-point of the "18-year gap." Released in 1990 and 1991, *Rosencrantz and Guildenstern Are Dead* and *Prospero's Books* both consciously posit their seminal plays as cultural artifacts that are simultaneously renewed (in the sense that possibilities are revealed that were not previously evident) and debased (in the sense that no production is viewed as worthy of the cultural statues of the play-text) when performed. This direct acknowledgement of the play as a cultural artifact gives way to a focus on the direct and personal relationship between the individual artist and the play that characterizes *Looking for Richard*, *A Midwinter's Tale*, and *Shakespeare in Love* in the mid–90s: their mutual self-reflexivity examining the personal connections that the dramatist establishes with the play-text in the realization of the production. Finally, we see a re-emergence of this subgenre at the end of the first decade of the 21st century as a site of cultural satire in *Hamlet 2* and *A Bunch of Amateurs*. Although all are directed by different auteurs, the tone and emphasis of these films seems to be equally a function of their socio-cultural or socio-historical context and the individual efforts of the auteur.

Rationale and Chronology of Films

These findings suggest the necessity of reexamining many of the films which constitute the acknowledged "canon" of adaptations of Shakespeare's plays in the cinema with an emphasis on Hutcheon's "How?" parameter (the elements of the seminal play that the film has incorporated) and a concomitant emphasis on Hutcheon's "Where/When?" parameter (the influence of the contemporary socio-cultural and social-historical contexts on the film). They also suggest the necessity of reexamining films which are acknowledged to be influenced by Shakespeare's plays, but are not considered part of the acknowledged "canon" of Shakespeare in the cinema, again with an emphasis on Hutcheon's "How?" and "Where/When?" parameters.

The list of films to be examined is as follows:

"Canonical" Films

Film Title	Year of Release	Director
Othello	1923	Buchowetzki
A Midsummer Night's Dream	1935	Dieterle and Reinhardt
Romeo and Juliet	1936	Cukor
Henry V[14]	1944	Olivier
Hamlet	1948	Olivier
Macbeth	1948	Welles
Othello	1952	Welles
Richard III	1955	Olivier
Kumonosu djô[15]	1957	Kurosawa
Gamlet	1964	Kozintsev

Film Title	Year of Release	Director
Chimes at Midnight	1965	Welles
The Taming of the Shrew	1967	Zeffirelli
Romeo and Juliet	1968	Zeffirelli
Korol Lir	1970	Kozintsev
King Lear	1971	Brook
Macbeth	1971	Polanski
Ran	1985	Kurosawa
Henry V	1989	Branagh
Hamlet	1990	Zeffirelli
Much Ado About Nothing	1993	Branagh
Hamlet	1996	Branagh
Richard III	1996	Loncraine
Romeo + Juliet	1996	Luhrmann
Titus	1999	Taymor
Hamlet	2000	Almereyda

"Non-Canonical" Films

Film Title	Year of Release	Director
Forbidden Planet	1956	Wilcox
The Lion King	1994	Allers and Minkoff
10 Things I Hate About You	1999	Junger
She's The Man	2006	Fickman

"Un-Canonical" Films
(Direct Representations)

Film Title	Year of Release	Director
The Tempest	1908	Stow
A Midsummer Night's Dream	1909	Kent
Re Lear	1910	Lo Savio
Il Mercante di Venezia	1910	Lo Savio
Twelfth Night	1910	Kent
Richard III	1910	Benson
The Taming of the Shrew	1929	Taylor
As You Like It	1936	Czinner
Warui yatsu hodo yoku nemuru[16]	1960	Kurosawa
Hamlet	1969	Richardson

(Subtextual Representations)

Film Title	Year of Release	Director
The Godfather	1972	Coppola
The Godfather: Part II	1974	Coppola
Tempest	1982	Mazursky
Strange Brew	1983	Moranis and Thomas
King Lear	1987	Godard
The Godfather: Part III	1990	Coppola

The "Canonical" list has been set by common critical agreement. The "Non-Canonical" list represents works that have attracted significant critical attention. The "Un-Canonical" list includes films which have generated little or no discussion in critical literature regarding their relationship to their seminal plays. These represent Shakespeare's plays directly or through subtexts, and demonstrate that the subject of Shakespeare in the cinema encompasses a broader range of material than is currently acknowledged.

Viewing the list of films in chronological order by release date reveals an interesting fact. Regardless of whether films on the list are the work of an acknowledged auteur of Shakespeare in the cinema, part of the acknowledged canon of representations of Shakespeare in the cinema, or are one of the films acknowledged as merely influenced by Shakespeare's plays,[17] they all tend to reflect influences particular to the period when they were made. Brook and Polanski's films, released within a year of each other (and less than five years after Stoppard's play of *Rosencrantz and Guildenstern Are Dead*), are both heavily influenced by Jan Kott's *Shakespeare: Our Contemporary*, whereas Taymor and Alymereda's films are released within a year of each other and are both works of millennial cinema. The majority of the films released in the 1970s and 1980s all utilize contemporary, rather than Elizabethan, English, and displace the play from a Renaissance setting to a contemporary or futuristic setting. This last point is especially compelling, for it suggests that Hutcheon's "How?," or the decision as to which elements of the seminal play are to be appropriated, may be as much a function of Hutcheon's "Where/When?," or the socio-historical or socio-cultural context of the film, as a function of a decision by an individual auteur. This suggests that cinematic approaches to Shakespeare are equally influenced by the socio-cultural context of their production and consumption as they are by the artistic decisions of an individual auteur. This suggestion is explored in the following chapters.

Chapter Outline

The succeeding chapters are devoted either to specific periods of time, in order to reveal the influence of an adaptation's socio-historical contexts, or to a reevaluation of the works of recognized auteurs, in order to reveal the influence of their socio historical contexts on their adaptations.

Chapter 1 examines representations of Shakespeare's plays in silent cinema, and considers the impact that the contemporary characteristics of cinema as a medium had on the films. During this period, the inability to aurally represent speech coupled with conventions concerning the length of feature films[18] were controlling parameters surrounding adaptations of Shakespeare's plays in the cinema. Filmmakers responded creatively to these limitations, and this chapter explores the effects of their responses.

Chapter 2 examines sound representations of Shakespeare's plays in mainstream cinema that were released prior to the beginning of World War II, and explores the relationship of these films to their contemporary cinema. Slapstick comedy, visual spectacle and recognizable stars were predominant elements of 1930s cinema, and filmmakers emphasized these elements in their approaches to Shakespeare's plays.

Chapter 3 examines the works of Olivier and Welles. Although they are traditionally considered rival actor/managers, it is shown that there are surprising similarities in their approaches to the works they dramatize. Both successfully integrate techniques specific to cinema in their approaches, and both utilize visual countertexts to query and expand upon Shakespeare's plays.

Chapter 4 examines those films by Kurosawa that are considered part of the "canon" of adaptations of Shakespeare in the cinema, detailing how their contemporary socio-cultural and socio-historical context impacts their construction. While his films have had wide circulation in the West, it has not been fully realized that, in constructing his first and second representations of Shakespeare's plays, Kurosawa responds not only to a Shakespeare tradition unique to Japanese culture, but also to 20th-century issues in Japanese society. The discussion further shows how Kurosawa, in constructing his third adaptation of Shakespeare's plays, responds not only to a uniquely Japanese Shakespeare tradition and contemporary Japanese issues, but also to prevalent international issues.

Chapter 5 utilizes a similar approach in an examination of the two films by Kozintsev that are considered part of the "canon" of representations of Shakespeare in the cinema. In his adaptations of *Hamlet* and *King Lear*, Kozintsev utilizes properties specific to cinema; specifically, the use of voiceover narration and the cinemascope frame, and general properties of visual iconography, to imply a critique of life in the Soviet Union in the mid–20th century.

Chapter 6 considers the relationship of Zeffirelli's representations of Shakespeare to the mainstream cinema of the 1960s and early 1990s. Zeffirelli's privileging of the visual image over the play-text reflects a contemporary emphasis in 1960s mainstream cinema of the visual image over the spoken word.[19]

Chapter 7 focuses on the "wave" of adaptations of Shakespeare in the late 1960s and early 1970s, which were clearly influenced by the writings of Jan Kott in *Shakespeare: Our Contemporary*. The works of Richardson, Brook and Polanski confront Kott's notion of "the grotesque" in disparate manners, but all find a cinematic vocabulary for its expression.

Chapter 8 examines the 1970s and 1980s, a period in which no mainstream direct adaptations of Shakespeare's plays were attempted. This discussion challenges two critical orthodoxies. The first posits this time period as the "18-year gap"—a period of time in which Shakespeare was thought (by some) to have simply disappeared from mainstream cinema,[20] and the second posits that only films which use Elizabethan English and non-contemporary settings can be admitted to the "canon" of Shakespeare in the cinema. The chapter shows that several mainstream films based on Shakespeare's plays were produced during this time period. It also shows that the strategy used to adapt Shakespeare's plays during this time period had, in fact, been used in mainstream cinema for some time.

Chapter 9 redirects emphasis to the work of an individual auteur by examining the emergence of the films of Kenneth Branagh in the late 1980s and early 1990s, and their orientation to their mainstream contemporary cinema. Branagh aligns his representations of Shakespeare with mainstream popular cinema, and achieves popular success in doing so.

Finally, Chapter 10 focusses on a "wave" of films that became prevalent in the mid 1990s, in which Shakespeare's plays were represented in order to express concerns contemporary to the coming millennial moment. Although the 1990s has been generally characterized as "The Branagh Era," the representations of Shakespeare in the cinema that emerged in the second part of the decade were qualitatively different from the works of Branagh. In addition to challenging critical orthodoxies, as in previous chapters, this discussion provides a particularly clear example of the connection between a cultural moment and the films that emerge from it.

CHAPTER 1

Silent Shakespeare

In *Shakespeare in the Cineplex*, Samuel Crowl describes the period following World War II as "the great international phase in Shakespeare's absorption into film by directors as diverse as Laurence Olivier, Orson Welles, Akira Kurosawa, Grigori Kozintsev and Franco Zeffirelli" (1). This position is contradicted by John Collick in *Shakespeare, Cinema and Society*, where he notes that (more than 30 years prior to the release of Olivier's *Henry V*) "between 1907 and 1912 there was an international boom in Shakespearean film production" (42). While others have established the history of Shakespeare on film, discussion of silent films often is used as a frame for discussions of other sound adaptations of the same seminal play.[1] There has been little discussion of the paradox created by silent film versions—the representation of supremely verbal poetic texts in almost purely visual terms—and little detailed analysis of the dramaturgy or scenography of these early films. The approach of silent cinema to Shakespeare's plays was determined by technological and conventional constraints (chiefly the inability to record sound, and the average length of early films). Filmed adaptations of Shakespeare made prior to the availability of sound recording technology show a pattern which suggests that any given play was not viewed as an entirety by an adaptor, but rather as a resource containing an array of elements which could be employed in the ensuing production. In *Shakespeare on Film*, Judith Buchanan notes that "Shakespeare was recognized as a plunderable source of filmable material almost as soon as the new medium recognized itself as such" (22). Pre-sound representations of Shakespeare in the cinema are remarkable in that they obviously rely on the familiarity of their intended audience with the text they purport to represent. In essence, early adaptors isolated elements of the text that they felt would be most attractive to a general audience and structured the resultant film around these elements.

Percy Stow's 1910 film of *The Tempest*—also referred to as "The Clarendon Tempest" (McCombe 142)—rejects Shakespeare's employment of the classical unity of time and adopts a linear cause and effect narrative approach that is punctuated by massive narrative ellipses. According to John P. McComb in "'Suiting the Action to the Word': The Clarendon Tempest and the Evolution of a Narrative Silent Shakespeare," this was done in order that the "adaptation could speak to both those who were already consumers of Shakespeare and to those who were dependent on the film to provide an introduction" (152). Judith Buchanan also notes that this film "did not have its genesis in a stage production. Rather, it was conceived as an autonomous piece of cinema" (*Shakespeare on Film* 27). The film begins not with a representation of the tempest, but rather with a depiction of Prospero and the infant Miranda (appropriately dressed in Renaissance garb) being placed into a rowboat and sent off to sea (an event reported but never dramatized in the play). They arrive at the island and Prospero initially discovers Caliban. In this production Caliban is not a monster; he is a "wild man," wearing a shaggy beard and rags, whose foraging is interrupted by the appearance of Prospero on the island. Where Shakespeare's play describes an early period of relationship between Prospero and Caliban in which there is mutual camaraderie and affection, Stow's film portrays Prospero as immediately drawing his sword and subjugating Caliban into his service upon meeting him.

This defines the singular status of Caliban as the only character in this film who is controlled by the threat of the physical violence of the sword. Ariel is liberated from the tree by Prospero's staff, and the majority of manifestations of magic in this film are performed by Ariel under Prospero's command, suggesting a dichotomy between those who are manipulated by magic and those who are manipulated by the direct threat of violence. Ferdinand, for instance, is lured into Prospero's cell by repeated apparitions and disappearances of Ariel which goad Ferdinand into a game of "hide and seek," the object of which is to bring him before the magician. When Ferdinand arrives at the cell, he is confronted by Prospero and draws his sword, only to be disarmed by Prospero's magic.

This is in stark contrast to an earlier scene depicting a reported event in Shakespeare's play: Caliban's attempt on Miranda's "virtue." There is no attempt at forcible rape depicted in this scene. Caliban approaches Miranda and appears to be speaking to her softly. At the point when Caliban places his hands on Miranda's shoulders—without apparent force—Ariel appears and transforms into a monkey. This action confounds Caliban, thereby allowing Miranda to escape. In this scene, Caliban's rags and bestial appearance contrast both with Miranda's pure white gown, and with Ariel's fairy costume, which recalls those worn by ballet dancers. As Ariel often dances in this film, and is played by a young girl, there seems to be a deliberate strategy to contrast various states of sexual awareness between characters. Miranda's virginal gown suggests her propriety in awaiting a correct partner. Ariel's age suggests a pre-sexual state which is one of "pure spirit." Similarly, Prospero's obvious asexual old age is associated with his ability to control magic, while Caliban's physical bestiality suggests a wanton sexuality.

The film bears this differentiation in their characters out in the scene depicting the tempest. Prospero's cell is a cave which appears to have a "portal" carved into the rock. Prospero uses this portal to visualize the tempest, which is conjured here using tropes of stage magic that an early 20th-century audience would easily recognize: as Prospero waves his wand there is a flash of smoke and several doves fly away. As the characters view the ship being tossed by the waves, Miranda is transfixed by the event, which suggests the play's depiction of her as deeply concerned for the sailors on the ship so battered by the storm her father has conjured. Caliban's gestures suggest pure, unreasoning terror here: he seems to have no comprehension that this event is a result of Prospero's magic and is controlled by it.

The portrayal of Caliban here suggests an appropriation of the trope of "the wild man," which Hayden White suggests, in *Tropics of Discourse*, is characteristic in modern European thought (43). This film's portrayal of Caliban is interesting in that it preserves the relative proportion of time spent on Caliban in the play, but completely abandons the elements of Prospero's early attempts to civilize Caliban, and of Caliban's "rebellion" with Trinculo and Stefano in tow. The choice of the sword as the tool of subjugation is again problematic here. In the film's final scenes, Ariel appears to Alonso and company who have been washed up on the beach, conjures up a sumptuous meal for them, and then removes the meal to their amazement. At this point, Prospero steps forward and is reconciled to the party. Again the tool of subjugation is magic, as it has been with every character in this film except Caliban. This may suggest a view of the intellectual inferiority of those who conform to the trope of the wild man: where "civilized" men will obviously understand that they are no match for the power of magic and will make no attempt to retaliate once they are disarmed, "uncivilized" men somehow require the threat of immediate violence to comprehend their subjugation. In *Tropics of Discourse*, Hayden White argues that the tropes of "the wild man" and "the noble savage" have historically been imposed on other cultures by Europeans in order to justify an agenda of European cultural domination (183–196), and further argues that "the noble savage" is used to reflect the state of "the wild man" after he no longer poses an obstacle to this agenda. White believes that European cultures tended to perceive other cultures as animalistic, but perceived themselves as possessing spiritual as well as animalistic elements (189). The dichotomy between the animalistic and the spiritual is represented in Stow's film. Caliban is animalistic, Ariel spiritualistic, and Prospero is a human being who represents characteristics of both. Stow's film, made at a time in which the British Empire was one of the planet's foremost colonial powers therefore reflects tropes of colonialism that are traditionally associated with Shakespeare's play.

Charles Kent's 1909 film of *A Midsummer Night's Dream* also utilizes the trope of representing a fairy or spiritual creature as a little girl in a ballet dress. Puck is depicted as a little girl in this film, and twirls and pirouettes while performing her magic just as Ariel would a year later in Stow's film. Both films were conceived as "autonomous pieces of cinema" (Buchanan, *Shakespeare on Film*, 124), focus on relatively few elements from the play and utilize title cards to indicate ellipses. *The Tempest* begins with the depiction of Prospero being ousted from Milan, depicts the early life of Prospero, Miranda, Ariel, and Caliban on the island, then jumps ten years to present Caliban's attempt on Miranda's virtue, the tempest itself, the wooing of Ferdinand and Miranda, and concludes with the final reconciliation. *A Midsummer Night's Dream* begins with a title card explaining the dilemma of Lysander, Hermia, Demetrius and Helena, and then provides a brief scene showing the couples sneaking off into the woods. A title card then introduces the "rude mechanicals," explaining that they hope to perform before Theseus and his bride at their wedding. The film then proceeds to a brief depiction of the events in the forest overnight, concluding with the return of the reconstituted couples and the restoration of Bottom to his compatriots. The wedding and the performance of Pyramus and Thisbe are not depicted in this film.

The strategy of dramatization used here differs from that used in Stow's film of *The Tempest* in the relationship their directors establish with the unities of their seminal plays. *The Tempest* completely abandons Shakespeare's presentation of the events of the play in "real time," stretching the narrative over a period of a decade while depicting key highlights to maintain the basic structure of the narrative. Conversely, *A Midsummer Night's Dream* seems to assume that its audience will have a high degree of familiarity with the play, and therefore privileges the development of individual scenes over the exposition of the narrative. Bottom is extensively privileged in this production not only in the amount of time the film assigns to his narrative, but also in the sophistication of the pantomime utilized to depict his character. Bottom is never directly introduced in this film, rather, a title card introducing the players as a group appears early in the film, followed by an extended pantomime of Act I, scene ii of Shakespeare's play. Although Bottom is never directly identified, it is clear from the pantomime that he is attempting to dominate the entire production to the obvious annoyance of his fellow performers. In order for the pantomime to convey meaning within the context of this film, the audience must be sufficiently familiar with the play to recognize this scene. The sheer amount of time used in the film to depict this scene (in relation to the number of plot points it develops or anticipates in the film's narrative) indicates that it has been included by Kent for two reasons: firstly, to amuse the audience with Bottom's arrogance and grandstanding, which may be recalled from the text of the play, and secondly, to develop character through solely visual means. The length of the scene, combined with Kent's use of close-ups and the dramatic emphasis on Bottom, indicates that Kent is attempting to establish Bottom's character without any textual assistance from title cards, or aural assistance from dialogue. Kent is endeavoring to create a purely visual language to represent Shakespeare on film. Close-up shots fill the frame with their subject, usually obscuring the context of the mise-en-scène; Kent's use of them here communicates the importance of Bottom without the use of aural sound or visual title cards.

Costume in this film is consistent with early 20th-century theatrical conventions of the depiction of ancient Greece, as is the setting in the scenes depicting Athens. Interestingly, the forest creatures in this film also wear basic Athenian garb, with some "forest" elements (such as leaves, small vines, etc.) added to their costumes as flourishes. Hermia and Helena's dresses, however, seem to belong to a much later period, possibly the late 18th or 19th century. The dresses function as a labeling device: all of the forest creatures in this film (including Puck) are female, and only four of the play's denizens of the forest (Titania, Puck, and two anonymous "fairies") are credited. Presumably the later period costume facilitates reading on the part of the audience by preventing them from confusing Hermia and Helena with the fairies. However, this costume choice also may serve a symbolic function similar to that of Miranda's dress in Stow's film of *The Tempest*; where in one scene Miranda's white dress is a marker of difference between herself and the tatters worn by the "bestial" Caliban. The dresses worn by Hermia and Helena in Kent's film may emblematize their entrapment by "civilized" mores around marital sexuality, whereas in the fairy realm these mores are not recognized. As there are no males in the forest in Kent's film, Lysander, Demetrius, and the rude mechanicals can wear nominally Athenian costumes without such a contrast being necessitated.

In the same year that Stow's *The Tempest* was released, Gerolamo Lo Savio demonstrated that representation of Shakespeare in the cinema had already become an international practice with the productions of *Re Lear* and *Il Mercante di Venezia* by Film d'Arte Italiana. Robert Hamilton Ball's assertion that, between 1908 and 1911, "on the continent ... there was a definite and conscious movement ... toward the 'art film'" (90) is corroborated by the press kit accompanying the DVD release of *Silent Shakespeare*, in which Luke McKernan notes that this production company "was ... devoted to the production of art films, by which was meant the filming of classic stage productions with famous actors, often (as here) with rich stencil coloring, painted directly onto the film" (4). Although both of these films utilize hand tinted color, *Re Lear* utilizes this color to indicate changes in personal states. In this film Lear, played by "the most distinguished tragedian in Italy, Ermete Novelli" (Ball 120), wears a crimson robe over a drab brown garment when we first see him on his throne. When Lear's authority is challenged, (initially when Goneril beats Oswald, and later when Regan places Kent in the stocks), Lear casts off his crimson robe in order to depict the loss of his authority. Similarly, Lear's madness on the beach at Dover in this film is approximated by a scene depicting both The Fool and Kent as they struggle with Lear in order to place his robe back on: Lear now refuses to wear the robe. Later an escalation in Lear's madness will be shown as he attempts to sweep the sand off of the beach using a broom. When Cordelia's men request that Lear follow them to meet her, he agrees, standing astride the broom and skipping along with them in the manner in which a child might skip astride a hobby horse: The Fool's assertion that Lear has "madest thy daughters thy mothers"[2] is visually reflected in this film with the image of the old man reduced to the behavior of a child, skipping astride a hobby horse to meet with his daughter.

The Fool in this film appears on screen with both Cordelia and Kent, the stage tradition of doubling The Fool with Cordelia being eschewed here in order to depict a far more intimate type of tragedy than that presented in Shakespeare's play. The characters of Albany, Edward, Edmund, and Gloucester do not appear in this film at all, resulting in what Ball refers to as "the complete elimination of the Gloucester plot" (122). Although it initially might seem convenient to argue that the 16-minute length of this film precludes their appearance, Frank Benson's *Richard III*, at 23 minutes, presents a full cast of characters. The effect of this narrowing of the dimensions of *King Lear*'s plot is to intensify the sense that humanity is preying "on itself/Like monsters of the deep"[3] by confining the scope of this play to the immediate family. The Goneril and Regan of this film are not the scheming sisters of the play; they are openly contemptuous of Lear and laugh at him when depriving him of his authority. The injustices depicted by this film are solely at their prompting. Although Oswald is given enough screen time in this film to prompt the audience to consider him a significant villain, Lo Savio isolates his character by placing him in a horned helmet, surrounded by other characters wearing helmets with wings. This association of Oswald with the cuckold's horns here deflates Oswald's potential status as a villain, regulating him to the position of one of Goneril's minions.

Where Lo Savio reduces the national tragedy of *King Lear* to a family melodrama, his film of *Il Mercante di Venezia* has the unfortunate effect of relegating Shylock to the status of a two-dimensional villain. Ball observes that there is "nothing about Jessica's theft of money and jewels from her father" (125) in this film, and the effect of this omission is that Shylock's malice seems utterly motiveless here. Lo Savio's Lear seems to embody the characteristics of a stock character of Victorian melodrama; according to Barbara Weiss in *The Hell of the English: Bankruptcy and the Victorian Novel*, one stock character of Victorian melodrama was the "'good old man,' often the father of the heroine, who is forever tottering on the brink of ruin" (58). Conversely, his Shylock seems to embody the characteristics of "the villain" that is a centerpiece of the same tradition; according to Kristen Guest, in "The Subject of Money: Late-Victorian Melodrama's Crisis of Masculinity," the villain as a stock character is often motivated by "materialism" (635–657) rather than inherent malignity. Shylock is introduced with a title card referring to him as "Shylock, the Jew." Interestingly in this film, although the same title card explains that Lorenzo is in love with Jessica who is Shylock's daughter, it is never suggested that Jessica may be possessed of any of Shylock's moral failings. This implies either that Shylock's failings are a result of his character rather than his religion, or that by adopting Lorenzo's lifestyle Jessica is freed of her father's moral influence.

The film is explicit in describing Shylock's ultimate undoing as a result of his attempt to shed a drop of Christian blood, which would immediately indicate that the film exemplifies a racist ideological viewpoint of Jewish people, and a sexist ideological viewpoint of women—Jessica's status as Jewish or Christian is determined through her relationship to a more powerful male. However, Lo Savio problematizes his film in a provocative manner. Although Shylock is portrayed as a duplicitous character throughout, his duplicity is easily matched by that of Antonio and Bassanio. When

Shylock negotiates the loan with Antonio and Bassanio his manner is pleasant, servile, and accommodating. Whenever Antonio and Bassanio turn their backs or leave the room, however, Shylock gleefully grins and laughs, indicating that he believes he has them where he wants them. The clause in the contract regarding "the pound of flesh" is presented to Antonio by Shylock as something of a joke in this film. The three men read the clause, laugh, and then Antonio and Bassanio sign the contract while Shylock grins menacingly behind their backs, indicating that he has duped them into signing this clause that he is serious about enforcing. When Antonio and Bassanio leave Shylock's house, however, we find that their negotiating the loan is part of the ruse by which Lorenzo gets Jessica to leave Shylock's house. Lo Savio's film omits Jessica and Lorenzo's robbery of Shylock's ducats and Leah's ring, which Jessica trades for a monkey. In this film, therefore, although Shylock's behavior is aligned with that of Bassanio and Antonio in terms of its duplicity, the extremes to which Shylock pursues his intents (duping Antonio into signing the clause and seeking his death in the court) render him as a villain.

If Lo Savio is making a racist statement in this film, the behavioral differences he depicts between races are of degree rather than kind. It should also be noted that Lo Savio's identification of "Shylock, the Jew" as a stock villain in his socio-historical context would have been anachronistic. Jews were granted full and equal rights under Italian law in the 1790s under Napoleon; although these rights were rescinded when Napoleon was defeated, they were regained throughout Italy in the period between 1848 and 1870. With the unification of Italy in 1861, the Jews were emancipated and the ghettos of Florence and Rome were abolished. In 1904, the Great Synagogue of Rome was built. The Prime Minister of Italy at the time of the film's release was Luiggi Luzzatti, Italy's second Prime Minister of full Jewish ancestry (a third prime minister, Sidney Sonnino, had a Jewish father). Although the presentation of Shylock as a stock villain whose behavior is not inconsistent with the behavior of the film's protagonists would seem to indicate that Lo Savio does not make an overtly racist statement, it is difficult to determine the actual degree of racist sentiment in this film.

As in his film of *Re Lear*, Lo Savio's *Il Mercante di Venezia* isolates one element of Shakespeare's play and centers its narrative around that element: in the former, Lo Savio focuses on the family conflict, and in the latter he focuses on the contract between Antonio and Shylock. The appearance of Portia in this film is utterly subservient to this element. It is mentioned in a title card that Bassanio wants the loan to marry her; however,

Portia does not directly appear on screen until we are given a scene depicting her horror at the fate awaiting Antonio, and her resolve to help him. According to Ball, although "about two thirds of the original film remain today" (123), it is "probable that this film eliminated entirely the casket plot and the ring plot" (125) as well. Although Lo Savio is reductive in his approach, his films do maintain something of the narrative structure of the plays which ostensibly inspire them: Lo Savio's Lear reconciles with Cordelia only to die in despair after her murder, and his Shylock's plot on Antonio's life is defused through Portia's intervention in court.

Charles Kent's 1910 film of *Twelfth Night* is far more reductive in its approach, for it is focused almost entirely on the "gulling" of Malvolio. Viola's shipwreck and separation from Sebastian are swiftly depicted in order to move the narrative to Olivia's house, where we are then shown Olivia's entourage. No one in Olivia's entourage, except Malvolio, is identified by name, although the complete text of the forged letter is related to us through title cards. Malvolio is overjoyed at the news that Olivia loves him; the major portion of the screen time in this film is utilized by a depiction of Malvolio's rapture in the foreground, while Olivia's unidentified entourage eavesdrop in the background, their heads peering through bushes while they snicker at Malvolio. As in his *A Midsummer Night's Dream*, Kent utilizes the close-up shot combined with pantomime to convey Malvolio's character solely through visual means, and to stress the importance of Malvolio in his film. A brief sequence depicts Viola and Sebastian being reunited, and Malvolio tearing up the letter and furiously storming off stage. Although Shakespeare's play is reduced to several short scenes encompassing one slightly longer sequence here, all of the actors are meticulously dressed in Renaissance garments, including frilled collars and sleeves. Malvolio does not violate any norms of apparel in this film, as he does in Shakespeare's play. A title card informs us that he simply becomes even more pompous than usual when under the delusion of Viola's love for him.

Sir Frank R. Benson's 1911 film of *Richard III*, interestingly focuses on thematic rather than specific elements of the play's narrative. Benson's film accomplishes this by conspicuously returning to stage-craft and using obvious back-drops to represent locations. Benson spent the majority of his career reviving Shakespeare on stage, and in 1888 assumed the position of manager of the Stratford-Upon-Avon Shakespeare festival. Benson was one of the foremost Shakespearean actor/managers of his time, and he structures *Richard III* around a visual disparity between blatantly theatrical sets and actual exterior location shooting. Benson uses the disparity in his visual strategies to indicate a dichotomy between public and private deeds. Public deeds are undertaken in this film on an obvious, and full stage; private deeds are undertaken in this film at locations.[4] Furthermore, the stage used was that of the Shakespeare Memorial Theatre in Stratford; Judith Buchanan notes that, in "1911, it was still a far more technically complicated task to light a theatrical venue sufficiently to produce a satisfactory film image than it was to relocate the theatrical event to a film studio lit for the purpose" (*Shakespeare on Film* 30) which indicates that Benson's visual strategy here is deliberate.

Benson preserves the majority of characters from Shakespeare's *Richard III* and stages much of the action with the majority of characters present as witnesses. Benson also provides some interesting embellishments to the play. The film opens at the aftermath of the Battle of Tewkesbury, the scene from *3 Henry VI* modified here to posit Richard as the sole murderer of Prince Edward (who in the play is stabbed by Richard, Clarence, and King Edward). The murder of Prince Edward takes place after the battle has finished when the Prince no longer poses a threat. Benson then follows the play in his depiction of Richard's murder of Henry VI, which takes place in the tower while they are alone. Richard stabs the king in the chest; the king collapses, and Richard waits until the king stops breathing, then stands astride the corpse and stabs him twice again in the chest in a simultaneous display of bloodthirstiness and cowardice.

The film progresses in this pattern of alternation between public and private scenes. The wooing of Lady Anne is accomplished with about 20 people on the stage, whereas Clarence's murder—again a vicious stabbing—takes place when he is alone in the tower. King Edward's decision to pardon Clarence is not revealed until after Clarence has been murdered, and is again revealed in open court. In this film, manipulations are the stuff of public moment, whereas murders are the stuff of private moments. Richard prevents the coronation of the two boys, plots the execution of Hastings, is crowned by the Lord Mayor, and orders the execution of Lady Anne in open court. Also reserved for private moments is Richard's obvious glee whenever his latest scheme proves fruitful.

The public order of Lady Anne's execution and the private murder of the two princes represent a turning point in this film, after which Richard is no longer associated with public space. The court is obviously sickened by his decision to execute Lady Anne, representing an initial loss of his power. We are not directly shown the murder of the two princes; we are rather shown the remorse of the murderer in the aftermath of the event, as he tenderly and reverently carries their bodies out of the tower. When

Richmond arrives he is initially alone on stage; soon, all of the nobles who formerly surrounded Richard surround Richmond. Richard's final private moment in this film depicts the ghosts of all of those he has murdered, materializing and dematerializing until the final ghost—that of Buckingham—brings Richard's standard down. The final event depicted in this film is the public death of Richard at Bosworth field, the private haunting and public killing at the conclusion of this film mirroring the public and private murders that began the film.

Dimitri Buchowetzki's 1923 film of *Othello* contextualizes the events it depicts with a scene provided by the filmmaker to establish motivations for Iago's behavior that are not clearly established in the play. In Buchowetzki's vision Othello is idealized by the citizenry of Venice and Cyprus as their savior, large crowds following him wherever he goes through the film's grandiose settings. In *Shakespeare on Silent Film: An Excellent Dumb Discourse*, Judith Buchanan notes that "as a product of a national industry that valued the expressionist potential of architectural design, the set for *Othello* is tremendous: it includes a grand set of courtyards, arches, staircases, and balconies" (246). The effect of these settings is to "contextualize the domestic drama within a larger social and political framework" (*ibid.*, 247). The film begins with a large crowd gathering to welcome Othello back from the wars. Iago—described by a title card as possessing a "serpent's soul" and played by Werner Krauss, who would have been recognizable to the contemporary audience through previous roles which included Dr. Caligari and Robespierre (*ibid.*, 241–242)—waits with Roderigo and explains that he expects to be made Othello's lieutenant at the ceremony that will follow. It is clear from the outset of the film that this is the slight that Iago seeks to redress; his humiliation is both public, as he is forced to stand in front of the crowd alongside Cassio while the Duke demands that Othello reveal his choice, and private, as he has been gloating to Roderigo that he expects to be chosen as the lieutenant. As Desdemona is not yet at this point married to Othello, it is clear that Iago is spurring Roderigo on as a means of manipulating Roderigo to murder Cassio.

Othello is clearly presented as a Saharan African in this film; during the second crowd scene which depicts the public outcry that Othello not be arrested for having married Desdemona, he announces himself (by title card) as the son of an Egyptian Prince and a Spanish Princess, prompting the Duke and the public to applaud the marriage. Othello's arrival in Cyprus is accompanied by a similar gathering of a large crowd bearing beating drums to honor his arrival. During the night of liberty decreed by Othello to celebrate his nuptials, the film again privileges the celebrations of the crowd, depicting entertainments such as sword swallowing amidst the general revelry. Throughout the film Buchowetzki employs the crowd as a form of chorus which punctuates both Othello's fortunes and his decline. This decline is depicted by Buchowetzki as having several stages: Othello initially goes into a catatonic state and merely stares blankly ahead as a title card proclaims, "Now farewell the tranquil mind." Othello's stupor is punctuated by scenes depicting the crowd first remarking that there are more Turks now making for Cyprus, and later wondering why Othello is not being sent to save them from the Turks.

Othello's paralysis is broken here when Roderigo, prompted by Iago into singing a love ballad to Desdemona before her window, is mistaken by Othello for Cassio. He now runs uncontrollably out into the hallway and meets Iago. According to a title card, Othello demands that Iago tell him who was singing, choking Iago as Iago manages to croak the half-word "Cass...." Othello retreats to his bed, and his dream is represented by Bukowetzki with a superimposed image of Cassio and Desdemona kissing over his head. Iago hears his cries, and runs to Othello in his bed, "comforting" Othello in a scene which depicts the degree to which Othello has been rendered infant-like by Iago. Iago gathers Othello in his arms, strokes his hair and rocks him back and forth while Othello kisses Iago's hand in return. Iago then fluffs Othello's pillows and fans Othello with the handkerchief that Othello gave to Desdemona, waiting for Othello to recognize it.

The use of the handkerchief as an example of Iago's talent for manipulation is further demonstrated in his relationship with Emilia; he uses her obvious infatuation with him to manipulate her into stealing the handkerchief, which in this film is given to Desdemona by Othello at the time of their marriage. Othello clearly tells Desdemona that because of the "magic in the web of it ... to lose or give it away were such perdition as nothing else could match." Despite Desdemona's later repetition of this curse (depicted with a title card in both instances) to Emilia, Emilia willingly steals the handkerchief and surrenders it to Iago in exchange for his displays of affection. Once Othello is led to believe that Desdemona has given the handkerchief to Cassio, he rips it apart with his teeth.

The film is sufficiently detailed in its treatment of the play to allow for significant plot changes. So, in the ending when Emilia tells Othello the truth regarding the handkerchief in response to Desdemona's murder, Iago's ability to control Othello is lost. As Iago enters the chamber, a title card represents Othello attacking Iago: "Spartan dog, more foul than anguish, hunger or the sea. Look on the tragic loading of this bed. This is *thy* work!" Iago is then stabbed to death by Othello, and Emilia is not harmed by either of them. Confronted by Cassio and the officers of the Duke, Othello stabs himself, crawling back into the bed to die beside Desdemona's corpse. The final shot of this film depicts Cassio relating the news of Othello's death to the citizens of Cyprus, accompanied with a final prayer requesting mercy for Othello's soul. By mirroring its opening's public welcome and celebration of Othello with the public display of mourning for his loss at its end, this film underlines a moral point: despite his destruction of his general, Iago never achieves the public affirmation of his status that has prompted his actions from the beginning.

With its incorporation of motifs depicting Othello as a kind of culture-hero and Iago as an almost sexualized manipulator, Buchowetzki's *Othello* seems the most accomplished of the silent films discussed here in its adaptation of one of Shakespeare's plays; however, it must be noted that by the 1920s conventions for silent filmmaking and distribution now dictated a length of two to three reels for "feature" films. A length of one reel was considered the standard for distribution at the times of release of the other films discussed: at nine minutes[5] *Il Mercante di Venezia* would have been considered a film of normal length in 1910, whereas James Keane's 1912 *Richard III*, at 59 minutes in length, would have been considered an abnormally long film. As conventions regarding length changed over the course of a decade, Bukowetzki, by sheer virtue of screen time alone, was able to represent far more of the plot specifics of Othello than the other filmmakers discussed here. All of their films, however, use their contemporary cinematic techniques in an attempt to engage their seminal play while imposing contemporary tropes and motifs onto it. Stow's *The Tempest* attempts to utilize a linear narrative to dramatize, in silent film, a plot that Shakespeare dramatized using embedded recounted narratives, and reflects the European cultural trope of "the wild man." Kent's *A Midsummer Night's Dream* focuses on the most central and humorous elements of Shakespeare's play in its highly sophisticated use of pantomime to depict a familiar subject, yet also, in its depiction of the fairies, reflects the European cultural tendency to associate a virginal feminine state with one of spiritual purity. Lo Savio's use of hand-painted color in *Re Lear* uses a visual property specific to film to dramatize an emotional change signaled by dialogue in Shakespeare's play, and further utilizes a stock character from Victorian melodrama to illustrate the character of his protagonist. Conversely, Lo Savio's depiction of Antonio and Bassanio's attempt to negotiate the loan as a ruse for facilitating Jessica's elopement suggests an ambivalence in their character demonstrated in Shakespeare's play by a subplot wholly absent from Lo Savio's *Il Mercante di Venezia*. Like *Re Lear*, however, *Il Mercante di Venezia* relies on an identical Victorian archetype to illustrate the character of its villain. Although Kent focuses his film on one incident in Shakespeare's play in *Twelfth Night*, his use of a mise-en-scène and a deep space composition to place Malvolio in the foreground and Olivia's entourage in the background represents a filmic solution to a problem of representing this scene without sound. Finally, Benson's *Richard III* uses non-realistic modes of stagecraft to suggest a disparity between public manipulation and private murder, depicting how Richard's loss of control in the public realm parallels his shift from private victimizer to private victim of apparitions. Although bound by limitations imposed by technology and their contemporary storytelling conventions, these films all attempt to find a cinematic "voice" for their presentations of their seminal plays.

The silent tradition of Shakespeare in the cinema was truly international: *The Tempest* and *Richard III* were British productions, *A Midsummer Night's Dream* and *Twelfth Night* were American productions, and *Re Lear* and *Il Mercante di Venezia* were Italian. Although Crowl, in *Shakespeare at the Cineplex*, seems to credit Olivier and Welles with inaugurating the "international" period of Shakespearean film production (1), it should be remembered that international productions predated their works by three decades. The silent tradition of Shakespeare in the cinema also established a central tension which all future directors of films of Shakespearean plays would need to resolve: the tension between the word and the visual. The means by which each succeeding socio-historical period resolves this tension defines the characteristics of each resultant film.

CHAPTER 2

The Classical Hollywood Period to World War II

Although there is a tendency in popular culture to arbitrarily distinguish between "pre-sound" or "silent" cinema, and "talkies" or "sound" cinema (and a further tendency to consider silent cinema as inferior to sound cinema in complexity and execution), the development of sound technology in the late 1920s did not completely revolutionize filmmaking. The addition of recorded dialogue merely made a previously unavailable signifying system available to what many filmmakers considered a primarily visual medium. (It should also be noted that the term "silent cinema" is in itself something of a misnomer; the conventional practice in projecting films was to provide a musical accompaniment.) For example, Sternberg—who would become famous for directing Marlene Dietrich in several "women's films"—was quoted as stating that he considered himself to be foremost a visual artist. The world's most popular filmmaker at the advent of sound technology, Chaplin, felt that the addition of recorded dialogue would limit film's effectiveness as a medium, and did not release a film utilizing conventional recorded direct dialogue until 1940.[1] When recorded dialogue became available to cinema, 1930s mainstream cinema remained a primarily visual medium which utilized recorded dialogue within the constraints of established conventions, which included the frequent utilization of carefully cultivated "star images," and the presentation of narratives in a manner which clearly conformed to established genres and subgenres of storytelling, such as slapstick comedy or costume drama—a subgenre of the historical film which, according to Robert Rosenstone, "uses the exotic locale of the past as no more than a setting for romance and adventure" (51).

Two of Chaplin's three partners in founding the United Artists Company, Douglas Fairbanks and Mary Pickford, demonstrated the fact that the transition from silent cinema to sound cinema was not instantaneous. As many theatres had not yet installed sound equipment, Fairbanks and Pickford filmed their 1929 adaptation of *The Taming of the Shrew* in both silent and sound versions. Their film, as well as the other Shakespeare films of this transitional period, was also conceived within the parameters of mainstream Hollywood costume drama, and also employed slapstick comedy.

Pickford—referred to as "America's sweetheart" or "the world's sweetheart" in the press—was the most recognizable female star of this period, and it is her star image which the film foregrounds. The opening credits give Pickford top billing by first accompanying her name with an image of her brandishing a whip, followed by an image, accompanying Fairbanks' name, of him laughing and swaggering. The third image we see is that of Shakespeare, with the accompanying phrase "in William Shakespeare's *The Taming of the Shrew*." This is not the only strategy that the film uses to foreground the demands of its star power over those of its seminal play. With a running length of 66 minutes, the film dispenses with the play-text's subplot involving the courtship of Lucentio and Bianca, focusing entirely on the relationship of Katherine and Petruchio. The film also dispenses with the Christopher Sly induction that Marjorie Garber (57–59) finds crucial to the play, providing instead a frame of a Punch-and-Judy show. In this puppet show, Judy first tells Punch, "I'll kiss you," and then hits him. Punch then picks up a stick and says, "Here is my fools-cap and staff…. I'll tame you" and then swats at Judy with the stick. Judy's immediate response to this is to say, "Oh you're wonderful" and kiss Punch.

Under Sam Taylor's direction, this *Taming of the Shrew* employs a strategy of subverting expectations throughout. The expectation that seems to follow from the Punch and Judy show is that Petruchio will tame Katherine, and she will find Petruchio wonderful as he swats her; Taylor's film, however, will show that quite the opposite is the case. The expectation that an audience would have of Mary Pickford would be that of "America's sweetheart" or "the world's sweetheart," which would have prepared audiences for a passive-submissive portrayal of Katherine. Our introduction to Katherine is preceded by our introduction to Hortensio and Bianca: a long dolly shot takes the viewer away from the Punch and Judy show through a sumptuous Renaissance set that depicts a vibrant and lively social scene in which pipers play and onlookers merrily go about their business. A series of dissolves first isolates Baptista's home and then Hortensio and Bianca, who—believing themselves unobserved—are kissing. The camera is then moved back on a dolly to reveal that Baptista is observing Hortensio and

Bianca. Taylor's reliance on dolly shots to connect the Punch and Judy frame to Baptista's home articulates the structure of the film and underlines the craft which goes into its making. Although Taylor's reliance on conventions of slapstick comedy and star image, and the heavily cut text he utilizes, may tempt critics to question the "seriousness" of his approach, the unwieldiness of early sound camera equipment suggests that these dolly shots are part of a meticulously planned visual strategy. The dolly shots do not only connect the frame to the main action, they effectively bring us into a state of confrontation with the main actors.

Baptista's admonishment that he will "not bestow [his] youngest daughter until [he] has a husband for Katherine" is immediately followed by a jump cut to a glass door which loudly shatters as an object flies through it. A crane shot reverses the camera down the stairs, revealing that the door at the top of the staircase leads to Katherine's room. As Katherine's attendants frantically run from the room, the camera ascends the staircase once again, to reveal all of the breakage in the room, which looks as if every one of the objects within it has been smashed. The camera cranes back slightly again to frame the doorway, revealing the emergence of Katherine glaring directly into the camera, and brandishing a whip. To a contemporary audience watching this larger-than-life sized image of spectacle on a big screen, the subverted expectation of "America's sweetheart" would have been shocking, even though Katherine's uncontained hostility and rage had already been signaled, in a titillating shape, by the image of Pickford brandishing a whip in the credits.

Fairbanks, conversely, is introduced very much within the confines of his star image. His Petruchio swaggers in a manner entirely consistent with his performances in *The Three Musketeers*, *The Mark of Zorro*, and *The Thief of Bagdad*. Fairbanks' Petruchio is introduced wearing a cap with an enormous feather just as Fairbanks' *Robin Hood* wore, and underneath the cap, he wears a bandana just as Fairbanks' *Black Pirate* wore. As Petruchio reacts to Hortensio and Grumio's warning with an emphatic "Have I not in my time heard lions roar/Have I not heard the sea, puff'd up with winds," they react to his bombast with a knowing wink, suggesting that they realize his swagger outweighs his substance. This is again suggested when Grumio mournfully shakes his head in reaction to Petruchio's exaggerated and over-determined laughter after stating, "And do you tell me of a woman's tongue." This technique of juxtaposing a visual image directly against an element of the play-text proves to be an integral element of Taylor's dramatic strategy, which often relies on the qualification of spoken utterances by visual contradictions.

The initial wooing scene demonstrates this clearly. Petruchio introduces a disguised Hortensio to Baptista as Licio, announcing that he has brought Hortensio/Licio to be a tutor to Katherine and Bianca. Hortensio/Licio goes up to Katherine's chamber, and as Petruchio negotiates a dowery with Baptista a loud crash is heard, followed by a long shot showing Hortensio/Licio being thrown out of the door of Katherine's room and tumbling down the stairs. As Katherine's door slams shut Petruchio states, "Ah, how I long to have a g-r-r-r-r-r-r-r-r-r-r-r-apple with her." Like Petruchio's confident laughter, the exaggerated and over-determined rolling of the "r" in the word "grapple" immediately suggests that Petruchio's swagger outweighs his substance, as the association of boastfulness with incompetence is a standard comic trope. Taylor's employment of slapstick, although consistent with cinematic norms of this period, communicates information about Petruchio, Katherine and their relationship that could not be directly stated due to social conventions.

In "The Taming of the Shrew—Listening to Silence," Frances E. Dolan notes that although Petruchio's whip carries on an established stage tradition in depicting his character, the provision of Katherine with her own whip gives them "a curious kind of equality as they face off, whip to whip." At their first meeting, Katherine glares at Petruchio from the top of the stairs and menacingly cracks her whip; Petruchio returns her gaze, laughs ecstatically, and cracks his whip in return. Interestingly, Pickford's Katherine reacts to this by first staring at his whip, then staring back at hers, and then hiding her own whip behind her back, which possibly indicates her recognition that Petruchio's whip is larger than hers, and that she will need to contest him by utilizing other means. When Petruchio calls her "Kate" while approaching her, she is angered and draws her arm back to flog him. Petruchio takes advantage of her momentarily open posture to throw his arms around her and kiss her. Her reaction is initially to punch and kick him; however, she stops struggling enough for him to give her a long kiss, and then throws him back into the wall. Her reaction is dazed, subverting the trope by which the resistant female is made compliant by the first kiss, by presenting Katherine as far more disorientated than yielding. Her disorientation, coupled with her initial reaction to the whip (a symbol of something they share in common) suggests that on some level she realizes she has found a match in Petruchio, and is unsure of how to negotiate the relationship.

The complexity of Taylor's depiction is further demonstrated in his depiction of Petruchio's reaction to their wooing. Katherine's utterance "If I be waspish, best beware my sting" is accompanied by a vicious slap which she delivers to Petruchio's face. Not only does he not seem to register any pain, he laughs merrily as she repeatedly slaps him in the face without effect. As he tells her that she is "pleasant, gamesome, passing courteous; But slow in speech, yet sweet as spring time flowers" each pause in his line is accompanied with a vicious slap in his face from her. As Katherine's physical force has been established as being sufficient to throw a grown man through a doorway and down a flight of stairs, it seems unlikely that her inability to make Petruchio register physical pain here is due to any lack of ability to inflict it. Petruchio's imperviousness to her slaps here represents the film utilizing Fairbanks' star image as an icon of masculine strength. The association of Fairbanks with Zorro, Robin Hood and similar characters renders Petruchio impervious to what easily dominates the other men in this film.

This is further confirmed by what follows. Petruchio finally physically restrains Kate and forces her to sit in a love seat beside him, his arm wrapped around her torso while he clamps his hand over her mouth as she attempts to bite him. At this point Baptista enters the room behind them, and from his perspective Katherine appears to be resting her head on Petruchio's shoulder. Petruchio then rises and proceeds to inform Baptista of how he has won her love. Katherine draws her whip and proceeds to flog Petruchio with all of her might from behind while Petruchio registers no pain and does not miss a beat as he speaks to Baptista. Katherine is not so much dominated by Petruchio here as she is in the play; rather, she is utterly disorientated and frustrated by her inability to intimidate Petruchio, as witnessed by her floor-stamping and hair pulling as she runs from him after the whipping has no effect. He approaches her and she slaps him yet again, but again acquiesces as he kisses her. He leaves her breathless and again overwhelmed, calling, "We will be married o' Sunday" as he rides off.

As Petruchio departs, Katherine glares at him and states, "Look to your seat Petruchio, or I throw you/Katherine shall tame this haggard;— or if she fails,/Shall tie her tongue up, and pare down her nails." (As Dolan points out in "The Taming of the Shrew—Listening to Silence," this soliloquy does not occur in Shakespeare's play, but rather was given to Katherine by Garrick in Act I of his 1754 production of *Catherine and Petruchio*.) It is clear that Katherine here has recognized Petruchio as her equal, and that in her view any "taming" which is to occur needs to be done by her to him. Her reactions to his whip and to his kisses suggest that, in Taylor's presentation, Katherine has no objection to the wedding or their union at this point. She has found her match; what remains to be negotiated is the dynamic (or the terms) of their relationship, and what remains to be decided is exactly whom will be tamed by who.

The wedding scene implies that Petruchio will have the upper hand. Fairbanks' costume here seems more influenced by 1920s surrealism than by the description provided in the play: Petruchio's shirt is torn and has only one sleeve, his pants are patched with a striped pattern down one leg and a checked pattern down the other, and most noticeably, he wears an old boot on his head, upside down at a 45-degree angle. Taylor dramatizes the wedding scene in similar terms, showing Petruchio loudly munching on an apple and feigning ignorance of the process when the priest beckons him to the altar. Petruchio is obviously amused at Katherine's escalating annoyance as every line of the wedding ceremony is punctuated with a loud munch of the apple, and as he exchanges the ring for the rotten apple core at the crucial moment. When Katherine is asked if she will take Petruchio, her silent fuming is interrupted by Petruchio stomping hard on her foot, causing her to shout, "I do-o-o-o-o-o-o-o." However, as the "I" vowel sound and the hard "d" consonant sound in her shout are barely audible, it is unclear as to whether this is merely a scream of pain or an indication that she really wishes to marry him, is too proud to do so, and is prompted to do so by his stomping. Either reading seems viable.

Taylor's strategy of slapstick augmented by lines from Shakespeare's play remains consistent through to the scene at Petruchio's mansion, in which the situation is resolved. Katherine, having fallen in the mud alongside Petruchio's pigs in the courtyard, warms herself by the fireplace, muttering, "Look to your seat." Petruchio eavesdrops upon this unbeknownst to her. It would seem that Petruchio has the upper hand; however, Taylor soon provides a reversal of this scene. Petruchio, having carried Katherine up to the bedchamber (but dropping her back on her feet in order that she is forced to walk over the threshold) sneaks out to get some food. He doesn't realize that Katherine has also sneaked out of the chamber, and is eavesdropping on him. Petruchio delivers his soliloquy as in Act IV, scene i of the play in which he details his plan to tame her; while Katherine, out of his view, listens. As Petruchio states, "This is a way to kill a wife with kindness," Katherine nods knowingly, smiles, and winks to the camera. What follows is a reversal of the initial wooing scene.

Where Katherine had previously been paralyzed into inaction by her inability to dominate Petruchio, Petruchio is now increasing frustrated by his inability to provoke any reaction out of Katherine. Petruchio's first ploy is to pointedly make a great deal of noise as he reenters the bedroom while Katherine attempts to sleep. He slams the door, trips over a stool, throws it across the room, and coughs loudly while Katherine pretends to be sound asleep. Frustrated at her lack of response, he begins to sing at the top of his lungs. Far from any display of annoyance, she responds to this serenade with a warm round of applause. Frustrated, he opens one of the double windows to their bedroom allowing a deluge of rain and wind to assault the room. Katherine pretends to greatly enjoy this and opens the other window. Lines from Act IV, scene v are displaced to this scene, albeit in a fashioned altered by Taylor's purpose of showing Petruchio's increasing lack of control over the situation. As Petruchio looks out of the bedroom window, saying, "How bright and goodly shines the sun," an interposed cutaway shot has just shown that it is the moon he is, in fact, looking at. After some brief confusion, Katherine states, "What you will have it named, even that it is; and so it shall be still for Katherine."

In Shakespeare's play, Hortensio comments, "Petruchio, go thy ways; the field is won," indicating that this acquiescence on Katherine's part indicates that her taming has been accomplished. In Taylor's film, however, this acquiescence only serves to further frustrate and disorient Petruchio during his first night with his new wife. The early wooing scene depicted Katherine's increasing frustration at her inability to deter Petruchio from his course of action; the later wedding night scene depicts Petruchio's increasing annoyance at his inability to control Katherine in her course of action. She was disorientated at his lack of submission to her dominance; he is disorientated at her submission to his dominance. After pacing back and forth across the room in frustration, he grabs one of the bedsheets and says, "What's this, a spot?" Katherine immediately proceeds to the bed and rips all of the bedclothes from it, strewing them on the floor.

At this point Taylor's wedding night scene moves entirely into the slapstick humor of the Punch and Judy show. Petruchio takes a long drink to calm his nerves, as Katherine makes herself comfortable in the bedclothes strewn on the flow, resting her head against a pillow propped up on the wall. Petruchio yanks the pillow from under her head, causing her to painfully bump her head against the wall. She rises, and a tug of war over the pillow ensues. This leads to a shoving contest, and Petruchio begins to laugh again as Katherine gets increasingly frustrated. Petruchio gives Katherine a violent shove, and she lands hard, seated on the floor. Petruchio's manic laughter prompts Katherine to throw a stool at Petruchio. The stool hits him on the head, and he collapses, moaning. Horrified at what she has done, Katherine runs to him and kneels beside him, crying, "Oh Petruchio, Petruchio, beloved Petruchio." With a huge bruise and cut on his forehead he mutters, "I that have heard lions roar, the rage of an angry boar" as Katherine helps him to bed. (This direct refrain of lines from his introductory scene, where Petruchio seems fearless and impervious to any threat posed by "a woman's tongue," here ironically indicates his acknowledgement and amazement that he could be physically dominated by a woman. Lines are not merely cut in this production, they are also displaced into scenes not anticipated in the seminal play, in order to create new ranges of possibility and meaning.) Seeing his pain, Katherine throws her whip into the fireplace and embraces him tenderly, soothingly saying, "Here." Smiling at her, Petruchio says, "the sun is shining bright," and smiling back at him, she replies, "Aye, the blessed sun."

A fade out and fade in transition brings us in media res to Katherine's famous speech as she states, "Thy husband is thy lord, thy life, thy keeper..." to an astonished group sitting around a dinner table, which includes Baptista, Grumio, Gremio, Hortensio, and Bianca. Petruchio looks at her adoringly; however, any sense that he has tamed her is swiftly diminished by the huge bandage on his head and the blatant wink that Katherine gives to Bianca as she recites the words "serve, love, and obey." Bianca responds by mouthing the word "Oh," nodding her head, and smiling. It is clear at this film's conclusion that it is Petruchio who is tamed, and that Katherine is humoring him by allowing him to appear as the master of the house to the assembled company.

Stephen Buhler (54) has noted that Taylor wished to present Pickford not as America's Sweetheart but rather as a representative of "the New Woman" in her first sound film. It is also significant that Pickford's star power in fact surpassed that of Fairbanks at this point in their respective careers, and that they were widely celebrated in the media as a famous married couple. In Taylor's vision, a true happiness is found in marriage only when the male partner becomes submissive to the female. The final scene ironically displays Petruchio in his final reversal; at his first entrance, he wore a bandana while strutting around the room and loudly proclaiming his dominance over women. In the final scene he is seated, wears an emasculating bandage around his head where the bandana would have been, and smiles silently while Katherine addresses the party. Katherine has not been tamed; rather, through taming Petruchio, she has learned to be dominant within the constraints of the social role of a wife and mother. It is Petruchio's reduction to an infantilized state, as brought about by the impact of a stool to his cranium, which has brought out her maternal instinct, not the assertion of his dominance. Shakespeare's play is presented here, yet subverted. Happiness is not found after Katherine is forced to live under Petruchio's power, it is found after Petruchio is forced to live under Katherine's power.

Although Taylor's film can be called contemporary in its attempt to align its seminal play to reflect the shifting roles of men and women in the early part of the 20th century, the mise-en-scène of the film clearly evokes the Italian Renaissance. Buhler notes that Fairbanks and Pickford "were drawn to this play ... for its visual potential: the sunlit streets of Padua; the sumptuous palazzo of Signor Baptista.... The design is indeed sumptuous, as realized by William Cameron Menzies ... and Laurence Irving" (53–54). The exterior sets of the piazza and Petruchio's home are equally as ornate as the sets of Baptista's home. The peasants who attend the Punch and Judy show and stroll the piazza are clearly wearing Italian Renaissance costumes. The exterior and interior shots of the cathedral are elaborate and ornate, adding a sense of spectacle to the film by showing off sumptuous locales. These elements match the sense of spectacle engendered by Fairbanks' and Pickford's outsized performances, and all of them together permeate the film with an exotic quality. This approach to mise-en-scène was characteristic of Hollywood approaches to Shakespeare's plays during the 1920s and 1930s. Grandiose locales and other conventions of costume drama were unilaterally employed in order to provide audiences with the ornate, exotic scope of escapist cinema, which was so popular at the time of the film's release.

It is not surprising, then, that a similar approach to mise-en-scène characterizes Dieterle and Reinhardt's 1935 film of *A Midsummer Night's Dream*. Although this film was advertised upon its release as "Max Reinhardt's production of *A Midsummer Night's Dream*," publicity material clearly shows Dieterle and Reinhardt working in tandem on the set. Anthony R. Guneratne ("The Politics of Adapting Shakespeare" 44) and Judith Buchanan (*Shakespeare on Film* 128) suggest that Warner Brothers intended this film as a "prestige" production and didn't expect that the film would recover its investment; however, promotional material preceding the film's release shows that it was being marketed as an event that would signal a breakthrough in popular cinema from which there would be no return.

If this film was intended to privilege Reinhardt's vision over Jack Warner's, and to be a film that would "break the mold" of contemporary cinema, then the casting strategy utilized by Warner Brothers seems curiously inconsistent with their goal. Victor Jory, a well-known screen "heavy," was cast in the part of Oberon. James Cagney was interestingly cast against type in the part of Bottom. Cagney was normally associated with gangster roles such as that of Tom Powers in *The Public Enemy*; however, his popularity at the time of release would have attracted audiences to the film. Similarly, Joe E. Brown was one of Hollywood's top ten moneymaking stars at the time of the film's release, and, as a well-known comedian, was cast in the role of Flute. Mickey Rooney, a well-known child star due to the *Mickey McGuire* series of films, was cast in the role of Puck. Although this film is usually associated with Reinhardt's Hollywood Bowl stage production of the play, the casting strategy employed suggests that *A Midsummer Night's Dream* was conceived far more as a mainstream Hollywood film production than it was as an adaptation of a stage play.

From the opening credits of this film onward, an alternating pattern of theatrical and cinematic conventions emerges. After following the theatrical (or operatic) practice of an overture, a series of title cards which posits the film in terms of its relation to the theatre appears. "The Warner Brothers have the pleasure to present A Max Reinhardt production" is written on the first title card, followed by "A Midsummer Night's Dream" on the second title card, and "by William Shakespeare" on the third. The next title card gives the names of the five stars in order of billing following mainstream Hollywood conventions of the star system: James Cagney, Joe E. Brown, Dick Powell, Mickey Rooney, and Victor Jory. After these main credits, however, we are presented with a second set of credits type set in a similar manner to folio editions of The Complete Works of Shakespeare, giving information such as "Hermia, in Love with Lysander" and "Theseus,[2] Duke of Athens" rather than simply giving the name of the character and the actor portraying her or him. Cinematic conventions again are privileged over theatrical conventions, however, when we are presented with a close-up shot of a paper proclamation announcing the acting contest, the shot tilting down a long scroll. The principal players in the film who are associated with the acting contest are Cagney as Bottom and Brown as Flute: the players who have received first and second billing, respectively.

The filmmakers surely anticipated that Elizabethan verse might be difficult for their intended audience; unlike *The Taming of the Shrew*, in which this situation is addressed by reducing the number of characters and lines in the play to less than 25 percent of those in the seminal play, Dieterle and Reinhardt's film utilizes a number of interesting strategies for clarifying relationships and situations. During the opening sequence, in which a multitude of extras sing a patriotic song while clothed in anachronistic Athenian robes (in the later wedding sequences the costuming strategy will shift to medieval garb), a "waving" contest between Lysander and Demetrius as they vie for Hermia's attention is staged. In the same sequence, a pantomime showing Demetrius' obvious annoyance at Helena's attempt to place a garland on his head is also staged. During the portion of the opening sequence in which a love song is sung, close-up shots of Lysander and Hermia singing the song to one another establish their bond; whereas, shots of Lysander and Demetrius are inter-cut when the crowd begins to sing a battle song to establish their rivalry. Later, as the four of them argue in the forest, layered sound tracks are used to reduce their separate disputes into a single unintelligible cacophony, thereby establishing the chaos created by Puck and Oberon's interventions to great comic effect.

Cinematic techniques effectively convey a sense of wonder throughout the diegesis of this film. Sparkling lights are superimposed over the primary images, giving a sense of tiny fairies constantly dancing in the air in the scenes when Oberon and Titania are present. The special effects sequence which realizes the fairy ballet is remarkable by standards of the time; the fairies materialize from the mist and ascend a luminous spiral into the sky. Bottom's transformation is presented on screen using a series of lap dissolves to represent his metamorphosis from a man into an ass, and Titania is backlit to give the sense of an ethereal glow to her hair. Oberon is lit with his face half in shadow to convey a sense of menace to his character. Yet the techniques of theatrical practice are also in evidence. There is a gnome orchestra which initially plays for the Changeling Boy. The gnomes are omnipresent through the forest sequence suggesting an implied orchestra pit. One extended ballet sequence accompanies the materialization of the fairies, and another accompanies their later dematerialization while Oberon and Titania undertake a stately march toward one another. In accordance to theatrical practice, the film contains a ten-minute intermission. *A Midsummer Night's Dream* is the progenitor of many subsequent representations of Shakespeare in the cinema which would represent neither cinema nor theatre exclusively, but would rather represent a point of nexus between the two.

One trope well represented in Dieterle and Reinhardt's film which overlaps both stage and film traditions in the classical Hollywood period is that of the stately march. It is employed three times: first comically, as Titania, Bottom and Titania's attendants march to their love nest accompanied by Mendelssohn's wedding march; then solemnly, as Oberon, Titania and all the fairies of the forest march to celebrate the cessation of their dispute; and finally joyously, at the awakening of the newly established couples and their return to Athens to be married.

This trope is also well represented in George Cukor's 1936 film of *Romeo and Juliet*, which opens with two stately marches which combine drums and a chorus of "Alleluia's" in much the same way that Reinhardt's film followed its framing sequence with an opening march of singing Athenians. In Cukor's film two parades converge upon each other, one comprised of Capulets and the other of Montagues. The two families are marching to church in formal parades, and although members of each family glare at each other across the street from time to time, the elders of either family seem determined to keep the peace.

Other strategies also serve to align the two films. Dieterle and Reinhardt's use of the frame of the scroll to provide context for the action of the film is paralleled by Cukor's decision to frame his film with a tapestry come to life. We are shown an establishing shot of a tapestry; the tapestry portrays an image of a chorus standing on a stage, holding a scroll. This dissolves into a shot of an actor playing a chorus, standing on stage, holding a scroll, reciting the prologue. Cukor's credits also posit his film at a nexus of cinematic and theatrical conventions. The first title card reads "Leslie Howard and Norma Shearer in," and features a woodcut of Shakespeare in the lower right corner. The second title card gives the name of the film, and the transition between all title cards is achieved by having each succeeding title card roll down the screen in front of the previous card like a curtain or a scroll. Cukor also follows a strategy similar to those of Taylor and Dieterle and Reinhardt in casting his film. Romeo was played by Leslie Howard, who at the time was recognized as a romantic lead, and whose performance in *The Scarlet Pimpernel* associated him with foppery that masks a large capacity for decisive action. Howard's performance in *The Petrified Forest* also associated him with romanticism or intellectualism accompanied with a willingness to give one's own life for the benefit of his beloved. Juliet was played by Norma Shearer, whose performance in *The Divorcee*, among other films, established her persona as that of a woman who would resist social mores regarding sexual relationships. Tybalt was played by Basil Rathbone, who in the period prior to the first Sherlock Holmes mystery was established as a sinister, sword-wielding villain with impeccable diction and pronunciation. Mercutio was played by John Barrymore, who was recognized as the patriarch of the Barrymore clan and the greatest Hamlet and Richard III of his time.

Unfortunately, Howard, Shearer, Rathbone, and Barrymore were 42, 36, 44, and 54 years old at the time of filming, rendering the appropriateness of the studio's choice in casting them questionable. In "Romeo and Juliet," Emanuel Levy notes that Cukor was rumored to have difficulty controlling Barrymore's alcoholism during production. In "Screen Saver," Noah Isenberg notes that Thalberg hired Professor William Strunk of Cornell University, telling him, "Your job is to protect Shakespeare from us." Despite the hiring of Strunk, the film is disrupted by the portrayal of Peter by Andy Devine, a gifted comic actor whose performance style (he is perhaps best known for his performance as Link Appleyard in *The Man Who Shot Liberty Valance*) was unfortunately incompatible with Elizabethan dialogue. (One is also led to wonder how diligently Strunk was instructed to enforce his protection of the play, given that Friar Laurence doesn't appear until the mid-point of the film, Romeo's first speech to Juliet at the balcony is cut from 25 lines to eight lines, and his second is cut from seven lines to three.)

However, the film includes some impressive and interesting moments. Romeo and Juliet are both introduced to us with pastoral images. Juliet is feeding a deer when we first see her, and Romeo is observing a shepherd tending to sheep. These pastoral images exist in sharp contrast to Verona, which is portrayed in the film as a bustling Renaissance metropolis, much as Padua was depicted in Taylor's film: people energetically go about their business and street acrobats perform for passerby. An interesting effect is achieved in aligning Mercutio with this cosmopolitan energy. Although Barrymore's performance seems deliberately over the top, Mercutio is consistently depicted as a person in need of the attention of an audience. When he is not mugging for his friends—as in the Queen Mab speech—he mugs for an audience of women who congregate on a balcony above his favorite courtyard. His death is preceded by a final depiction of these women in the courtyard; they seem to have lost their energy, and Mercutio seems to have lost his. This moment of malaise in the courtyard occurs immediately after Romeo and Juliet's wedding, which is transformed from Shakespeare's secret ceremony in Friar Laurence's cell to a full church service accompanied by the chanting of a choir on the soundtrack, dissolving to shots of bells ringing, and various pastoral images of suns rising and streams flowing. This visual strategy seems to suggest that the pastoral world of the film and the metropolitan world of the film conflict with one another.

The casting of Howard as Romeo also has interesting implications for the Capulet's ball scene. An extended dance scene is presented in which Romeo is rapt as he first sees Juliet. Romeo here is the passive onlooker. This is Juliet's "coming out" ball at which she is supposed to be introduced to her future husband, Paris. Juliet meets Paris on the dance floor but her gaze immediately shifts to the standing Romeo, and she begins to leave the dance floor, moving toward him. Romeo only approaches Juliet at the conclusion of the dance scene when it's clear to him that she also notices him. Juliet is the instigator of their relationship.

Two weeks following the release of Cukor's *Romeo and Juliet*, Paul Czinner's film of *As You Like It* was released. Like Cukor's film, Czinner's also featured frequent non-diegetic singing on the soundtrack, and was filmed on an equally grand scale: Russell Jackson notes, in "Filming *As You

Like It: A Playful Comedy Becomes a Problem," that the forest set was, at 300 feet long, the largest set ever constructed in a British studio. Czinner was married to Elizabeth Bergner, who had performed the role of Rosalind more than 600 times on the German stage before being forced to flee the Nazis. Although, at 39 years of age, Bergner was an established stage star,[3] Czinner's film seems a precursor of things to come in many ways: the score was written by a composer named William Walton, the film was edited by a filmmaker named David Lean, and Orlando was played by an actor named Laurence Olivier.

Czinner's film anticipates in significant ways the approaches later utilized by Olivier and Welles in bringing their adaptations of Shakespeare to the screen. Although, like Dieterle and Reinhardt and Cukor, Czinner uses standard mainstream film grammar, his film occasionally ventures into the realm of non-realistic filmmaking through its employment of stage conventions. Although Bergner wears exactly the same outfit to signify Ganymede as she had during the stage run of the play, the tunic and tights that Rosalind wears here to disguise herself as Ganymede are not nearly as effective in concealing her gender in close up shots as they were to the third balcony.[4] If Rosalind truly is the love of Orlando's life, in the close proximity and realism which cinema implies it seems unlikely that he would not recognize her. Although also effective on stage, on film the deep voice that Bergner uses to affect Ganymede would convince the majority of people in the audience of nothing more than the fact that Rosalind had developed a bad cold. The majority of Bergner's film roles had been in German productions, at that point in her career, which implies that the British audience for Czinner's film would have familiar with Bergner because of her association with the stage, and with the role of Rosalind. This suggests that the intended audience for Czinner's film was expected to be familiar with the play, and that the ineffectiveness of the Ganymede's costume and voice in concealing the identity of Rosalind shatters the realism of the film in order to achieve a humorous effect.

In addition to this potential for irony in the depiction of Rosalind/Ganymede, Czinner employs many uniquely filmic techniques to shatter the realism of this film. Czinner employs rapid swish pans to depict the dialogue detailing the three declarations of "And I for Phebe/And I for Ganymede/And I for Rosalind/And I for no woman." As the characters are placed from screen left to screen right in the order of Silvius, Phebe, Rosalind/Ganymede, and Orlando, the effect at each refrain is for the camera to quickly pan right from Silvius to Phebe, to quickly pan right from Phebe to Orlando, and then to quickly pan back left from Orlando to Rosalind/Ganymede; the latent "gag" in the scene here underscored by the movement of the camera. For his final sequence, Czinner's cast moves back inside the city gates from the forest for the business preceding the nuptials, which is followed by a public song of joy on the soundtrack in accordance with the conventions employed by Dieterle and Reinhardt and Cukor. Czinner's camera dollies away from the crowd through the city gates, which swing closed to reveal that the legend "Epilogue" is mounted on top of them. Rosalind stands in front of this tableau, and delivers the epilogue. As she does so, a series of dissolves is utilized to present her costume as transforming at will from that of Rosalind to that of Ganymede, and back again. Although in many ways the most "filmic" of the works under discussion, Czinner's film utilizes techniques specific to film to find analogues for the theatrical experience. Rosalind's walk from the realism of the town set to the theatricality of the epilogue set anticipates the journey that Olivier's *Henry V* would soon take from the realism of the Globe Stage to the theatricality of his film world.

Just as conventions surrounding release length allowed filmmakers who represented Shakespeare's plays to encompass the entire narrative of a given work as opposed to focusing on specific elements, the availability of recorded dialogue in films allowed filmmakers to represent Shakespeare's poetry more completely than had been possible through title cards. Representations of Shakespeare on film, however, were not automatically freed from the economic context of filmmaking; rather, they were constructed in a manner consistent with the prevailing conventions of mainstream Hollywood filmmaking. Star image, opulence in mise-en-scène, and insertions of song and dance sequences not found in the seminal play are conventions imposed upon these four films by the production context in which they were made. These conventions facilitate the intended audiences' readings of these works as contemporary films rather than antiquated plays. Ironically, the film that is the most reductive in its approach to its seminal play is the most strikingly effective; Taylor's *The Taming of the Shrew* manages to find a highly effective balance between its seminal play and its contemporary conventions. Dieterle and Reinhardt's *A Midsummer Night's Dream* remains an effective film by contemporary standards. The special effects techniques employed are aesthetically beautiful while also dreamlike in quality, and the pantomimes employed outside of dialogue are effective in clarifying relationships in addition to being quite amusing. If rigid adherence to the convention of star image in many ways limits the effectiveness of Cukor's *Romeo and Juliet*, its juxtaposition of the pastoral against the metropolitan and its specific use of Leslie Howard's star image still render it worthy of discussion as an attempt to adapt Shakespeare to the cinema by using the tropes of the "classical Hollywood period." Czinner's *As You Like It*, although again limited in its effectiveness by its use of the stage convention of clothing Rosalind in a tunic and having her speak in a lower voice when disguised as Ganymede, again proves worthy of interest in its audacious violations of the conventions of cinematic realism in a manner that precurses the films of Olivier and Welles.

All of these films utilize grandiose, spectacular sets, elaborate costumes, and associate themselves through star image with traditions of the costume drama or the theatre. The use of Fairbanks in *The Taming of the Shrew* and of Leslie Howard in *Romeo and Juliet* associates these films with costume dramas contemporary to their release, whereas the association of Reinhardt with *A Midsummer Night's Dream*, and Czinner and Bergner with *As You Like It* associates these films with mainstream, spectacular theatrical productions. The sense of adventure and romance located in an exotic locale is reflected in individual performances in each of these films. Petruchio's exaggerated and over-determined rolling of the "r" in the word "grapple"; Theseus' consistent vocalization of the trilled "r," Dieterle and Reinhardt's use of the operatic conventions of the overture and intermezzo, Howard's exciting and extended sword fights with both Basil Rathbone and Ralph Forbes (Paris), and Mackenzie Ward's egregiously exaggerated jester's headdress (as Touchstone) all are consistent with the extremes and exaggerations of behavior that characterize the costume drama. All four films are consistent in their resolution of the tension of the visual and the word. The exotic proportions of each production mandate that the visual is ascendant in each film; however, each film also deliberately points back not only to its roots in the word, but also to its roots in the theatre. Although *The Taming of the Shrew* utilizes the grandiose sets and exaggerated performance style of the costume drama, the third name and image we see in the film are those of William Shakespeare, whose likeness is displayed in the third title card during the opening credits. The film also begins with a depiction of a Punch and Judy show being shown in a puppet theatre in a public space, clearly aligning the film with an anachronistic mode of theatre. *A Midsummer Night's Dream* is spectacular in its set design and in its use of special effects, yet begins with a close-up shot which tilts down so the audience may read a royal proclamation, utilizes an overture to announce the film is soon to begin, and an intermezzo which is played while a title card indicates that an intermission has been reached. *Romeo and Juliet* also uses sumptuous sets, art direction, and a gowned formal waltz that does not appear in the play; however, the film begins with a tapestry that comes to life and depicts the chorus standing on a stage while reading the induction from a scroll. *As You Like It* was filmed on a set representing the Forest of Arden that was not only realistic, but what was then the largest set ever constructed in Britain. However, its final shot depicts a camera dollying back through a gate which closes to reveal a sign that says "Epilogue," as Bergner emerges on screen to deliver the epilogue in soliloquy, directly to the camera. Although each of these films privileges the visual and appeals directly to its contemporary audience, each film acknowledges its relationship to the textual and to the theatre.

CHAPTER 3

Olivier and Welles

Olivier and Welles are frequently considered as near rivals by critics. For example, Stephen Buhler argues that both auteurs were attempting to revitalize a declining actor/manager tradition by displacing that tradition from theatrical repertory companies to cinematic repertory companies, with each of them occupying the actor/manager position in their respective companies (96). Buhler further argues that "Olivier constantly looks back at theatre; Orson Welles constantly glances at Olivier as a rival claimant to the Shakespearean mantle" (*ibid.*). This overly simplistic analysis is seemingly reinforced by the fact that these directors tended to operate from opposite extremes of the continuum of mainstream cinematic auteurs. Olivier's adaptations of Shakespeare in the cinema were well financed. Welles' Shakespeare films were made on shoestring budgets, and Welles would frequently take on acting assignments in other directors' films in order to finance his own. There may also be a tendency to align Olivier's films with a tradition of "classicism" with roots in the British theatre, whereas Welles is often considered a "maverick"[1] in his approach to film and the theatre. In attempting to construct this "rivalry" narrative, Buhler fails to appreciate that the approaches taken to Shakespeare's plays by Olivier and Welles bear striking similarities.

Silent cinema found its initial voice for the representation of Shakespeare's plays by focusing on a central element of a given play that would be widely recognized, and dramatizing that element. Sound films made prior to the Second World War had found strategies to represent Shakespeare's plays through the deployment of "star" images and through the use of medium specific properties. Regarding Czinner's *As You Like It*, Russell Jackson, in "Filming *As You Like It*: A Playful Comedy Becomes a Problem" has noted that critical discussion at the time of its release was framed "largely in terms of the appropriateness of adapting Shakespeare ... [and]

the extent to which it might be expected to succeed as popular entertainment." In other words, the critical and financial reaction to pre–World War II sound film adaptations of Shakespeare is in many ways attributable to a sense of film as an "upstart" medium unequal to the task of representing the greatness of this source material. Olivier and Welles avoided this trap by utilizing a strategy of contextualizing Shakespeare's plays with countertexts that serve to query and critique the seminal play. Olivier's *Henry V* and Welles' *Macbeth* preoccupy themselves with the nature of the dramatic illusion. Olivier's *Hamlet* and Welles' *Othello* present their protagonists as characters who naively believe that their actions and fates result from their exercise of individual agency; however, the destinies of their main characters are arbitrarily mandated by the demands of a play that the characters fail to perceive themselves as immersed in. Both *Hamlet* and *Othello* also present their mise-en-scène as a non-negotiable labyrinth through which their protagonists unknowingly propel themselves toward their respective fates. Olivier contextualizes *Richard III* within the performance history of its seminal play, depicting Richard in his rise as a master dramatist, and in his decline as a dramatist who has lost his audience. Welles structures *Chimes at Midnight* around texts[2] that provide conflicting information regarding the details and meanings of historical events.

Olivier's first attempt at representing a Shakespearean play in the cinema earned him the distinction of being the first auteur of the cinema to produce a Shakespeare film that was simultaneously a critical and financial success. The film's positive reception by critics is largely due to the audacity of Olivier's approach whereas its generation of revenue is aligned with timeliness: *The Chronicle History of King Henry the Fift* [sic] *with His Battell Fought at Agincourt in France* was filmed from 1943 to 1944 and released in England in November 1944 (shortly after the D-Day invasions). Olivier approaches the seminal play by embedding it in a cinematic depiction of a dramatization of *Henry V* at the Globe Theatre, thereby sidestepping the objection of depicting Shakespeare's work in an inadequate and upstart medium. Olivier here provides us with an illusion of cinema as wholly conjoined with the theatrical experience: sets are constructed and lenses are utilized which provide cinematic analogues for a live performance. For example, in the scenes depicting the Battle of Agincourt, the use of landscape photography might threaten the illusion that what unfolds is aligned with theatre rather than cinema. Zoom lenses are utilized, thus giving the background a "compressed" appearance that implies a theatrical "backdrop" to an obviously "real" landscape. This visual strategy cannot be characterized as simply "looking back to the theater" (Buhler 96) because Olivier is here utilizing properties specific both to film and to theatre to create a new form of hybrid experience. In utilizing this approach to cinematography Olivier also avoided a common objection to both Dieterle and Reinhardt's and Czinner's films. In "Filming *As You Like It*: A Playful Comedy Becomes a Problem," Russell Jackson argues that the painstaking realism with which the sets of Dieterle and Reinhardt's and Czinner's films were constructed created "a new kind of hyper-reality" in which the viewer senses that they are witnessing a "believable unreality." Olivier's film, dramatized within the frame of a theatrical performance at the Globe, eschews the "self-consciously elaborated 'realism'" employed by Reinhardt and Czinner.

There is a critical consensus that *Henry V* is a propaganda film, and is not unlike Eisenstein's *Alexander Nevsky* in eliciting unqualified admiration for its hero. Like Eisenstein's portrayal of Nevsky, Olivier's character of Henry V is presented as morally infallible. Michael Manheim's observation, in "The English History Play on Screen," that "Olivier cuts most of the action revealing the violent side of Henry's nature—his threats before Harfleur, his hanging of Bardolph, his command to kill the prisoners" (122) is consistent with Olivier's depiction of an entirely bloodless battle of Harfleur: "We are flooded with cinematic contrivances insisted upon by the popular heroic film: cuts from advancing horsemen, to spruce drummers, to archers with bows raised, to the king with his sword on high ready to give the command to shoot, to a magnificent tableau of battle itself ... culminating in the hero's victory over the evil knight. All these effects invite the film audience to relish the victory and its splendid achiever. But all these effects add to the effect of something manufactured to please" (Manheim 124).

In *Alexander Nevsky*, Eisenstein's Huns are graphically depicted at an early point in the film as throwing naked babies into a fire. Of *Henry V*, Alan Stone, in "For God and Country," writes, "So the audience will share his righteous anger, Olivier has the French act first, attacking the boys and the luggage. He presents this episode as led by the cowardly French dauphin, who thus becomes the embodiment of the evil enemy." Although Stone continues to dismiss Olivier's *Henry V* as "a treacly fairy tale," Mannheim believes that it uses the guise of a propaganda film to provide a sophisticated discourse on using the devices of the Machiavel in order to rule effectively: "His Henry is ... the perfect embodiment of the new Machiavellian prince—not a figure to be hated, feared, and scorned ... but one who could strengthen and preserve the state ... in his efforts to create the image of a victorious wartime leader for a country at war in a noble cause, Olivier ... created what is probably the sole instance in drama of what Machiavelli really had in mind—and he did it by means of the medium most suited to the creation of illusionism" (125).

Combining the views of Mannheim with those of Jackson reveals a fresh insight: Olivier's *Henry V* utilizes the dramatic illusion of a theatrical performance in order to subtly query the ideological illusion of the "good" Machiavellian leader. Although Olivier's film presents Henry V as "the great good King" whose appearance is without blemish and whose victories are without bloodletting, in the final analysis this King is an actor in makeup who coughs nervously before entering the stage to play his part. In "Diachronic Design in Olivier's *Henry V*" (an unpublished paper presented at the 2009 annual PCA/ACA conference) Howard Schmidt discusses Olivier's insistence on the visual disparity between the physical appearances of the two characters played by him. The first is the appearance of the actor portraying Henry V on stage, whose face is conspicuously covered with heavy stage makeup and whose hairstyle includes sideburns which extend about an inch below the tops of his ears. The second is the idealized image of Henry V we see once the film has rejected the confines of the Globe Theatre setting, whose makeup is now naturalistic and whose hairstyle now includes bangs and is cut far above his ears. This disparity between the actor we see backstage and the idealized King we see presented on the stage suggests that Olivier's film, although normally associated with wartime propaganda, utilizes the frame of the production of the Globe ultimately as a means of querying the propaganda behind the image of "the great good king." Where Machiavelli advised his prince to portray an illusion in order to consolidate power, Olivier here implicitly dramatizes the process by which princes who consolidate their power portray illusions in their popular culture. Olivier's *Henry V* demonstrates and critiques the ability of the propaganda apparatus to conjure idealized images in the minds of the members of the audience. In many ways, this critique anticipates Welles' juxtaposition of disparate texts in order to reveal the propaganda apparatus behind "official historical records" in *Chimes at Midnight*.

Like Olivier's *Henry V*, Welles' *Macbeth* challenges many of the conventions of realist cinema that were current to its 1948 release, in order to instigate reflection on the nature of the dramatic illusion. Welles utilized the set of a serial entitled *The Perils of Nyoka* as the mise-en-scène of this production, and further exploited this overdetermined mise-en-scène by utilizing equally overdetermined properties and costumes. (The influence of German Expressionism is clearly shown by Macbeth's crown, which is a huge wooden square punctuated with spikes that jut upwards from each of its four corners; the passages and halls of his castle, which are indistinguishable from a cavern; and his huge wooden spear, which connects to a circular hub from which wooden spikes radiate.) The effect of the overdetermined mise-en-scène, costumes and properties is to permeate the film with a sense of theatrical artificiality which is central to Welles' interpretation of *Macbeth*.

The film begins with the Weird Sisters over the cauldron as depicted in Act IV, scene i of the play. However, the Weird Sisters are not preparing a potion, they are preparing a voodoo doll of Macbeth. Similarly, at the close of Welles' film Macbeth's death is depicted with a rapid cut to the image of the voodoo doll being beheaded. When Macbeth conjures the Weird Sisters in order to ascertain how great a threat MacDuff poses, the apparent naturalism of the horizon behind Macbeth is subverted by lightning that casts reflections of trees against a cyclorama. As these reflections appear behind Macbeth's back, he cannot see them. This lighting effect augments a countertext in this film in which Macbeth believes himself to be an autonomous character attempting to gain control over his destiny, when he is in fact entirely a creation of the Weird Sisters, and his actions are entirely determined by their manipulations.

The disparity between Macbeth's autonomous self-definition and his reality as a pawn of the Weird Sisters is reinforced through the set design of the film. The majority of the screen time in this film is set in the courtyard of Macbeth's castle, the dimensions of which Welles consistently defines and reinforces throughout the film through a series of establishing shots. Macbeth's throne sits on a platform opposite the entrance to the courtyard space, giving an impression of a proscenium stage or space for actors. Every course of action that Macbeth undertakes in this film is initiated when he is within this courtyard space. Here, he acts as a type of dramatist in order to direct the events regarding his destiny. Conversely, those occasions which reveal that his attempts to control his fate have proven ineffective are set in the caverns which radiate from the courtyard space. He retreats when confronted with the reality that he is far more directed than a director. This movement from the courtyard as the locale of his director status to the caverns as the locale of his directed status is reflected in Welles' staging of Act V, scenes vi-viii. Macbeth is prominent in the courtyard space until he realizes that Burnham Wood has indeed come to high Dunsinane, at which point he retreats into the caverns pursued by MacDuff. He emerges once more into the courtyard, where he finds that MacDuff was "untimely ripped" from his mother's womb. A long shot of the Weird Sisters, now revealed to Macbeth to be in a position to observe him, coupled with their reiteration of the phrase "untimely ripped" causes him to realize the extent to which he has been manipulated by them. This realization spurs him to a final retreat into the cavern, where in a last attempt to regain control of his destiny he decides to fight MacDuff, and is killed. The pre-eminence of Weird Sisters as the authors of his being and destiny is ultimately reinforced by their final utterance "the charm's wound up" as the screen fades to black, suggesting that all of the events of the film have occurred under their control.

Released five months prior to Welles' *Macbeth*, Olivier's *Hamlet* presents a similar visual and aural countertext to that utilized by Welles. Olivier's film begins with a pre-credit logo presented on a title card, accompanied with the sounds of an orchestra tuning up, again—as in *Henry V*—aligning his film with a theatrical experience. After the credit sequence, which depicts Elsinore as an island surrounded by an angry sea, we are presented with an image of a model that depicts the design of a set representing the platform at Elsinore, which dissolves to a visual text and Olivier's reading of Act I, scene iv, lines 23–28. We again dissolve to the platform at Elsinore which shows us the body of Hamlet being borne by an honor guard, accompanied by Olivier's reading, "This is the tragedy of a man who could not make up his mind." These visual and aural countertexts at the film's onset establish that Hamlet's destiny, like Macbeth's, is entirely preordained and—as implied by the orchestral tuning, the set model, and Olivier's choice of the word "tragedy"—is a matter of dramatic necessity.

In "Olivier, Hamlet, and Freud," Peter Donaldson has suggested a Freudian reading of this film in which he reads "Hamlet's final 'success' as a kind of self-destruction" (123). Donaldson's use of the term "success" here refers to resolution of the Oedipus complex and the establishment of a differentiated personality. In the context of post–Second World War culture, a far more nihilistic reading of Olivier's film seems warranted in which the central conflict is not Oedipal but rather between Eros and Thanatos, a central theme of the period.[3] The initial scene in which Hamlet's body is first presented, the first appearance of the ghost of Hamlet's father, Hamlet's abortive suicide attempt and the final bearing of his body are all depicted in the ramparts of the castle. The bulk of the action of this film is depicted in the lower chambers of the castle. Hamlet appears incongruous in a Renaissance-styled tunic, tights, and carefully coiffed haircut which together stand in stark contrast to the medieval robes and affectations worn by the majority of the other inhabitants of Elsinore, which, in this film, stands in roughshod isolation from the rest of the world. Hamlet's effeminate personality in this film indicates an underdeveloped ego which is incapable of dealing with threats to the psyche, either interior or exterior. Although in his mode of dress Hamlet most closely resembles his idealized self, Horatio, we find late in the film that his dress also resembles that of Osric, whom he perceives as a buffoon. Hamlet's doom in this film is preordained by his lack of psychological insight into himself and his situation; a situation analogous to that which many artists and filmmakers felt faced humankind in the immediate post-war period. Olivier's Hamlet fails to make up his mind because he is incapable of comprehending his mind.

In "Hamlet, Macbeth and King Lear on film," J. Lawrence Guntner suggests that the elaborate camera movements through archways, stairways and the halls of Elsinore represent the audience's journey through Hamlet's convoluted and incomprehensible psyche (118). Olivier's visual strategy in *Hamlet* insists on the recurring motif of a journey up and down stairs. Shots are often reframed to indicate a shift in point of view.[4] Ophelia at one point—through the use of a dissolve—appears to materialize into an archway out of thin air. The sequence depicting Hamlet's instructions to the players features extensive use of cameo lighting.[5] These elements, coupled with the mist that enshrouds the ramparts of Olivier's Elsinore, give this *Hamlet* the sensibilities of a dream. Although the pre-credit sequence and the initial shots and titles announce the artifice of the theatre, Olivier's *Hamlet* moves from the theatre to a sophisticated utilization of cinematic techniques, which again proves Buhler's analysis of Olivier's visual strategy to be overly simplistic at best.

Also heavily influenced by post-war thought, Welles' 1952 film of *Othello* again presents its audience with a would-be master dramatist who is naively unaware that his attempts to assert his autonomous agency merely serve to direct him to a preordained fate. Although there are no characters in this film—supernatural or otherwise—directing Iago to unwittingly ensnare himself in his attempts to ensnare Othello and Desdemona, Welles presents us with a pre-credit sequence depicting the funerals of Othello and Desdemona, and the caging and hoisting of Iago up onto the ramparts of Cyprus. This pre-credit sequence, coupled with many shot-reverse shot patterns of both Othello and Iago through bars, window frames, and nets throughout the course of the film suggest again that Iago's attempts to empower himself through his manipulation of Othello and Roderigo merely accelerate him toward a pre-determined conclusion which he cannot avoid. This is further confirmed by Welles' presentation of Iago's utterance that he will "make the net that shall enmesh them all." Although Iago is referring to Othello, Desdemona, Cassio, and Roderigo, the large steel cage that the audience is already aware of through the pre-credit sequence as Iago's future prison hangs over Iago's head in the shot. Our awareness of the cage that is unseen by Iago as he finalizes his plans to destroy the other characters confirms our sense that he is unwittingly destroying himself, and that his fate is unavoidable.

Where Welles presents Dunsinane as a clearly defined space in *Macbeth*, Cyprus is presented in *Othello* as a virtually impenetrable maze, with doorways leading to underground rivers, walkways that intersect back upon themselves, hidden underground passageways, and twisting stairways which align Welles' Cyprus with Rossellini's *Stromboli*.[6] In Rossellini's 1949 film, Karin—like Iago—is entrapped by her efforts to empower and extricate herself from a disenfranchised position. A former Lithuanian socialite, she agrees to marry a fisherman in order to escape life in an internment camp at the end of the Second World War. Far from liberating her, her decision consigns her to a barren, brutal and isolated life on the island of Stromboli. In "No Place Like Home: Stromboli," according to Mike Hertenstein, "in *Stromboli*, the calculating Karin has made a miscalculation, and ends marooned on a forbidding, virtually desert isle." Like Rossellini's Stromboli, Welles' Cyprus is presented as an intensely elemental place—Rossellini's Stromboli is a barren rock topped by an active volcano, whereas Welles' Cyprus is constantly buffeted by high winds and waves, as is the platform at Olivier's Elsinore. Regarding *Stromboli*, Hertenstein notes, "One of the most devastating images we get in the film is the shot of Karin, who already feels trapped in Stromboli, racing to nowhere among the mazelike passageways of the village." Similarly, John Collick notes, in his brief analysis of Welles' *Othello* in *Shakespeare, Cinema and Society*, that Othello's world has "dissolved into labyrinths and fragments" (133). Collick later notes, in reference to Olivier's *Hamlet*, that Elsinore is represented in Olivier's film "as a large, chiaroscuro labyrinth ... [which] traps the protagonists in a maze of walls and staircases" (135). This suggests that Welles is utilizing a contemporary trope of entrapment in a maze in order to query the play's presentation of Iago as a would-be master dramatist. Just as Karin's efforts to improve her situation increasingly entrap her, and Hamlet's efforts to ensnare Claudius eventually destroy him, Iago's efforts to ensnare Othello ultimately lead to his own entrapment.

Like his other two Shakespeare films, Olivier's 1955 film of *Richard III* announces its theatrical pedigree at the onset, listing David Garrick and Colley Cibber, among other of the play's adaptors from over the centuries in the credit sequence. Olivier's *Richard III* also—like *Henry V* and *Hamlet*—shifts from the techniques of the theatre to those of the cinema.

After the opening sequence, which depicts the coronation ceremony from *3 Henry VI*, the camera trucks through a doorway to reveal an extreme long shot of Richard, standing by Edward IV's throne. The camera assumes a static position at eye level, observing Richard in the background, much like a member of a live theatre audience would. As he speaks, Richard approaches the camera, and once more retreats into the background, while the static position of the camera emphasizes the sense that the audience is witnessing a live theatre performance. Richard approaches the camera a second time; as he walks forward, the extreme long-shot he is initially filmed from is transformed into a mid-shot, and from that point in the sequence the camera—and the audience—follows Richard. Every new scene in which Richard appears will feature him in an establishing mid-shot, reinforcing the audience's sense that the medium of cinema has allowed the boundary of the proscenium arch to be crossed. Like Welles' presentation of Iago in *Othello*, Olivier presents Richard as a master dramatist who addresses the audience directly in soliloquy, advising us as to how he intends to develop his plans. During a scene in which Richard strolls along a balcony relating his plans to us, cinema evolves into meta-cinema as Richard casually opens windows in the foreground to allow the audience to see through them into the background (which depicts Edward IV accusing Clarence of treason) and assess the impact of his schemes. In this moment, Richard not only is an actor responsible for communicating the play to us, he is the cinema director responsible for conveying the image to us.

In *Filming Shakespeare's Plays*, Anthony Davies argues that Olivier here presents Richard as a "grotesque parody" (78–79) of his Henry. Manheim, in "The English History Play on Screen," argues that this Richard represents the Machiavellian prince who is to be "hated, feared and scorned" (125). In "Olivier's *Richard III*: A Reevaluation," Constance Brown states that Olivier intended *Richard III* as a portrait of tyranny (134); the appropriateness of this allegory is demonstrated by the historical realities of Hitler's rise to power. The examples of Riefenstahl's *Triumph des Willens* and *Olympia* demonstrate the effectiveness of Hitler's manipulations of media in facilitating the rise of fascism. Ann-Marie Barry writes, "At the beginning of *Triumph of the Will* when Hitler emerges from the clouds and, standing, rides through the city in his open car, sunlight dances on him. Low-angle close-ups of his hand outstretched in the Nazi salute are particularly effective as light seems to emanate *from* them" (295). The visual strategy of Riefenstahl's film here seems to suggest that Hitler is a deity associated with the sun. Olivier's cinematography supports this association of political power with the ability to propagandize. Richard's rise is associated with his "control of the camera." After Buckingham's revolt, Richard has no soliloquies that are directly addressed to the audience. His decline is emblematized by his loss of control of the medium which allows him to function as a propagandizer. *Richard III* also demonstrates the influence of film noir in its foreshadowing of Richard's eventual doom, at the moment that he believes he has realized his bid for power. As Richard is proclaimed king he descends from a balcony using a bell-rope. The bell begins to chime as Richard demands that Buckingham and Catesby, his former partners in scheming, kiss his hand and descend to their knees to genuflect at him. An ominous chord is repeated on the soundtrack as Richard revels in his achievement, unaware that behind him, the bell rope is dancing around in a position directly behind his neck. Like Welles' Iago and his own *Hamlet*, the moment of Richard's success also initiates the moment of his doom.

Welles' *Chimes at Midnight* establishes countertexts as a means of querying Shakespearean plays in a much more radical fashion. The film juxtaposes three disparate texts against one another. Ralph Richardson's voiceover narrations from Holinshed's *Chronicles* represent what might be called "an official historical record." Welles' drastically reconfigured adaptation of five Shakespearean plays constitutes the primary narrative structure of the film, which is related to us from the perspectives of both Prince Hal and Falstaff. However, a visual countertext further supplies a third perspective which presents the consequences suffered by people who, willingly or unwillingly, obstruct the dominant political agendas of the sociohistorical period represented in the film.

The juxtaposition of these perspectives is established within the first five minutes of the film. We initially hear a wistful tune played on a recorder accompanied by a visual image of a pristine, snow-covered landscape dominated by a bare tree in the foreground. Falstaff and Shallow warmly reminisce as they approach and enter Shallow's house. The ethereal beauty of the landscape is supplanted by a sense of warmth as Shallow and Falstaff sit in front of the fire. As they proceed from the landscape to the fireplace, the two characters enact a drastically idealized and abbreviated version of Act III, scene ii from *2 Henry IV*, which ends while Falstaff smiles and says, "We have heard the chimes at midnight, Master Robert Shallow," to which Shallow enthusiastically replies, "That we have, that we have, that we have. In faith, Sir John, we have." This elegiac prologue sequence is immediately followed by the credit sequence, where the wistful music of the recorder on the soundtrack gives way to the energetic music of drum and flute. We are then presented with a series of shots not found in any of Shakespeare's plays: a shot of the Boar's Head tavern, followed by men riding swiftly on horseback, and a column of soldiers struggling to march against a harsh, winter wind. We are then shown a shot depicting five hanged prisoners swaying on a gallows while men stand on the ground below them menacingly brandishing clubs; this shot is accompanied by the title, "Narration Based On Holinshed's Chronicles Spoken By Ralph Richardson." This image couples the perspective of the official historical record with oppression and brutality directed against those who oppose the agenda that it represents. A narrative disparity is thus created between the idyllic winter depicted in the prologue sequence and the harsh and brutal winter presented in the credit sequence. This narrative disparity is the structural principle of the film.

The battle sequence represents the second, and the major, depiction of the consequences suffered by those who oppose their contemporary dominant political agenda in the film. Previous to the battle sequence, Welles has already shown Falstaff's conscripts to us. Although the narrative structure of the film is concerned chiefly with the personal histories of some ten people, it is only Falstaff and his entourage that we see throughout the course of the battle sequence. Although this battle sequence forms the structural and emotional center of the film, the four characters in the diegesis of the film that have the most to win or lose depending on its outcome are nowhere to be seen. What we do see, amid graphic depictions of the fates of the anonymous soldiers in this battle, are brief and repeated shots of Falstaff, Bardolph, Pistol, Nym, and the page scurrying to avoid danger. In the aftermath of Shrewsbury, we are again presented with a voiceover narration from Holinshed coupled with images of the traitors from Shrewsbury being hanged.

A further narrative disparity is established in the film by a restaging of the prologue sequence which renders the initial staging, which seemed evocative of warm remembrances of things past, unreliable. The second presentation of the scene is realistic in nature as opposed to the idealized nature of the prologue version. Three men, Falstaff, Shallow, and Silence, as opposed to two in the original version, now sit in front of the fireplace. Whereas Shallow had previously been presented as giddy and enthusiastic in the prologue's dramatization of Act III, scene ii of *2 Henry IV*, he is here presented as an inane and irritating man who prattles on about insignificant matters to Falstaff's obvious annoyance. Shallow has also developed a truly irritating habit of poking and clawing at Falstaff, and playing with Falstaff s hat. The effect of this disparity is to undermine the authority of the narrative's version of historical events by revealing the contradictions it conceals.

The authority of "the official historical record" is similarly undermined at the film's conclusion. As Falstaff's huge coffin is wheeled out of the courtyard by Bardolph, Pistol, Nym, and Poins we hear the final imposition of Richardson's narration on to the action of the film. Holinshed speaks glowingly of Hal—"humane withal, he left no offense unpunished, nor friendship unrewarded. For conclusion, a majesty was he that both lived and died a pattern in princehood, a lodestar in honour, and famous to the world always." Previously, the interpolations of Richardson's narrations onto the soundtrack accompanied images of the hanging of traitors. Falstaff's death of a broken heart certainly represents a friendship unrewarded, thereby directly contradicting Holinshed's hagiography. Falstaff's fate is also directly linked here to the pattern of brutality and repression that those marginalized and victimized by the struggle to consolidate and maintain personal and political power experience.

Olivier and Welles, in their Shakespearean adaptations, seem far more interested in finding a cinematic language with which to query Shakespeare's plays in an exploration of larger issues than they do with merely translating their dramatic and narrative functions to celluloid. The narrative frame of the performance in *Henry V* and the opening of *Hamlet* serve a Brechtian function of asking the audience to consider what follows as a performance, in order to allow their audiences to relate the content of the film to their current situations, whereas the depiction of Richard as a dramatist in *Richard III* shows the process underpinning his Machiavellian manipulations. The narrative frame of the witches constructing the voodoo doll in *Macbeth*, and the pre-credit sequence in *Othello*, serve a function similar to Stoppard's famous coin toss—they announce to the audience that an arbitrary world of fixed outcomes is being entered. *Macbeth* utilizes Shakespeare's play in a deliberate meditation on the nature of theatre and the dramatic illusion, whereas *Othello* displaces Shakespeare's play from the context in which it was created by using visual inter-textual references to align the play with post Second World War mainstream culture. As discussed, *Chimes at Midnight* uses a visually performed text to challenge the authority of several canonized written texts.

Douglas Lanier has argued that Peter Greenaway's film *Prospero's Books* privileges the visual and performative dimensions of *The Tempest*, placing its textual nature at the service of the former, rather than placing the former at the service of the latter, with the result that Greenaway's film is "foregrounding the ways in which cinema as a visual and performative medium exceeds the formal capabilities of a written text" (182). Olivier's and Welles' films share almost exactly the same relationship with their seminal plays that Lanier describes as existing between Greenaway's film and its seminal play, and deserve recognition as equally audacious in their approach to Shakespeare's plays as are Greenaway and Stoppard.

CHAPTER 4

Kurosawa

In addition to crediting Olivier and Welles with inaugurating the "international" period of Shakespeare in the cinema in *Shakespeare at the Cineplex* (1), Samuel Crowl also reads *Kumonosu djô* (*The Castle of the Spider's Web* or *Throne of Blood*), *Warui yatsu hodo yoku nemuru* (*The Bad Sleep Well*) and *Ran* as a continuation of this period (manifested in international mainstream cinema) into the late 1950s and early 1960s (*ibid.*). Crowl further reads the works of Kozintsev and Zeffirelli as indicating a continuation of this period into the 1970s, and suggests that it ended with the release of Polanski's *Macbeth* (*ibid.*). The works of Kurosawa, however, are vastly different in genre and tone from the works of Olivier and Welles, just as the works of Kozintsev and Zeffirelli are equally different in genre and tone from each other and from Kurosawa. The disparity between the approaches utilized by these auteurs suggests that Crowl's classification of the works of these five filmmakers into a single and specific category arbitrarily imposes a trend of continuity on works which are the products of distinct socio-historical contexts, and are intended for the consumption of distinct audiences.

In *Shakespeare, Cinema and Society*, John Collick argues that Kurosawa's three representations of Shakespeare are influenced by a unique and indigenous tradition which resulted from the introduction of Shakespeare's plays to Japanese culture in the 19th century (161). According to Collick, "Japanese intellectuals were able to 'read' Western culture according to their own codes of meaning with little interference from colonial ideology. Once we recognise this ... it underlines the crucial fact we must bear in mind when dealing with Kurosawa's films: Shakespeare in Japan is, and always has been, an essentially Japanese tradition" (*ibid.*). Regarding the theme or motif of the disparity between the cultural mythology of feudal Japan and the historical realities of feudal Japan,[1] Collick argues:

Honour and obligation, ethics that are stressed time and time again in Japanese culture, rarely stood in the way of a retainer who felt himself to be unjustly treated by his master. The phrase ge koku jo (literally, "the low defeats the high") was coined in this era and was used specifically to refer to the slaying of a lord by one of his own samurai who wished to take his place ... in the culture of the era, the mark of a true Japanese hero was his sincerity to his ideals, to the lord of the clan and, ultimately, the symbolic figure of the Emperor.... Unfortunately the treachery and Machiavellian diplomacy that had characterised Japanese politics for seven centuries left little room for such ingenuous honesty. Consequently the sincerest heroes in Japanese culture are also the most tragic [152].

Kurosawa's *Kumonosu djô (Throne of Blood)* depicts Washizu[2] initially as the "low" who defeats the "high" in order to ultimately become the defeated "high." His treason and eventual death are presented simultaneously as a part of a social cycle and as part of a mythical inevitability. In *Filming Shakespeare's Plays,* Anthony Davies writes: "*Macbeth* is a drama about the power of choice, and the exercise of that power. *Throne of Blood,* on the other hand, is a drama about inevitable prophetic truth, and the film is more accurately titled *The Castle of the Spider's Web.* Where Macbeth has choice, Washizu has only destiny, and this distinction between Shakespeare's play and Kurosawa's drama is forcibly announced at the beginning and the end of the film, by the chanting chorus which rings out the inevitable fate of ambitious men and proclaims it to be a truth which transcends particular circumstances of history" (155). In order that his contemporary Japanese audience would perceive the events depicted in *Throne of Blood* as achieving a mythical stature, Kurosawa utilized temporal ellipses in the narrative diegesis of the film. The first image is that of a heavy mist dissipating to reveal the desolate patch of ground on which Washizu's fortress once stood. We are informed by a chanting chorus that he was "murdered by ambition" and that his spirit is "walking still." The mist again gathers, and again dissipates to reveal an exterior shot of the first castle at the commencement of the film's main action. Concerning the film's conclusion, Davies states, "The panning shot across empty, mist-shrouded desolation is identical with the opening shot of the film's action, and it is accompanied in the same way by the unmelodic drone of the chorus" (*Filming Shakespeare's Plays* 158–159). The effect of these identical opening and closing shots is to collapse the audience's perception of the difference between their contemporary historical period, and the historical period in which the action of the film takes place. Kurosawa's use of a gathering and dissipating mist to indicate a temporal ellipse has the effect of situating the diegesis of his film in a mythical, rather than a historical past.

Just as Kurosawa collapses the passage of time between his contemporary historical period and that of the film's main action, he also collapses the passage of time within the film's main action while preventing his audience from engaging its willing suspension of disbelief. The initial battle during which Washizu distinguishes himself as a warrior is never directly depicted in the action of the film. Instead, the progress of the battle is reported to Kunihara[3] by messengers, with the result that the audience is presented at this point not with a narrative presentation of the progress of the battle, but rather with a narrative presentation of a narrative presentation of the progress of the battle. "The sequence of messengers who arrive to report on the battle is punctuated by horizontal wipes across the frame to indicate time lapses" (Davies 162), heightening the audience's sense that what it is witnessing is not intended as an illusion of reality but rather as a depiction of a story.[4] Kurosawa further collapses time within the diegesis of *Throne of Blood* by dividing the film into recognizable segments. As Robert Hapgood notes, in "Kurosawa's Shakespeare Films," "four 'acts' are indicated by fades followed by comments by Washizu's retainers, marking in turn his accession to North Castle, his possession of Forest Castle, and finally his declining fortunes" (239). Washizu's retainers function largely as an interior chorus which reminds us throughout the course of the action that everything taking place within the main action of *Throne of Blood* occurs within the frame of a corresponding exterior chorus.

Kurosawa also emphasizes that his film is a work of narrative art through his choice of performance conventions. As Davies observes, in *Filming Shakespeare's Plays*:

> There is a very subtle development of the opposition between stasis and movement in the characterizations of Washizu and his wife, Asaji.[5] The conventions of movement through which each of these characters is revealed are drawn from separate artistic traditions. Asaji ... seldom moves in the frame, but when she does, it is with smoothness and control ... her movement, gesture and expression are highly conventionalized within the choreographic discipline of the Noh drama.... The movements of Washizu, on the other hand ... rise ... from the depictions of the Yamato-e picture scrolls. Washizu moves like an animal. He paces up and down, he breathes heavily, he flexes his facial muscles rhythmically and bares his teeth [160].

As it can be further argued that Washizu's exaggerated but rhythmic gestures are also reminiscent of Kabuki theatre, *Throne of Blood*'s two main characters, then, are both presented within easily recognizable yet distinct performance paradigms, and the audience is therefore encouraged to view the film as a work of narrative art. Interestingly, at the moments of their respective breakdowns, both Washizu and Asaji abandon the performance paradigm that had previously been associated with them. When Asaji begins to frantically wash her hands using an invisible bowl her gestures and voice stylizations assume the frenetic quality that has previously been associated with Washizu. Similarly, as the dying Washizu takes his final steps toward his soldiers, with an arrow through his throat, his expression is immobile, and he briefly walks in the smooth and contained manner formerly associated with Asaji.

Although *Throne of Blood* functions chiefly on a mythic level, in "*Macbeth* on Film: Politics," E. Pearlman notes that Kurosawa injects some comment regarding feudalism into the film's array of meanings:

> The society of Throne of Blood is also deeply corrupt. Unlike Macbeth, where the witches invade a basically healthy universe, Kurosawa's universe is devoid of political virtue. The present master of Forest Castle, Kunihara, has become its lord not by inheritance or election but by murdering the last occupant of the office. In one emblematic scene a group of soldiers discuss the decay of Washizu's castle. The castle is shaking, they assert, because "the foundations have long been rotting. Even the rats have begun to leave." The allegory tells us that not only the castle but feudalism itself, is rotten.... The society is characterized ... by narrow self-interest, distrust, constant fear, and the easy recourse to violence [257].

Although Pearlman's observations are correct, Kurosawa's use of performance, narrative structure, and cinematic technique would situate *Throne of Blood* as a critique not of feudalism in its operation as a socio-historical economic system but rather of a romanticized or mythologized view of feudalism. In dramatizing *Throne of Blood* within the confines of a mythical past, as opposed to a historical past, Kurosawa suggests that the past is both not as glorious as the audience might like to pretend it was, and not as dissimilar to the present as the audience might like to think it is. The political climate of *Kumonosu djô*'s 1957 release was dominated by the ruling Liberal Democratic Party, which Ian Buruma, in "The Re-Birth of Japanese Democracy," characterizes as "a large conservative coalition party..., funded to some degree by the U.S., ... put in place to marginalize all left-wing opposition." The imposition of the LDP into the democratic political system that had only been established early in the same decade, at end of the U.S. military occupation of Japan, resulted in "the opposition dwindl[ing] into an impotent force, mere window-dressing to a one-party state." Buruma also notes that "one-party rule breeds complacency, corruption, and political sclerosis," and that the system which flourished as a result of the LDP's domination of Japanese politics functioned as follows: "LDP faction bosses took turns as prime minister, palms were greased by various business interests, more or less capable bureaucrats decided on domestic economic policies, and the United States took care of Japan's security (and much of its foreign policy, too)." The contemporary climate of the LDP "monopoly on power," which was imposed by "factional bosses, many of whom were from established political families, and most of whom relied on shady financing" would have generated nostalgia for imperial Japan, which had become defunct only 12 years earlier. The corruption depicted in *Kumonosu djô* would have deflated nostalgia for the romanticized or mythologized view of feudalism by depicting that system as plagued by the same issues plaguing contemporary politics.

In an article entitled "The Bad Sleep Well," David Sterritt notes that Kurosawa had stated, "It has always seemed to me that graft, bribery, etc., at the public level, is one of the worst crimes that there is," and that Kurosawa had also been quoted as wanting to make a film "about corruption" which would publicly reveal the people who "hide behind the façade of some great company or corporation ... how dreadful they really are, what awful things they do." According to Sterritt, when preparing his next film that was influenced by Shakespeare, Kurosawa had stated, "I wanted to make a movie of some social significance." There is a general consensus that *Warui yatsu hodo yoku nemuru (The Bad Sleep Well)* is Kurosawa's attempt to represent *Hamlet* in the cinema. There seems to be an equally general tendency to avoid discussion concerning how this film engages *Hamlet* in order to present a contemporary social critique. In "Kurosawa's Shakespeare films," an article which purports to discuss all three of Kurosawa's Shakespeare Films, Robert Hapgood divides his discussion between *Kumonosu djô* and *Ran*, mentioning *The Bad Sleep Well* chiefly in two paragraphs which supply a brief inventory of ways in which the film appropriates some of the themes and motifs of Hamlet (242). Anthony Dawson, in "Reading Kurosawa Reading Shakespeare," directly announces that he will not be addressing *The Bad Sleep Well* because as it is "set in 1960 corporate Japan, [it] raises different questions" (159) than those posed by Kurosawa's two other Shakespeare films. John Collick, in his lengthy discussion of Kurosawa in *Shakespeare, Cinema and Society*, fails to acknowledge *The Bad Sleep Well* as an adaptation of one of Shakespeare's plays. The tendency to marginalize *The Bad Sleep Well* from discussions of representation of Shakespeare's work in the cinema probably exists for the same reasons that Coppola's *Godfather* trilogy is rarely incorporated into these discussions. Coppola's and Kurosawa's relationship to the plays they reference in creating these films is problematic in that both directors rely on the audience's recognition of the motifs and themes that they have displaced from the seminal play in order to offer a critique of their contemporary culture.

Robert Hapgood's observation, in "Kurosawa's Shakespeare Films," that "Kurosawa pushes Shakespeare to extremes" (243), is evidenced from the beginning of *The Bad Sleep Well*. Shakespeare's play begins with a report of a wedding immediately following a portent of a strange eruption to the state; whereas Kurosawa's film begins with a wedding during which the portent erupts. Kurosawa's wedding, however, is not that of his Claudius to his Gertrude; rather, Kurosawa's Hamlet (Nishi[6]) is marrying Keiko (Kurosawa's Ophelia and daughter to Kurosawa's Claudius: Iwabuchi) with both the blessing of and a threat from Tatsuo (her brother and Kurosawa's Laertes). In addition to Kurosawa's conflation of the Claudius and Polonius lines, his "strange eruption to the state" is embodied by the appearance of an unsolicited wedding cake. The wedding cake is a facsimile of the corporation's office building and has a red rose planted in one of the seventh story office windows. We later find that the cake was secretly sent by Nishi and that the window with the rose planted in it indicates the window that his father jumped out of while committing a forced suicide at the command of Iwabuchi. Whereas in Shakespeare's play the ghost signals a call to the son for revenge, in Kurosawa's film the cake signals that the call has been answered and revenge is underway.

Although the reporters, police and district attorneys in *The Bad Sleep Well* have no immediate counterparts in Shakespeare's play, they are deployed by Kurosawa to illustrate the appropriation of another one of Shakespeare's themes. In Shakespeare's play, Claudius mentions that the court of Denmark has "freely gone with this affair along" during his wedding speech, indicating that the court may be complicit in his crime to the extent that the circumstances surrounding Old Hamlet's death and Claudius' sudden marriage to Gertrude should have indicated some foul play to its members. In *The Bad Sleep Well* the police, district attorneys, and reporters are well aware of the kickback scheme and are doing everything they can to bring the ironically named "Public Corporation" to justice. What prevents justice from being done is the misapplication of the practice of Seppuku, a ritual suicide traditionally employed to prevent Samurai from falling into enemy hands, here utilized by Iwabuchi to prevent his corporate officers from reporting their kick-back scheme to the police or press. Seppuku is deployed by Kurosawa here as an analogue to Shakespeare's "leprous distilment." Iwabuchi's orders of ritual suicide are frequently poured into the porches of his officer's ears to elicit their deaths in order to further his agenda. Here again, as in *Throne of Blood*, practices of the romanticized or mythologized past are aligned with the corruption of the contemporary period.

Where Kurosawa has conflated his Claudius with Polonius, his Hamlet has become conflated with both Rosencrantz and Guildenstern. In Shakespeare's play, Rosencrantz and Guildenstern are ordered by Claudius to use their bond of friendship to spy on Hamlet. Kurosawa has Nishi infiltrating both Iwabuchi's office (by taking a job as his secretary) and his home (by marrying his daughter and moving in) in order to spy on Iwabuchi. Kurosawa's Nishi differs from Shakespeare's Hamlet here in that where the latter's "son of a dear father murdered/Prompted to [his] revenge by heaven and hell/Must, like a whore, unpack [his] heart with words," the former's son of a father forced to suicide has implemented his plan in which he kidnaps two disgraced officers of the "Public Corporation," preventing their suicides but imprisoning them in an underground vault. In one scene Nishi gleefully recounts the crimes he has committed (kidnapping, fraud, marriage by false pretense) in order to bring his father's murderer to justice, stating that he is willing to do what the authorities are unable to: become evil himself in order to oppose evil effectively. Shakespeare depicts a second-guessing prince who misses his opportunity for revenge because he does not wish to send his father's murderer to heaven. Kurosawa depicts Nishi's sense of justice as so absolute that his ultimate goal is not to bring about Iwabuchi's death, but to turn both Iwabuchi and himself in to the authorities once he has compiled sufficient evidence of Iwabuchi's guilt (after holding a press conference in order to make the secret corruption of the "Public Company's" officers public knowledge[7]). In "Contemporary Kurosawa: *The Bad Sleep Well* and *High and Low*," R.D. Finch writes:

> In *The Bad Sleep Well* Kurosawa explores the distinction between justice and revenge. He asks the viewer to judge how far one should go to exact retribution, and if a wronged person is justified in harming the innocent (here Nishi's bride, who actually is in love with him) to punish the guilty (her father and his associates). He also shows the conflict Nishi feels between his use of others as cat's paws and his dawning recognition that they too are human beings with feelings. Kurosawa doesn't really answer the questions he poses so much as examine the effect on Nishi and others of his obsessive need to get revenge and to erase the shame he feels has befallen his family.

Shakespeare's play ends with the deaths of Claudius, Hamlet, and Laertes, the ascendence of Fortinbras to the throne of Denmark, and the assurance that Hamlet's story will be preserved and broadcast by Horatio "lest more mischance/On plots and errors, happen." Where Shakespeare's play allows for a reading in which Fortinbras will redeem the corrupt polity and the story of Hamlet might provide a moral lesson for those who may in future undertake plots, Kurosawa seems to offer a challenge to his seminal play. Nishi is ultimately found to be morally superior to Iwabuchi in that where Nishi forms a genuine bond of love and respect with Keiko, Iwabuchi drugs her in order find out where Nishi can be found. Nishi seems destroyed more from Keiko's inability to comprehend the evil her father is capable of than from any lack of resolution or ability in confronting evil on his own part. Nishi's inability to prevent Iwabuchi and the officers from injecting him with grain alcohol and leaving him in a car on the train tracks is due to the simple fact that he is outnumbered and therefore easily overpowered physically. Keiko and Tatsuo's mutual decision to disown their father and leave him might imply a kind of death and punishment (he is obviously too old to have any more children, so their departure will ensure the end of his line). However, Kurosawa informs us, near the film's conclusion, that Iwabuchi isn't the real enemy, and is, in fact, subject to an order from the president of the "Public Company" to commit suicide himself if Nishi makes the details of the kick-back scheme public. Itakura, Kurosawa's Horatio figure, is unable to report Nishi and his cause aright to the unsatisfied because, having failed to establish their real identities, as they planned to do at the press conference, Itakura is now unable to legally establish an identity as either Nishi or Itakura. In Kurosawa's response to *Hamlet*, therefore, any moral lesson is lost—silenced by the corruption Nishi and Itakura had hoped to expose.

Kumonosu djô and *Warui yatsu hodo yoku nemuru* were financed by the Toho Company and Kurosawa's own production company; their primary distribution was intended to be the Japanese marketplace. Released in 1985, *Ran* was financed by an international partnership of Japanese and French creditors, and was distributed by Orion Pictures in the U.S. To recoup this international investment, Kurosawa, in adapting *King Lear* to the cinema, dramatized the play in a manner that would engage the sensibilities of both Japanese and international audiences. *Ran* successfully mediates Shakespeare's most nihilistic vision with the socio-historical priorities of its intended audiences, while presenting its own vision in a qualified, rather than a completely nihilistic, manner. The conclusion of Kurosawa's *Ran* is complex and ambivalent, despite the "humankind on the precipice" reading that seems to be favored by North American and European critics. Stephen Buhler describes *Ran*'s conclusion as follows: "Tsurumaru is left alone. He steps, tentatively and dangerously, toward the cliff. The void ... overwhelms us with its emptiness, its silences, and, in Kurosawa's vision, sheer beauty. The space of tragedy is infinite, both everything and nothing." (173). John Collick similarly writes, "The blind man is tapping his way towards a cliff edge. He stumbles and jerks back from the gulf. The scroll of Buddha falls from his hand to lie, opened, on the ground. The camera then draws back, showing the tiny figure in the midst of a barren landscape" (186). In an unpublished paper entitled "An Earthly Lament," Janet Melo-Thaiss proposes that this signifies "an apocalyptic vision of humanity perched on the edge of a meaningless void ... a world dominated by chaos and despair" (4). Although all three critics assert that Tsurumaru is on the edge of a cliff,

Tsurumaru is actually on the rampart of his family's ruined castle, and (due to his blindness) does not realize that he is witnessing the funeral procession of the man who has blinded him, murdered most of his family, destroyed his castle, and who is indirectly responsible for the death of his sister.

Although Collick claims that Kurosawa here depicts Tsurumaru as a character "trying to withdraw from reality" (186), it is arguable that Tsurumaru is one of the few characters in the film who has a realistic orientation to the world around him (an appropriation of Shakespeare's motif whereby Gloucester cannot emotionally "see" the intentions of Edmund until he is physically blinded). When Hidetora is brought to Tsurumaru's hut, Tsurumaru recalls Hidetora's cruelty, stating, "I try to be like my sister. To pray to Buddha, and rid myself of hatred. But not one day do I forget! Not one night do I sleep in peace! I regret I cannot welcome you as befits the Great Lord. Luckily ... my sister gave me a flute. I will play for you. Lacking anything else, I give you hospitality of the heart. It is the only pleasure left to me." In sheltering Hidetora and playing the flute for him (in essence offering the man who has destroyed his family and blinded him all he has left to offer), Tsurumaru is demonstrating a form of compassion which encompasses both the idealism of Buddhism as practiced by Lady Sue (his sister and Hidetora's daughter-in-law) as well as an understanding of his own limitations as a human being. Although he realizes that he should try to forgive Hidetora, Tsurumaru's orientation toward the world is realistic, lacking the nihilistic ferocity of Jiro and Kaede, the naivety of Sue and Hidetora, or the idealistic arrogance of Saburo. The final shot of the film depicts him as still having the capacity to jerk back from the edge of the rampart, despite having been blinded, having his castle destroyed, and his entire family murdered. Although he has been seriously harmed by Hidetora's family, his ability to function as a human being with a realistic orientation toward the world, and his own experience, is intact.

Robert Hapgood notes that *Ran* is set in a specific historical period, "the Sengoku Jidai or 'Age of the Country at War' (1392–1508)" (235) . Near the conclusion of the film, in response to Kyoami's weeping, Tango states, "It is the gods who weep. They see us killing each other ... over and over since time began. They can't save us from ourselves." In "*Ran*: Gods as Audience, Audience as Gods," Vili Maunula states that Kurosawa suggested "that *Ran* was intended as "gods' view" of human struggle." One possible interpretation of *Ran* is that the frame represents the view of the gods, who are powerless to intervene in human affairs but are deeply affected by them. This suggests that *Ran* ends on a guardedly optimistic note, with Tsurumaru able to deal realistically with the world and not drop into the abyss, despite the distance that separates him from the image of the Buddha.

It is Hidetora who responds to every crisis that he is faced with in the film by attempting to withdraw from reality. In the opening sequence of the film, when Saburo makes a pointedly rude remark in order to imply that Hidetora's conciliatory attitude toward Ayabe and Fujimaki conceals an agenda to slaughter them and assume their lands (as Hidetora had previously done to Tsurumaru's family), Hidetora feigns sleep in order to avoid responding to the implication. When this strategy of avoidance fails, and Hidetora is yet again confronted with Saburo's rudeness (now supported by Tango), he banishes Saburo and Tango in an attempt to make the problem go away. Hidetora realizes his error when he learns that Taro and Jiro have forbidden any peasants from helping him on pain of death, yet refuses to go to Saburo and seek forgiveness despite being urged to do so by Tango. Madness, a different form of avoidance of reality, allows Hidetora to escape the battle at the third castle without being killed or committing suicide. On the heath, Hidetora retreats from Kyoami's description of a phantom army comprised of all of the people who Hidetora has murdered, and in Tsurumaru's hut, he shrinks from Tsurumaru's offering of music by literally crashing through a wall. While in the ruins of Tsurumaru's castle Hidetora shrinks from the mention of Saburo's name, claiming that it hurts his head, and he later bolts and runs from the ruins of the castle when he realizes where he is and that Sue and Tsurumaru are there with him. When Saburo finally finds him on the plain, Hidetora states, "What do you mean by Father? Wait…. I remember. I had three sons. Are you one of them? Saburo? It's you! I have no face to show you, no words to excuse myself. Give me poison to drink. I'll swallow it gladly…. No sweet lies; I've had my fill…. If only you can forget my cruelty to you. Forgive me. I am a stupid old fool." At this point, although Hidetora begins to face reality and to mend his relationship with his son, he has done so far too late.

Collick characterizes Hidetora's "madness" and "retreat from the world" as "wholly inappropriate weapons against the tragic violence of feudal Japan" (186). Related to Hidetora's avoidance and madness are Jiro's and Taro's dismissal of Saburo as rude when he first makes the hare analogy, later suggests that Hidetora is not well, and then directly confronts Hidetora. As "rudeness" is a social construction, the social rules of feudal Japan, as depicted here by Kurosawa, serve to perpetuate a system of treachery and violence rather than contain it. As the third castle burns, Taro states that Hidetora will have no choice but to commit suicide—again, as dictated by a social rule. Hidetora instead staggers out of the burning third castle and walks onto the plain. Due to his age, this takes a long time, during which Taro and Jiro's men stand lined up on either side of Hidetora, presumably unsure what to do with him, as there is nothing in the rules of their social system that addresses this situation.

Ran can be situated at an intersection of a Japanese Shakespeare tradition with 20th-century international cinema. Buhler has noted, "Welles' *Chimes at Midnight* has had an impact here" (173). The narrative structure Kurosawa employs in *Ran* certainly recalls the narrative structure used by Welles in *Chimes at Midnight*. Both films employ a two-part narrative structure demarcated by an extensive battle sequence that occurs at roughly the mid-point of the film. The respective battle sequences of both films precipitate pronounced changes in the state of their main characters (In *Chimes at Midnight* Hotspur dies, Hal initiates his process of "redeeming time when men least think I will," Henry IV's illness and decline begins, and Falstaff loses his vitality; In *Ran*, Taro is killed and Hidetora goes mad.) Like Welles' depiction of Shrewsbury, Kurosawa's depiction of the battle at the third castle represents a breathtaking cinematic achievement; in "Two-Dimensional Shakespeare: 'King Lear' on Film," Peter Holland describes that battle sequence as "an extraordinary depiction of carnage and bloodshed, counterpointed with the sight of Hidetora sitting distraught, inside the stronghold" (63). Words are inadequate to describe this remarkable sequence with its exquisitely balanced and composed images of archers lying dead in their turrets riddled with arrows, the vibrant colors of the banners that the soldiers use to identify themselves, the beauty of the flames that consume the third castle, and the delicate pink color of the smoke that erupts from the soldiers' muskets as they decimate Hidetora's entourage with gunfire. This battle sequence recalls Olivier's Agincourt in its depiction of the deployment of archers releasing volleys of arrows into the air, but unlike Olivier's sanitized and bloodless battle, Kurosawa's battle sequence shows a plethora of bloody corpses riddled with arrows. This sequence is initiated by Hidetora's retainer claiming—as he dies from his wounds—that "we truly are in Hell." The images that follow this appraisal certainly reinforce it. Unlike Welles' partially diegetic use of sound in his battle scene, Kurosawa's use of sound does not directly correspond with the visual images he gives us on screen. We instead listen to wistful music played by an orchestra that seems to be comprised almost entirely of strings, while the visual images of the battle are occasionally intercut with an image of grey clouds though which light breaks, which together again suggest the weeping of the gods at the carnage they are witnessing.

The images Kurosawa uses in this sequence recall the palate often utilized by Stanley Kubrick. Although—like Kubrick—Kurosawa never once reminds his audience that they are merely watching a film, Kurosawa's use of color and composition—like Kubrick's—is extremely stylized. *Ran*'s colors are invariably garish and vibrant, its compositions symmetrical and aesthetically pleasing. The effect of this visual strategy is to make the film beautiful to watch, which forces the viewer to contrast the aesthetics of Kurosawa's presentation with the elements of Kurosawa's narrative. Buhler agrees in characterizing Kurosawa's use of color as "vivid" (172) and "strangely beautiful" (*ibid.*), and poses the question "The strangeness of the beauty ... rests in the savagery and desolation of the events depicted: how can these sights so horrifying or heartrending be beautiful?" (*ibid.*). It is possible that Kurosawa is forcing the members of his audience to confront their own innate tendencies toward violence and sadism; by recognizing the horrifying sights as aesthetically pleasing, Kurosawa's audience may confront its own hypocrisy surrounding its predisposition to savagery.

Ran also frequently conflates the myth systems of feudal Japan with those of Western culture. Regarding the sequence of the battle at the third castle, Buhler writes, "Only at the moment when Taro, the eldest of Hidetora's sons, is killed at the order of Jiro, the middle brother, does the soundtrack provide the actual sounds and screams of war. Kurosawa has linked the West's most influential story of the final conflagration with its most enduring account of the Primal Murder, Cain's assault on Abel" (173). Buhler also notes that Hidetora's example of the bundle of arrows as a demonstration of family unity (one arrow is easily broken when its ends are bent toward one another; however, several arrows united in a bundle are much stronger and more resilient) represents "not only a rewrite of Shakespeare's daughters but a revision of a Japanese legend about Faithful sons" (172). When initially warning Jiro to beware of Lady Kaede's influence, Kurogane, in the following speech from *Ran*, characterizes Kaede in accordance with the terms of a recognizable Japanese myth: "There are many foxes hereabouts. It is said they take human form. Take care, my lord. They often impersonate women. In Central Asia a fox seduced King Pan Tsu and made him kill 1000 men. In China he married King Yu and ravaged the land. In Japan, as Princess Tamamo, he caused great havoc at court. He became a white fox with nine tails. Then they lost trace of him. Some people say he settled down here (*pointing at Kaede*). So beware, my lord, beware."

Kurogane's warning that Kaede is a shape-shifting fox is consistent both with Japanese legend and with Western mythologies concerning vampires, who can shift shape into wolves or bats. Later, Kaede attacks and seduces Jiro, (wearing her mourning robe—a garment associated with a shroud) exploding out of her earlier pattern of movement (which was consistent with the conventions of Noh drama), and easily overpowering Jiro despite the fact that he is much larger than she is (great strength being a core attribute of the Western characterization of the vampire). During this attack she nicks his throat with her knife, drawing blood, and during their ensuing sexual encounter she licks his throat clean of blood. Another element of the Western mythology of the vampire is their ability to hypnotize their victims, which in the context of *Ran* accounts for the ease with which Kaede manipulates Taro. When Kurogane murders Kaede, the wall behind her is literally coated with the blood that spews from the wound. This contrasts with the earlier depiction of Asaji in *Throne of Blood*. Whereas Asaji's decline is signified by a shift from one easily recognized Japanese performance paradigm (Noh) to another (Kabuki or picture scrolls), Kaede's dominance over Jiro is signified by a shift from an easily recognized Japanese performance paradigm (Noh) to a characterization deeply embedded in Western mythologies (Vampire).

Just as Kaede is initially presented within the formalized movements of Noh drama, to later burst out of these confines to assume characteristics of the Western Vampire, Collick notes that Hidetora's face is "made up to resemble the mask worn by actors playing the aged in the Noh" (185). Melo-Thaiss writes, "Kurosawa is concerned with more than the rot of feudal society. Given the consistency of Kurosawa's pessimistic view of the human character as well as the constant emphasis on humanity's inability to transcend its violent nature, Kurosawa moves beyond feudal Japan and uses history to comment on contemporary society" (11). *Ran* can be seen as an apocalyptic vision rooted in a critique of feudal Japan, which moves outwards from that specific context, incorporating elements of Western culture in a larger critique of contemporary society. Melo-Thaiss further notes "at the moment that Saburo seems able to transcend the flow of violence by rescuing Hidetora and fulfilling his father's desire for peace, he will become yet another victim of the inevitable cycle of human brutality. The futility of action is a bleak conclusion ... resulting in the depiction of humanity's inability to exert agency in the hopes of a meaningful existence" (12–13). Collick disagrees, stating, "*Ran*, despite the carnage and suffering, ends with an optimistic critique of the traditional concepts of transcendence, insanity and forgiveness" (181). *Ran* is apocalyptic in its presentation of Hidetora's failure to ensure that his dynasty will usurp Fujimaki and Ayabe through the cooperation of his sons against them. Yet, the film ends not with the funeral procession of Hidetora and Saburo, but with an image of the blinded Tsurumaru, alone atop the ramparts of his ruined castle, unwittingly witnessing the funeral procession of the man who had destroyed his family. Although his distance from the Buddha is emphasized in the final scene, it can be argued that this distance signifies the importance of being aware both of spiritual enlightenment and of the realities of human existence. Although damaged by his suffering, and aware of his anger, Tsurumaru is ultimately able to display compassion to Hidetora, despite Hidetora's crimes against himself and his family.

Kurosawa's strategy in representing Shakespeare's plays in the cinema seems to be one of simultaneously referencing and challenging his seminal play in order to provoke comparisons and contrasts between the play and his film. Ostensibly faithful to the narrative of *Macbeth*, *Kumonosu djô (Throne of Blood)* depicts its mythologized feudal Japan as irredeemably corrupt in order to dissipate its contemporary audience's nostalgia for imperial Japan. *Warui yatsu hodo yoku nemuru (The Bad Sleep Well)* attributes Nishi's defeat not to a lack of character or resolution on his part, but rather to his ultimately being physically outnumbered by the corrupt businessmen he wishes to expose at a crucial moment, suggesting that Japanese society has become so irredeemably corrupted that any attempt to oppose its corruption is futile. *Ran* depicts the eradication of Hidetora's line not merely as a result of the foolishness of age, but also of the patriarch's inability to contain the violent society he has spent his life engendering.

Kumonosu djô and *Warui yatsu hodo yoku nemuru* are clearly responses to the political context of the late 1950s in Japan. Kurosawa appropriates Shakespeare's plays to comment on his contemporary socio-historical period in which rampant corporate and governmental corruption had become an "unacknowledged norm." *Ran* was released some 25 years later, at a period in Kurosawa's career in which he was considered an internationally successful filmmaker[8] and appeals to an international film audience, by mediating Shakespeare's play with Japanese mythologies and an international perspective. At the time of the making and release of *Ran* the "Second Cold War" was still in progress and nuclear annihilation was an established concern in the popular culture of the period (*WarGames* and *Octopussy*, both released in 1983, were popular mainstream action films which were both based on the premise of a potential nuclear war). In this context, *Ran* presents a critique of humankind's tendency to—as Tango suggests to Kyoami after they have witnessed the deaths of Saburo and Hidetora—"prefer sorrow over joy ... suffering over peace ... [to] revel in pain and bloodshed ... [and] ... celebrate murder." Roger Ebert, in his "Great Movies" review of *Ran*, suggests the following: "*Ran* is set in medieval times, but it is a 20th century film, in which an old man can arrive at the end of his life having won all his battles, and foolishly think he still has the power to settle things for a new generation. But life hurries ahead without any respect for historical continuity; his children have their own lusts and furies. His will is irrelevant, and they will divide his spoils like dogs tearing at a carcass." Although Ebert's observations are correct, it should be remembered that, at the conclusion of *Ran*, it is Tsurumaru who is left standing after the other characters have "preyed on themselves/Like monsters of the deep." Although *Ran* is concerned with the probable annihilation of humankind, Kurosawa also admits, in the final depiction of Tsurumaru, a possibility that the apocalypse might be forestalled.

Crowl's classification of Kurosawa's work as continuing a period inaugurated by the films of Olivier and Welles is highly problematic as the approaches utilized by Olivier and Welles are vastly divergent from those used by Kurosawa. Olivier and Welles present an adapted version of the seminal play accompanied with countertexts that contextualize their reading of a Renaissance play. Kurosawa, however, completely displaces the narrative context of his films to feudal or contemporary Japan, presenting tropes specific to a Japanese cultural context in order to facilitate his audience's reading of his film. *Kumonosu djô* transposes the narrative of *Macbeth* into a feudal setting in which the code of honor that Washizu violates is the samurai code. *Warui yatsu hodo yoku nemuru* displaces *Hamlet* into a contemporary Japanese setting and utilizes the misapplication of the practice of seppuku (ritual suicide) as a comment on contemporary corruption. *Ran* displaces *King Lear* into a feudal Japanese setting while clearly commenting on the director's perception of his contemporary socio-political situation. This suggests that, far from continuing a tradition established by Olivier and Welles, Kurosawa's films of Shakespeare's plays represent a distinct and separate body of work.

CHAPTER 5

Kozinstev

As previously discussed, characterizing Kurosawa's work as indicative of the continuation of an "international period" in Shakespearian film production is problematic. Although the battle sequence in *Ran* appears to reference famous battle sequences presented by Olivier and Welles in their adaptations of Shakespeare in the cinema, the bulk of his representations of Shakespeare in the cinema directly address the concerns of a Japanese socio-historical context. Grigori Kozintsev's two adaptations of Shakespeare in the cinema are similarly problematic because of their integration into a very different socio-cultural context. In *Shakespeare on Film*, Robert Shaughnessy lists Kozintsev's *Korol Lir* as one "of the widely acknowledged masterpieces of Shakespearean cinema" (4). In "Hawke Ascending," Robin Wood describes Kozintsev's *Gamlet* as a "breath-taking achievement" (8) which is the only "cinematic adaptation of *Hamlet* that could be claimed as having the stature, as film, that the play has theatre" (*ibid.*). In "On the Road: Reclaiming *Korol Lir*," Yvonne Griggs argues that Kozintsev's films have been "appropriated by Western academia as ... 'classic' rendition[s] ... and [are] thus ... considered to belong to 'high culture' rather than 'popular culture'" (97). Griggs proposes a "genre-conscious" reading of *Korol Lir* in which the film is interpreted as belonging to the genre of the "road movie," and reads the film in terms of its relationship to films as diverse as *The Wizard of Oz, The Grapes of Wrath, Butch Cassidy and the Sundance Kid*, and *Bonnie and Clyde*. These readings, however, do not place the films in their immediate socio-historical context, or discuss how the films can be seen as responses to their immediate contemporary concerns.

The tendency in "Western academia" to perceive *Gamlet* as a "classic rendition" is possibly encouraged by the emphasis placed by Kozintsev on the issue of fidelity to the seminal play. *Gamlet*, released in 1964, and *Korol Lir*, released in 1970, give screenplay credit both to Kozintsev and Boris

Pasternak (winner of the 1958 Nobel Prize in Literature), although Pasternak had died some four years previous to the release of *Gamlet*. Pasternak's contributions to the respective screenplays date from his 1941 translation of *Hamlet*, and his 1949 translation of *King Lear*, which were intended for theatrical productions of both plays, directed by Kozintsev. According to Daniel Gronsky, in "Shakespeare in Translation: Foreign Film Versions of Shakespeare's Plays," the translations were "known to be both very faithful and very workable." In *Understanding Boris Pasternak*, Larissa Rudova notes that the translations were also constructed to "produce an impression of life, not literariness" (118). The aim of Pasternak's work was fidelity: not necessarily to the word of the play, but to the play as a foundation for a vital performance.

Pasternak had undertaken a career in translation because his career as an author and poet was not viable in Stalinist Russia. Similarly, Kozintsev's best work seems to have been accomplished during the "Thaw" initiated by the regime of Nikita Khrushchev: a period characterized by "some liberation of individual creativity in the Soviet film industry," according to Steve Shelokhonov, in his "Biography for Grigori Kozintsev." In an article entitled "Gareth Jones' 1933 Moscow Interview Notes with a Soviet Off[i]cial Denying the Existence of Any Famine?," Nigel Colley notes that Shakespeare's *Hamlet* had been both "effectively banned and banned personally" by Stalin. However, the "Thaw" under Khrushchev made a production possible. Like Kurosawa before him, Kozintsev utilized Shakespeare's plays to explore issues contemporary to his own cultural context and moment; unlike Kurosawa before him, Kozintsev was not free to be openly socially critical. Kozintsev's *Gamlet* conveys its critique of its cultural context and moment through implication rather that direct representation.

In a production in which the "faithfulness" of Pasternak's translation seems to be at the forefront, this film is strangely devoid of words for several minutes at its beginning. There is a pre-credit sequence composed of three shots. Firstly, we see a high-angle crane shot of the sea, with a cliff in the foreground on the right side of the frame. Secondly, we see another high-angle crane shot of the sea, now with no direct image of the cliff in the frame, but rather with the shadow of the cliff on the waves. Thirdly, we now see a high-angle crane shot of the sea with a shadow of a medieval castle on the waves. The first shot is accompanied by the sounds of the waves, and of gulls calling in the background; the second shot is accompanied only by the sound of the waves, but in the third shot gulls can be both heard and barely seen flying over the sea and away from the shadow of the castle. Although anachronistic in a Renaissance play,[1] a medieval stone castle perched on a cliff here establishes a central binary opposition in the film's setting: formless, relentless sea and barren rock. This opposition is confirmed by the shot which immediately follows the credit sequence. The credits are displayed against a background of stone; when the credits are finished, the camera pans left, revealing that the stone is part of one of the castle ramparts, and also revealing a gap in the stone wall through which any approach by sea may be observed. This shot begins a progression of shots beginning with the extreme close-up of some the rough stones used to build the castle walls, followed by two shots prominently displaying the castle's brickwork. Later in the film, as Gamlet[2] sits at the base of the cliff while observing the sea, the cliff and castle in the background will seem to be visually indistinguishable from one another, as if the castle has somehow grown organically out of the rock.

This binary opposition is further confirmed after the credit sequence as Gamlet rides toward the castle. As he approaches, there are a few small bushes and shrubs in the background, which become increasingly sparse as he gets nearer to the castle. As he approaches the castle, all vegetation has disappeared; there is only rock on the ground. Gamlet crosses a drawbridge to enter the castle, beginning another procession of shots which display the drawbridge being raised behind him, spiked gates being lowered behind him, and heavy doors being shut together behind him. These opening shots establish the castle as aligned with rock (an element of stasis), the now impassable land access to the castle as aligned with vegetation (an element of growth), and the formless and relentless sea as the only possible means of escape from the castle. Kozintsev may here be using the seeming stasis of the castle as a visual metaphor for life in Stalinist Russia, the landscape as a visual metaphor for land access to the rest of Europe that was barred by border checkpoints, and the sea as the only unmonitored (because it is completely un-negotiable without access to a ship) possible point of access to the outside world. Gamlet will spend much of this film observing the sea; does it here represent his only possible escape route? Pasternak's adaptation includes the dialogue in which Gamlet agrees not to return to Wittenberg, which is presumably the place he had come from at the beginning of the film, and the place he is now barred from returning to by the triple barrier of drawbridge, gate and doors. This reading is also supported by an image showing the moat after the drawbridge has been raised; the moat is at screen center and reflects the sun, while the drawbridge and the gate occupy screen left and screen right.

The interpretation of Kozintsev's setting for the film as a metaphor for life in Soviet Russia is also supported by his deployment of Shakespeare's dialogue. The first dialogue we hear in the film is a proclamation read by a soldier to a gathered crowd; the text of the proclamation, however, is taken from Claudius' first speech from Act I, scene ii of Shakespeare's play, in which he announces his marriage to Gertrude to the court. The soldier reads the proclamation to the crowd ending with the phrase, "taken to wife." Kozintsev then cuts to an interior of one of the great halls in the castle, in which courtiers (wearing frilled collars that seem absurd when contrasted with the clothing worn by the peasants) are speaking to one another, saying, "With a defeated joy/in equal scale/weighing delight and dole": lines that had been part of the speech just delivered to the crowd of peasants. Kozintsev then cuts to an interior shot of a meeting room, in which all of the lords of the castle are seated around a rectangular table. Claudius delivers the remainder of his speech to this group in an enclosed room. By presenting a speech traditionally delivered by one character in one setting as delivered by three different characters in three different settings, Kozintsev establishes three of the four disparate "voices" that will be present throughout this film. In the film *Gorky Park*, a detective speaks of a chasm in its contemporary Russian society (1983) that many fall into: the chasm "between what is said and what is done." Assuming that the situation that the detective refers to already existed in 1964, it can be argued that Kozintsev here establishes a further chasm: that between the monologic centre of power and the dialogic voices of the heteroglossia. The first "voice" we hear is the "official" voice, which communicates that information that is considered "fit" for the public's consumption. The second voice we hear is that of the courtiers: people who interact directly with those in decision-making power, and who secretly understand the machinations of the court, but who would jeopardize their own positions or lives by giving direct utterance to their suspicions or opinions. The third voice we hear is that of those in power; we hear not only their proclamations, we hear their reasons, agendas, and concerns.

The tone that Claudius uses in this scene sounds much more like a report to a committee than it does a royal proclamation. The room in which he delivers this address to his lords is ornate but small, with a single central rectangular table. When Claudius describes how "young Fortinbras … hath not failed to pester us with message," he grins knowingly, and occasionally rolls his eyes, suggesting that this is a meeting of persons of equal stature in which one holds a leadership role, rather than that of a king and his courtiers. Although Claudius is the only figure in the meeting who literally speaks (until he persuades Laertes to speak) the sense we have of this body is that they are a collective entity. This reading again seems supported by the depiction of the committee following Gamlet—who sits not at the table but on the periphery of the room, and who has left the room at the mid-point of the meeting—into the hall to request that he not return to Wittenberg. Again, Claudius speaks for the committee, but it is the group of people as a whole who have followed Gamlet into the hall and who now listen to his decision to stay; this group is very deliberately placed by Kozintsev across the back plane of the on-screen space, leaving Gamlet, Claudius, and Gertrude in the front plane. This committee room will be revisited by Kozintsev after Polonius is murdered. Gamlet will be brought into the room and questioned by Claudius in the presence of all of the persons in the room. A few will be dispatched to locate Polonius' body; however, the committee will remain to hear the decision that Gamlet is to be sent to England. These depictions support a reading that Kozintsev is here depicting Polonius' court as a metaphor for the Politburo; decisions are made by a central committee, and those who deal with those in power, but who are not directly in power, live a precarious existence in which much of what they perceive and understand must remain unsaid.

As this committee leaves we are introduced to the fourth "voice" which is prominent in this film. Many filmmakers who have adapted Shakespeare's plays have used voiceover narration in place of soliloquies to maintain suspension of disbelief as a character addressing the audience directly would violate conventions of realism/illusionism. Kozintsev here uses voiceover narration to reinforce the thematic structure of his film as well, suggesting that the "voice" of one's innermost thoughts or feelings is a voice that must never be publicly expressed in this court. Gamlet's first soliloquy, also from Act I, scene ii is delivered as a voiceover narration given while Gamlet walks through the hall maintaining an expression on his face which indicates that he is alert and responsive to his surroundings. Here we see another chasm, that between what is unsaid and what one allows the world to see. Although Gamlet is here experiencing strong emotions such as sadness, despair, and disgust, the expression he shows to the world shows him actively interacting with the courtiers. He is not merely masking his feelings; he is taking significant pains to project a persona that will counterbalance them to the outside world. This will remain consistent throughout the film; when Gamlet is "mad in craft" the assembled ladies of the court are horrified when he asks Ophelia, "Lady, may I lie in your lap?" His delivery of the fourth soliloquy, presented a few minutes before this scene, is entirely in voiceover. Gamlet's private thoughts are Gamlet's alone, and he must actively construct a persona to prevent others in the court from learning his private thoughts. He is often depicted as only partially successful in this effort. As he thinks, "Oh, what a rogue and peasant slave am I," his expression shifts to one of anguish, and it is obvious he is distressed. As he rubs his temples the surrounding courtiers watch him carefully; it is obvious that they realize that something is very wrong with him.

Just as the motifs of the voices, the committee, rock, water and land, are established at an early point, Ophelia's entrapment is also established early in the film. Our first view of her is during a dancing lesson in Polonius' chamber; the steps are mindless, mechanical, and repetitive. Laertes enters the room, stating, "My necessaries have embarked," causing Ophelia to run joyfully to him and embrace him. Kozintsev here again, with great economy, dramatizes the central thematic concerns surrounding one of his characters. Ophelia is a character who longs to spontaneously express her emotions, but is forced by this environment to adopt a joyless and carefully choreographed life. Ophelia is also played using a very high-pitched and faint voice which is far more suggestive of a girl or an early adolescent than a young woman. As Polonius tells her he wishes for her to end her relationship with Gamlet, she is seated on the floor, with her face at his knee level, as he is seated in an elevated chair. This depiction of Ophelia seems disparate from that of Gertrude in the earlier committee scene. Gertrude, in the former, seems depicted as very much among equals and sits at the table with the rest of the committee—it is Gamlet who is forced to sit on a chair on the periphery of the room. Here, Ophelia is in a clearly subservient position to Polonius. At the line, "think yourself a baby," Kozintsev cuts from the establishing shot framing the two of them at eye-level to a high-angle close shot in which Polonius dominates the right side of the frame to the extent that all we can see is part of his robe and his giant wagging finger, while on the left side of the frame we see all of Ophelia's face and most of her upper body. The use of composition, lenses, and dialogue here serves to infantilize Ophelia; she is a child at the mercy of the adults who surround her. The scene concludes as Ophelia leaves Polonius' side and resumes her maddeningly repetitive dance lesson.

The sense of stasis, repetition, and entrapment conveyed in this scene is reinforced by Kozintsev's cut to an image of a giant clock in one of the castle towers. Just beneath the face of the clock, several carved figures mechanically emerge from a door on the right side of the clock and disappear into a door on the left. The figures appear to be those of a Bishop or priest, a king, a lady fair, a knight, and a skeleton. The early presentation of Polonius among the central decision-makers of Claudius' court served to metaphorically align this court with Kozintsev's contemporary Politburo. The treatment of Ophelia by Polonius is visually suggestive of that of a king issuing orders to a princess, and is immediately followed by the image of archetypal medieval characters paraded across the screen in a circular (and therefore unending) rotation. The possibility that Kozintsev is using these images to metaphorically suggest that his contemporary Politburo is virtually indistinguishable from a medieval court is supported by other elements of his mise-en-scène. Just as images of Lenin and Stalin dominated public spaces prior to Perestroika, Polonius' chamber is dominated by a portrait of Claudius; however, his treatment of Ophelia in his private chamber suggests he has aspirations to be a king himself, and that the unity with which the Politburo presents itself may be illusory. Although no internal conflict in Claudius' court is depicted in Shakespeare's play, the murder of Trotsky and the purges instigated by Stalin characterized political life in Soviet Russia, and it is this contemporary context that Kozintsev is alluding to with his portrayal of Polonius as a would-be King.

Kozintsev further uses visual iconography in his depiction of the ghost, which is first seen on the ramparts of the castle in full armour with a huge cape flowing from behind it. However, armour, in this film, is only worn by the nameless foot-soldiers who are responsible for reading proclamations, opening and shutting gates, and monitoring the castle's defences. The members of the court and Claudius' inner circle wear elegant frilled garments, and are never seen in armour. During the Second World War, Sergei Eisenstein released his film of *Alexander Nevsky*, in which a legendary 13th-century Russian prince successfully repelled an invasion of Huns. The film was initially suppressed, and then released during Hitler's invasion of Russia as propaganda, for which purpose it was wildly successful. In the film, of which Kozintsev and much of his audience would have been aware, Nevsky is portrayed wearing full armour and a cape, much as Nevsky is depicted in a 2002 monument to him in St. Petersburg. The spectre of Gamlet's father here visually recalls the image of Nevsky—an iconic Russian leader who would have been equated with past glories. If Claudius and his inner circle are a metaphor for a polity that has ostensibly replaced an earlier political system but has, in fact, merely redistributed power within the existing system to suit its own interests, the ghost here may also serve as a metaphor for the usurpation of a mythic and glorious popular version of Russian history by the revisionism of the central committee. The Nevskys of the past are heroic only inasmuch as they are useful to the Lenins and Stalins of the present.

Kozintsev aligns Gamlet's predicament much more clearly with Ophelia's than in other film versions of *Hamlet*. For Kozintsev, the proposition that Gamlet is "not in madness but mad in craft" seems a matter for debate:

when confronting Gertrude in her chamber, we do not see or hear the second visitation of the ghost; we instead see Gamlet suddenly adopt an expression of shock and horror as a bright light becomes visible on his face and a loud crescendo of music is heard on the sound-track. With this deviation from his source Kozintsev seems to suggest the possibility that Gamlet is hallucinating. Our second experience of Polonius' chamber occurs when Ophelia tells him that she has been "so affrighted" by Gamlet's behaviour toward her; a caged bird figures prominently in this scene. This metaphoric association of Ophelia with a caged bird after she is frightened by Gamlet is made literal by Kozintsev after Polonius is murdered by Gamlet: Female courtiers dress Ophelia in a metal bustiere and metal hoop skirt which support her mourning garments; she is now literally the caged bird in this castle. Ophelia's mad utterances are given, in Kozintsev's vision, as she meanders through the castle and courtyards in the black mourning dress which is worn over the metal cage into which she has been placed. While she gives her utterances ("There's rosemary, that's for remembrance; pray, love, remember: and there is pansies, that's for thoughts") she collects lifeless twigs as emblems of the flowers she believes she is collecting. Gertrude's report of Ophelia's drowning is not given in Kozintsev's film; rather, we are first shown an image of a tree in full bloom hanging over a small body of water. The camera pans across the calm water until we see Ophelia, floating just below the surface, now in a simple shift. Mist is rising from the water, and Kozintsev cuts to an image of a gull flying out to sea. Images of the gull flying out to sea are sustained over several shots, as the music on the soundtrack becomes lighter in tone and is accompanied by the occasional ringing of bells. The shots of the gull flying out to sea are intercut with shots of Gamlet, standing at the top of the cliff, observing the gull. Whereas Gamlet's style of apparel had previously been consistent with that worn by the rest of the courtiers (albeit far less gaudy), he now also wears a simple shift which is similar in appearance to a monk's robe.

Kozintsev's use of the gull may serve as a metaphor for the soul having finally attained freedom; in Chekhov's *The Seagull*—constructed by Chekhov with a deliberate inter-textual relationship to *Hamlet*[3]—Trigorin delivers the following summary of his story to Nina: "A young girl grows up on the shores of a lake, as you have. She loves the lake as the gulls do, and is as happy and free as they. But a man sees her who chances to come that way, and he destroys her out of idleness, as this gull here has been destroyed." The seagull is aligned with freedom early in Chekhov's play, and later is aligned with being destroyed by one's own beloved. Ophelia's destruction is here aligned with her final freedom. Interestingly, Gamlet's final act in this film, after he has killed Claudius, is to leave the confines of the castle and the courtyards and return to his favourite spot on the cliff, and observe the sea, just as the film has depicted him doing on several occasions. Equally interesting here is the depiction of Claudius' death, which we do not directly see. Gamlet, after hearing from Laertes how the sword has been "un-baited and envenomed," stabs Claudius with the sword. Screaming, Claudius runs from the small chamber where the fight has been staged through the halls of the castle. His final act is also one of escape; and his doom, in Kozintsev's vision, appears to be caused by his tendency to act in his personal interests rather than in the interests of the state. The only freedom possible, in Kozintsev's vision, is through one's own destruction.

Although at the beginning of the film, Claudius is almost invariably presented with the committee, his later schemes—his decision to hide behind an arras and eavesdrop on Ophelia and Gamlet, his decision to send Gamlet to England, the plot on Gamlet's life—are almost invariably presented as "back-room" deals to which only one or a select few persons are privy. As Claudius plots against Gamlet's life with Laertes, they are interrupted by a messenger: Kozintsev stages this scene using a two shot of Laertes and Claudius while they sit at a table from a high angle. All that we see of the messenger is his two feet as they enter the shot in the distance, and they are in the shot for several seconds before Claudius and Laertes notice the messenger, suggesting that Claudius is not only an observer in this court, but is also an object of observation. The fight scene is staged in a room aside from the great halls of this castle with few members of the court in attendance. As Gertrude enters the room while the first bout is already underway, it is apparent that she had not been invited to the fight. It is equally apparent from her actions that she was aware of Claudius' poison scheme, and has decided to disrupt it by drinking the poison herself. Claudius is undone by his own scheming, which Kozintsev depicts as done without the consent or knowledge of the entire governing body. Kozintsev here seems to suggest that Claudius is almost as much a victim in this system as are Gertrude, Laertes, Hamlet, and Ophelia. Claudius' plot with Laertes is immediately preceded by a final shot of the mechanical figures emanating from the tower clock; when Laertes leaves his chamber after agreeing upon their plot to kill Gamlet, Claudius sees his own reflection in his chamber mirror, and, in disgust, throws a goblet of wine at the mirror, drenching his own reflection. The individual human being is shocked at the moral implications of his actions; however, the cog in the political machine is compelled to perform them.

Gamlet can be seen as a metaphor for the Stalinist Soviet Union in its depiction of Claudius as destroyed by his tendency to exceed his authority to act in his personal—and not the collective—interest. *Korol Lir* can, in many ways, be seen as a metaphor for the post–Khrushchev Soviet Union, in which many of Khrushchev's reforms were reversed by the Politburo under the leadership of Brezhnev; the Politburo under Brezhnev was deeply unpopular and relied on the authoritarian exercise of power to remain in office. Kozintsev's film was released early in 1971; seven years into Khrushchev's exile and the same year that Khrushchev died and was denied the dignity of a state funeral. William Taubman, in *Khrushchev: The Man and His Era* noted that a major Russian pollster found that the only years of the 20th century evaluated positively by Russians were those under Nicholas II and those under Khrushchev (650). Although the release of the film predated Khrushchev's death by several months, the story of a king who loses political power due to a disastrous mistake, is stripped of all of position and wealth, and is forced to live on the margins of society by successors who are ruthless and utterly self-interested would again have resonated with a contemporary Soviet audience.

Also like *Gamlet*, *Korol Lir* utilizes formal properties of cinema in order to emphasize thematic concerns. During the 1960s a variety of formats and techniques emerged, in international cinema, to address the perceived erosion of film audiences by television. Cinemascope was among several formats devised to give film a sense of the spectacular which television could not approximate, because of the sheer size, depth, and density of the Cinemascope image. (David Lean's film of *Dr. Zhivago*, coincidentally, was filmed in Cinemascope.) Kozintsev uses this format not merely to overwhelm his viewers with a sense of the spectacular, he uses it to place all of the action of the film into a wider context. In "Two Dimensional Shakespeare: 'King Lear' on Film," Peter Holland writes, "Kozintsev's choice of format carries with it an implication for the view of the play.... The shape of the cinemascope screen means that a figure is always and necessarily seen in a context, a surrounding place in which the figure lives, through which it moves" (62). Stephen Buhler further notes: "*Korol Lear* ... begins ... with a bleak landscape inhabited by the poorest of the poor.... Kozintsev ... emphasizes the larger social context of the action.... We see peasants and beggars labour up a hill in sight of the castle where Lear will divide his kingdom.... The king does not 'affect'—care for—any of his subjects; he merely wants their obedience to his demands. When Cordelia and Kent dare to deny his royal pleasure, he expels them not only from his regard, but from the body politic. Yuri Yarvet, as Lear, declaims his sentences against his daughter and adviser before the assembled citizenry" (165).

Kozintsev is consistent in emphasizing the larger social context for the actions of the main characters throughout the course of his film. Peter Holland observes both that "Edgar, transforming himself into Poor Tom, joins a long straggling line of the dispossessed, the poor naked wretches, the underclass of Lear's kingdom (62)" and also that Lear "appears on the battlements and the people throw themselves prostrate to the ground at the sight of their king" (63).

Yet the Lear that Kozintsev depicts is hardly the sort of person that anyone would feel compelled to lie prostrate before if they knew him on a personal level. Our first impression of Lear, as he enters the throne room giggling and joking with The Fool, is that he seems to be an inane and somewhat silly old man who does not appreciate the seriousness of the situation that he himself has created. This impression is reinforced by Lear's continued play with The Fool as a page reads Lear's royal decree. This Lear is irresponsible to a fault—embarking whimsically or impulsively upon courses of action that have drastic consequences for his subjects, but ultimately taking no responsibility for their implementation. Lear's redemption in this film is to become one of his subjects, and to experience life as they experience it. In early shots in the film Kozintsev depicts peasants walking through unique rock formations on their way to hearing Lear's royal decree; Lear, Edgar, Kent and Gloucester will later be seen walking through those same formations, as they are all reduced to the stature of peasants. Marks from dirt and scars that are seen on peasant's faces in these first shots will later be reflected by identical scars on Edgar and Kent's faces. In the hovel Lear, The Fool, and Tom are joined by a least a dozen peasants who have also retired there to escape the storm. When this Lear states that he has "ta'en too little care of this," he is confronted with the enormity of his irresponsibility en masse.

In "*King Lear*: Kozintsev's Social Translation," David Margolies notes that Kozintsev and Peter Brook were in regular correspondence while they were preparing their respective films of *King Lear* (237). Kozintsev's *Korol Lir*, as a cultural product of Soviet Russia under Breshnev, focuses on the broader social impact of a dysfunctional polity; whereas, Brook's film, as a cultural product of 1960s and 1970s England, focuses on deeply flawed individuals who are spiritually isolated from each other. Interestingly, Kozintsev and Brook seem, in many cases, to have applied different techniques to achieve similar goals. Brook emphasizes Regan's narcissism by depicting her murder of the First Servant with a close-up shot of her twisted face and arms as she flails at the off-screen Servant with a blunt object. Kozintsev emphasizes the narcissism of both Goneril and Regan by using the Cinemascope frame to depict the mass destruction of the battle between Corwall, Albany, and France. Against a background of burning buildings, cannons firing, and masses of peasants (including Cordelia and Lear) running away from havoc, both Regan and Goneril wander single-mindedly pursuing Edmund, oblivious to the din that surrounds them. Brook is minimal in his depiction of the blinding of Gloucester; we see Cornwall draw a knife and move toward Gloucester, and the screen abruptly cuts to black while we hear Gloucester's piercing shriek on the soundtrack. Kozintsev, conversely, is expansive in his depiction of the blinding of Gloucester. We see Gloucester thrown to the floor, and as he struggles to escape, we see Cornwall stride toward him, and raise a spurred boot. As the boot is swiftly kicked downward out of the frame we hear Gloucester's first scream. Gloucester is surrounded and continues to scream as his second eye is put out: Kozintsev cuts to Edmund and Goneril, who are together in one of the bedrooms upstairs. Gloucester's shrieks and cries for Edmund to help him are unacknowledged by either Edmund or Goneril. Where Brook isolates characters in the frame to depict them in confrontation, Kozintsev uses the frame to show characters in relation to one another, to demonstrate how actions are interconnected and have implications for all. Most interestingly, the method of blinding Gloucester as depicted by Kozintsev is that which Brook depicted in his famous 1962 stage production of *King Lear*.

Depictions of brutality, mass starvation, and mass destruction are characteristic of the second half of Kozintsev's film. The first half of the film is concerned with Lear's gradual loss of control, and how this loss of control is greeted with displays of restraint and formality which are in stark contrast with the latent rage and brutality of the second half. In the first half of the film lack of restraint and control is confined to Lear: he rages at Cordelia during the throne room scene, spits in Kent's face when told to "see better," and violently tears the map apart while disinheriting Cordelia. At the midpoint of the film, where definite signs of madness begin to manifest themselves in Lear, an inversion begins to take place. Lear's "reason not the need" speech, found in Act II, scene iv of the play, is delivered quietly and earnestly by Lear to himself, after Regan and Goneril have shut a door in his face, isolating him in a room. Immediately prior to the storm, Kozintsev provides a shot of the heath accompanied by the howling of wolves on the soundtrack. We then see several shots depicting wolves, bears, boars, and then horses running away from the oncoming storm, against which Lear—

according to Marjorie Garber in *Shakespeare After All*—calls for the apocalypse[4] (670). His curse seems realized in the events that are to follow. In addition to Cornwall's gouging of Gloucester's eye with a spur, and the collective removal of his second eye, the First Servant is stabbed in the back, Edgar dispatches Oswald by breaking his neck with a stick, and the strong winds of the storm are reflected by the throngs of panicked people running away from battles in the same instinctual manner that the animals had prior to the storm. As Lear and Cordelia are surrounded and unable to break free of the running crowds, he seems here a victim of the curse that he, himself, has wished on humankind while in his rage. The forces unleashed by the storm at his command have been turned upon himself.

Although the bodies of Lear and Cordelia are borne away together at the film's conclusion, it is unclear as to whether the storm unleashed by Lear's curse has fully spent itself, as Kozintsev here does not conform to the normal narrative and formal codes associated with cinema. In *Hollywood from Vietnam to Reagan,* Robin Wood writes:

> In western cinema, the dominant codes of narrative have been the linear ones: the proairetic (code of actions) and the hermeneutic (code of enigmas), whose function it is to carry the story forward and maintain the reader/viewer's curiosity ... an action is announced, and we know it will be developed and carried to a conclusion, that it will lead to further actions; at the same time, the play of enigmas will keep us guessing what will happen, focusing our attention on events, outcomes, solutions. We attend to what is actually before ... for what it will lead to: we are continually pointed ahead, given enough hints to formulate a general sense of probable developments but never enough to give us certainty or preclude surprises [304–305].

The conclusions of mainstream Hollywood productions usually depict a closure of both of these linear codes; the chain of actions is presented as exhausted, and the chain of enigmas is resolved. For example, at the conclusion of Branagh's *Hamlet*, the main characters have all died, leaving the Fortinbras line once more empowered; similarly, at the end of Polanski's *Macbeth*, Donalbain approaches the witches' cavern to renew a never-ending cycle of corruption after Macbeth is killed. In contrast, at the conclusion of *Korol Lir*, Kozintsev does not exhaust his chain of actions or resolve his chain of enigmas. Upon Lear's death Edgar merely leaves the action of the film, the camera following him as he walks against the backdrop of dislocated people and devastation caused by the previous battle. (The final words in the film are Kent's "My master calls me, I must not say no." Albany's final pronouncement is cut from Kozintsev's script.) One of the film's final images is that of Lear's Fool being kicked by a soldier while sitting on the ground, initially weeping but, after the kick, playing a whimsical tune on his flute. These depictions precipitate an entirely new chain of enigmas that Kozintsev's film does not address: Where is Edgar going? Who is going to be in charge? Given his relationship to Lear, why is The Fool engaged in this course of action? Why does the soldier kick The Fool? Other enigmas presented earlier in the film remain unresolved: Given that Regan shrank from Cornwall as he walked toward her and tried to take her arm while dying, why does she give his corpse a ravenously sexual kiss on the mouth?

These unresolved enigmas may serve a similar function to Kozintsev's use of the clock face in *Gamlet*. By withholding narrative closure from his audience, Kozintsev may be implying that the events of his film are merely part of a longer repetitive cycle in which the "huddled masses" are continuously faced with the consequences of the mistakes of the privileged and the empowered. Here, the "huddled masses" certainly seem charged with the responsibility of repairing the damage that the privileged and empowered have done. As Edgar leaves the action of the film, the people in the background are clearly dousing fires and re-erecting posts that formed the superstructures of destroyed buildings. Kozintsev's refusal to provide narrative closure may reinforce a socialist view of history in which the proletariat pays for the mistakes of other classes; however, there are no easily identifiable analogues for the bourgeoisie in this film. A possible explanation is that Kozintsev's film may be evocative of the "Brezhnev stagnation" which succeeded Khrushchev's term in office; a period of time in which the Politburo mandated massive military spending and arrests of dissidents, while shortages of goods plagued the Soviet economy. Edgar's walk out of the action of the film supports this interpretation: he walks away from Albany, Kent, and the corpses of Lear and Cordelia and views the common people attempting to cope with the devastating aftermath of a struggle caused by a disagreement amongst the members of an empowered family. Edgar's unwillingness to further support a class of people who attempt to keep themselves in power can here be read as a metaphor for Kozintsev's lack of support for a Politburo that kept itself empowered to the detriment of the citizenry it nominally acted in the interests of.

Like Kurosawa before him, Kozintsev successfully represented Shakespeare's plays in the cinema in a manner which reflected the priorities of his unique socio-cultural moment. Unlike Kurosawa, and in many ways due to the efforts of Pasternak before him, Kozintsev was able to do so in a manner which represented the integrity of the play as an entirety. Although much of *Kumonosu djô* is clearly based on *Macbeth*, there are significant departures as well: the MacDuff subplot is entirely replaced with a subplot depicting the gossip of Washizu's retainers and logically connecting to the assassination of Washizu by his own samurai. Although Kurosawa's *Ran* preserves the basic story structure and many of the central characters of *King Lear*, it also borrows freely from other sources and is ultimately an amalgamated text. *Warui yatsu hodo yoku nemuru* is barely recognizable as being based on *Hamlet*; although the plot structure and some basic character relationships are maintained, the narrative structure is almost completely revised. Nor do any of Kurosawa's adaptations attempt to engage with the poetry of Shakespeare's plays. Although Kozintsev is also an intercultural adaptor of Shakespeare's works, he manages to re-read his seminal plays within the context of his own cultural background, while preserving the identity of his films as adaptations of Shakespeare. In doing this, he also manages to embed popular filmmaking techniques into the thematic structures of the films he makes. Unlike the Hollywood "costume drama" Shakespeare films of the 1930s, Kozintsev's use of mise-en-scène, sound, editing, and cinematography is aimed at establishing specific meaning effects far more than it is with endowing his film with a sense of the exotic. Kozintsev manages to convey a sense of both elevation and of intimacy in these films; although their events are seen as being of national import, his characters always display complex personalities and motivations.

CHAPTER 6

Zeffirelli

Zeffirelli's place in the canon of "auteurs of Shakespeare on film" would seem assured, as he has completed three financially successful filmed adaptations of Shakespeare's plays to date (one of which has remained as the single most popular and most seen direct interpretation of Shakespeare's work on screen for 40 years). However, Zeffirelli's films seem to be among the least discussed filmed adaptations of Shakespeare's plays in academic literature or at professional conferences. This is a paradox, as his output (excluding *Otello* which is technically a filmed representation of a Verdi opera based on one of Shakespeare's plays) equals the respective outputs of Olivier and Welles (three films each), and the box office results of *Romeo and Juliet* still exceed the box office results of Branagh's *Much Ado About Nothing* or Luhrmann's *Romeo + Juliet*. In "Zeffirelli's Shakespeare," Ace Pilkington argues that this situation results from a tendency among critics to dichotomize filmed adaptations of Shakespeare's plays as the work of either "purists" or "popularizers," in which critics perceive Zeffirelli as having the best "claim to the dangerous title of popularizer-in-chief" (164). Pilkington further argues that the purist "case" against Zeffirelli concerns the extent to which Zeffirelli abbreviates the plays he represents[1] (165), Zeffirelli's tendency to re-allocate lines of dialogue in order to alter the tempo of a scene[2] (166), and Zeffirelli's tendency to rewrite the play by replacing "difficult" words[3] (167) or by adding entirely new dialogue.[4] Lewis Grossberger exemplifies the purist case in "Shakespeare Goes Hollywood" when he refers to Zeffirelli's approach to the screenplay as "axplay" (220), and in "Stanley Kaufmann on Films," we find a related purist objection to Zeffirelli when Kaufmann describes Zeffirelli's "game" in filming *Romeo and Juliet* as "flatter the young and swamp them in Beeyootiful Color" (33).

Although these objections are certainly supported by Zeffirelli's approach, they are as supported by the approaches applied by Olivier,

Welles, and Branagh as they are by Zeffirelli's. Branagh's *Henry V* retains only about 50 percent of the dialogue in the scene depicting the execution of Bardolph, which Branagh stages in a manner that elicits more sympathy toward King Henry than it does to the doomed soldier. Olivier's film of *Henry V*, however, dispenses with this scene entirely as Olivier is presenting Henry as a sanitized "great, good king." Welles, in *Chimes at Midnight*, picks lines from 5 different plays in order to construct his 113-minute film,[5] and, at the beginning of *Othello*, provides a brief voiceover narration intended to orientate the audience.[6] Branagh's film of *Much Ado About Nothing* opens with a sumptuous visual panorama of the Tuscan countryside, despite the fact that Shakespeare's play calls for the scene to be set "Before Leonato's House," and supplies a scene depicting Margaret and Borachio having sex on a balcony, visualizing an event reported in Shakespeare's play. Branagh's film of *Hamlet* replaces the play's setting of "Elsinore. A platform before the castle," with a pan left across the grounds of Blenheim palace shot in 70mm technicolor. Objections such as these need not be confined to the work of the aforementioned four directors: Luhrmann's widely hailed *Romeo + Juliet* utilizes a TV anchor as its chorus, depicts Mercutio at the Capulet's ball dancing in drag to Kym Mazelle's rendition of the 1976 disco hit "Young Hearts Run Free," and features Romeo ingesting an ecstasy pill on his way in to the Capulet's ball. Yet Luhrmann's approach was hailed for its audacity, Olivier's for its genius, Welles' for its cinematic technique, and Branagh's for its compromise between commercial savvy and political statement. In this light, the objections to Zeffirelli seem not only arbitrary, they seem unsubstantiated.

A far more likely explanation for this critical tendency to dismiss Zeffirelli's importance lies in an unequal application of the "auteur theory" to Olivier, Welles, and Branagh. Stephen Buhler has suggested that the careers of Olivier, Welles, and Branagh represent a continuation of the "actor/manager" traditions established by Garrick, Macready, Forrest, Kean, Irving and Wolfit (96), and that the three filmmakers have "appropriated" the "functions" of the "actor/manager" in order "to bring Shakespeare to film." Although Luhrmann has only completed one filmed adaptation of Shakespeare's work, the release of his film in 1996 associates this film with what Kenneth Rothwell, in *A History of Shakespeare on Screen*, calls "the age of Branagh" (246). Zeffirelli, as a filmmaker representing Shakespeare's plays during what Crowl posits as the "international period" (Crowl 3) of Shakespearean film production, is unlike his peers in that he is neither an acclaimed actor/manager, as were Olivier and Welles, and is not attempting inter-cultural adaptations, as were Kurosawa and Kozintsev. Zeffirelli's films are clearly intended for an international mainstream cinema audience, and (with the exception of *Hamlet*) make no blatant claim to the theatrical tradition of Shakespeare. Rather, *The Taming of the Shrew* and *Romeo and Juliet* conspicuously reflect a growing tendency in the international cinema of the 1960s to privilege the visual image over the word. *DigitialDreamDoor.com* provides a list of what it refers to as the "100 Greatest Movies of the 1960's"; the excerpt which follows indicates in **bold** font films on the list that are renowned for their sumptuous or unorthodox visual strategies and/or feature extended sequences without conventional dialogue.

1. **Lawrence of Arabia (1962, David Lean)**
2. **Psycho (1960, Alfred Hitchcock)**
3. Dr. Strangelove (1964, Stanley Kubrick)
4. **8½ (1963, Federico Fellini)**
5. **2001: A Space Odyssey (1968, Stanley Kubrick)**
6. **Once Upon a Time in the West (1968, Sergio Leone)**
7. To Kill a Mockingbird (1962, Robert Mulligan)
8. Midnight Cowboy (1969, John Schlesinger)
9. Bonnie and Clyde (1967, Arthur Penn)
10. La Dolce Vita (1960, Federico Fellini)
11. **The Good, the Bad and the Ugly (1966, Sergio Leone)**
12. **The Graduate (1967, Mike Nichols)**
13. **Breathless (1960, Jean-Luc Godard)**
14. Yojimbo (1961, Akira Kurosawa)
15. **Wild Bunch (1969, Sam Peckinpah)**
16. **Persona (1966, Ingmar Bergman)**
17. The Leopard (1963, Luchino Visconti)
18. L'Avventura (1960, Michelangelo Antonioni)
19. The Apartment (1960, Billy Wilder)
20. The Manchurian Candidate (1962, John Frankenheimer)
21. **Easy Rider (1969, Dennis Hopper)**
22. Last Year at Marienbad (1961, Alain Resnais)
23. **West Side Story (1961, Jerome Robbins, Robert Wise)**
24. Cool Hand Luke (1967, Stuart Rosenberg)
25. The Battle of Algiers (1966, Gillo Pontecorvo)
26. **Doctor Zhivago (1965, David Lean)**

Of the 26 films listed, 13 feature extended sequences without dialogue and/or are renowned for their sumptuous or unorthodox visual strategies. *The Taming of the Shrew* and *Romeo and Juliet* are products of a socio-historical context in which the verbal was being de-emphasized in favor of the visual. The period's youth culture increasingly used colored clothing as an indicator of personal expression, and its mainstream cinema relied on visual splendor as a means of positioning itself against television, which was displacing cinema as the predominant visual narrative medium. Zeffirelli's approach to Shakespeare's play was heavily influenced by these factors.

Another disparity between Zeffirelli and his predecessors can be demonstrated by a brief examination of casting techniques: when representing Shakespeare in the cinema, Olivier and Welles cast themselves as leads and frequently utilized little-known but highly skilled Shakespearean actors to fill out their casts. Zeffirelli's Shakespeare films utilize the system of casting by star image which is more typical of mainstream Hollywood filmmaking. Although Olivier's *Richard III* might seem an obvious exception in his casting of Claire Bloom (who had achieved stardom due to her appearance in Chaplin's *Limelight*) and Stanley Baker (who was an established screen villain), it is an exception that proves the rule. Olivier's cast also includes John Gielgud and Ralph Richardson, thereby presenting the "triple-crown" of 20th-century Shakespearean theatrical performance in one film (which in its credit sequence gives screenplay credit to several of the aforementioned traditional actor/managers). Similarly, Welles casts Gielgud as Henry IV, and uses Richardson to recite a voiceover narration from Holinshed in *Chimes at Midnight*. In casting alone, Olivier and Welles' adaptations are aligned with a perceived Shakespearean theatrical tradition, whereas Zeffirelli's adaptations are aligned with mainstream commercial practice. If this is one cause for the tendency of "purist" critics to charge Zeffirelli with offences against the play for performance practices which, when used by Olivier, Welles, and Branagh, prompt those same critics to praise them, the irony of the situation is increased when the response of commercial or "popular" film critics to Zeffirelli's work is considered. In his review of Zeffirelli's *Hamlet,* Roger Ebert praised the film for its robust, upbeat style and for its insight that "there was nothing fundamentally awry with Hamlet until everything went wrong in his life, until his father died and his mother married his uncle with unseemly haste. This is a prince who was healthy and happy and could have lived a long and active life, if things had turned out differently." Writing of Zeffirelli's *Romeo and Juliet,* Ebert has placed the film on his "Great Movies" list, and stated, in his October 19, 1968, review of the film: "I believe Franco Zeffirelli's *Romeo and Juliet* is the most exciting film of Shakespeare ever made. Not because it is greater drama than Olivier's *Henry V*, because it is not. Nor is it greater cinema than Welles' *Falstaff [Chimes at Midnight]*. But it is greater Shakespeare than either because it has the passion, the sweat, the violence, the poetry, the love and the tragedy in the most immediate terms I can imagine. It is a deeply moving piece of entertainment, and that is possibly what Shakespeare would have preferred."

Interestingly, writing at the time of the release of *Romeo and Juliet*, Ebert seems to intuit and respond to the critical tendency to view Zeffirelli's work less than favorably in comparison to the work of Olivier and Welles. The disparity between Ebert's reactions to Zeffirelli's approach and the reactions of contemporary adaptation scholars can be understood in the light of Sarah Cardwell's assertion that "the study of adaptation arose in an environment that valued literature over the newer arts of film and television" (72), and that "pluralist Film Studies of the 1980s and 1990s ... placed film within the broader context of culture" (84). In short, the critical tendency to underestimate Zeffirelli has far less to do with *what* films Zeffirelli makes or *how* he makes them; it is rather a function of *when* he makes them that prompts this reaction. At the release of *The Taming of the Shrew* and *Romeo and Juliet*, critical perspectives were more heavily biased by the issue of fidelity to the seminal play than they would have been at the time of the release of Luhrman's film, which is heavily inter-textual. In the absence of a clear connection to an actor/manager tradition, or of an obvious inter-cultural approach, contemporary adaptation scholars reverted to a position biased by the confines of fidelity criticism when responding to Zeffirelli, who was working in a contemporary cinema which privileged the visual over the textual.

Zeffirelli's use of Elizabeth Taylor and Richard Burton as the leads in *The Taming of the Shrew* capitalized on the popular success of Mike Nichols' film of *Who's Afraid of Virginia Woolf?*, which had been released the previous year and which had earned American Academy Award nominations for both Taylor and Burton. The association of Taylor and Burton with Nichols' film (which portrayed the physically and emotionally abusive relationship of a couple as manifested in an evening of drinking) and with their equally volatile off-screen relationship would have facilitated an audience's reading of the relationship between Katherine and Petruchio in Zeffirelli's film. Nichols' film was shot utilizing stark monochrome photography, whereas Zeffirelli's is sumptuous in its use of color.[7] The bulk of the action of Nichols' film takes place in a single, claustrophobic setting whereas Zeffirelli's film is constantly switching locations and using dynamic camera work to provide a sense of energy and movement. Nichols' film seems a social satire in which the values of its characters and the class of people they represent is condemned, whereas Zeffirelli's film, according to Jack

Jorgens in *Shakespeare on Film*, seems more a "release of Dionysian energies" (73).[8] Although Zeffirelli's casting technique seems on a surface level to reflect mainstream Hollywood casting strategies that had been in use since the 1930s, the purpose served by casting Burton and Taylor was far more complex than is usually given credit for with the description "casting by star image."

Zeffirelli's use of setting here is also much more complex than a superficial examination might immediately indicate. The setting of Zeffirelli's *The Taming of the Shrew* might initially recall the sumptuous settings of Taylor's *The Taming of the Shrew*, Reinhardt and Dieterle's *A Midsummer Night's Dream*, Cukor's *Romeo and Juliet*, and Czinner's *As You Like It*. Zeffirelli, however, was using actual locations, whereas his four predecessors were using manufactured sets. Zeffirelli's use of setting is, in fact, often the inverse of the realism/illusionism which characterized the "classical Hollywood period." Where Zeffirelli's four predecessors were using manufactured sets that were designed to appear realistic, Zeffirelli, in the early establishing shots of his film, used an obvious backdrop for the Padua cityscape. As an experienced scenographer, this was hardly a mistake on Zeffirelli's part; rather, it represents a directorial choice. Like Taylor, Zeffirelli presents a representation of the minutiae of life in Verona as a wonderstruck Lucentio first enters the city. Like Cukor and Reinhardt and Dieterle, we are then presented with a stately march into the Cathedral square, which is accompanied by a choir singing religious music over the credits. The cardinal steps into the square, blesses the crowd, and the scene immediately transforms itself from a solemn observance into a medieval festival which bursts from the square out onto the streets. The festival includes a skeleton raised on a staff, cross-dressing men, a lord of misrule being flayed with a broom and tossed above the crowd in a blanket, and a costume which parodies a rich man. Many of these festival depictions characterized medieval carnivals, and are still present in contemporary carnival celebrations. Zeffirelli is here signaling to his audience that the film to follow will be structured around carnival inversions, around situations meeting and becoming their opposites. Bakhtin characterized medieval carnival as being concerned with "the inversion of power structures, the parodic debunking of all that a particular society takes seriously (including and in particular all that which it fears)" (Morris 250). In this light, Jorgens' view of this film "as a release of Dionysian energies" (73) seems not only appropriate, it seems integral to understanding Zeffirelli's strategy in dramatizing the film.

This sense of carnival inversion is maintained through the early scenes of the film as we are introduced to Katherine, Baptista, Hortensio, and his retinue. The frightened men scurry away from Katherine; Baptista—nominally the representative of patriarchal authority here—nervously stutters his lines, while Hortensio speaks in an effeminate, high voice while wearing long hair and frills. The role reversal of Lucentio and Tranio adds to this sense of inversion, as Tranio jokingly brushes dust off of Lucentio's cloak after they've switched roles. Petruchio's lack of self-control and violent response to Grumio's insolence is presented in the foreground of a scene which depicts carnival revelers as the background of the action. At dinner, while Hortensio attempts to recruit Petruchio, the latter is far more interested in picking fleas from his dog's coat than he is in what Hortensio has to say. Once Petruchio agrees to aid Hortensio, he assures Hortensio, "I will not sleep ... till I see her," and immediately falls into a drunken slumber.

This pattern of carnival inversion is the structural principle of this film and also reverses standard critical interpretations of the play and its characters. Far from being chaste, Bianca is depicted as a flirt who quite enjoys the attentions of several men. When Petruchio enters Baptista's house he seems far more a thief than a potential son-in-law when he checks all of Baptista's goblets in order to ascertain their value. Grumio is often insolent to Petruchio, and at one point attempts to undermine Petruchio's attempt to deceive Baptista. Petruchio assures Baptista that, at his death, he will leave "all [his] lands and leases whatsoever to Katherine," but Baptista's glee and relief at this reassurance is undermined by a flatulent sound produced by Grumio blowing into a tube, as if Grumio is attempting to warn Baptista that Petruchio doesn't really have much in the way of assets. During the initial wooing scene, staged by Zeffirelli as a chase throughout Baptista's home intercut with scenes of the disguised Lucentio and Hortensio tutoring Bianca, Katherine's response to Petruchio shifts from the confrontational mode of behavior which had previously been associated with her, to an avoidant mode. Unsuccessful in dissuading Petruchio from his suit by use of force, Katherine tricks Petruchio into looking the other way and then sneaks out of the room.

Katherine escapes to a locked room which contains a huge bin full of raw wool, which she leaps into and rolls around in to the accompaniment of joyful music on the soundtrack, which establishes this as a favorite and "safe" space for her. As Petruchio invades this space through a trap door, Katherine attempts to place a large sack of grain on the door to prevent him from entering. Unsuccessful at this, Katherine then climbs up a ladder to a mezzanine or loft in the room and pulls the ladder up behind her to prevent Petruchio from following her. Later in the sequence, Petruchio crashes through a plaster wall in his pursuit of her. Katherine attempts to escape by walking along a rooftop; Petruchio catches her, and as the roof collapses under them they both fall into the bin of wool. Petruchio tells her that she is "pleasant, changesome, passing courteous, and slow in speech but sweet as springtime flowers"; while each utterance of a descriptor on his part is punctuated by a sharp crack on the soundtrack as she beats him with a piece of wood. Petruchio then takes the wood from her, and holds it to her throat while stating, "Will you, nill you, I will marry you." Katherine's "safe and free" space has now become the space of her entrapment, the wall that had separated Petruchio becomes an opening through which he gains access to her, and the stick that she attempted to fight him off with becomes the instrument of his domination of her. All through this film, people, places and things become their opposites.

This sense of inversion is further punctuated in the scenes depicting life at Petruchio's house. Leaving Katherine in the mud outside, Petruchio gleefully bursts into the house, laughing as he opens the casket containing his dowry, and flings coins to his servants. While doing this, he hums to the accompaniment of boisterous music on the soundtrack, and finally bursts into song with the lyrics "Where is the life that late I led, it's gone, it's gone, it's gone." Zeffirelli's staging of this scene and Burton's performance combine to suggest that the "life" that Petruchio is singing about is the life he led while in debt, from which the dowry has freed him. However, as Katherine enters the home Petruchio's tone becomes subdued to the extent that the last repetition of "it's gone" seems a bare murmur: his "freedom" from debt is accompanied by a loss of freedom as he enters domestic life. This sense is reinforced by Grumio simultaneously snickering and softly singing, "it's gone, it's gone, away," as he takes Katherine to the bridal chamber.

Petruchio's implementation of his plan to dominate Katherine precipitates yet another reversal. Petruchio emerges from the bedroom loudly berating the servants for their incompetence, spitting on Grumio after stating, "I spit on you that you should treat her thus," and then in a soft voice says to them, "This is the way to kill a wife with kindness," indicating out of Katherine's hearing that his wildly explosive persona is merely a guise he has assumed. The servants stare back at him with facial expressions that clearly register shock and disgust at the extremity of Petruchio's behavior and his gratuitous shouting (they are in the next room as he bellows for them). Katherine, weeping in her bed, suddenly grins and begins to chuckle to herself. The next morning Petruchio awakens to find his servants happily putting his house in order under Katherine's direction. He is no longer the master of this house, she is, and Grumio offers Petruchio a feather duster in order to punctuate the point.

The final reversal in this film would seem to be Katherine's final speech, which Elizabeth Taylor plays with complete sincerity, prompting controversy among critics who attempt to classify Zeffirelli's film as exclusively pro- or anti-feminist. Focus on Taylor's delivery of the speech itself often causes critics to neglect the context that Zeffirelli very carefully imbeds this speech in. Firstly, at the end of this scene when Petruchio exhorts Katherine by stating, "Kiss me, Kate," in Zeffirelli's staging, although Petruchio makes this request of Katherine, it is clearly Katherine who initiates this passionate and public kiss. In an earlier scene Petruchio makes the same request before they enter Baptista's house; Petruchio threatens to return to Verona if Katherine doesn't meet the request, and Katherine responds by stating, "I will give thee a kiss," then quickly giving Petruchio a swift peck on the nose. The scene that separates these two public kisses presents the wedding ceremony of Bianca and Lucentio. The scene contains an interesting shot in which Katherine, during the ceremony, observes two children fighting under a table, to be corrected by their parents. It is possible that Zeffirelli includes this shot to indicate that Katherine wants children, and recognizes that her battle with Petruchio must end to facilitate this. However, it is far more consistent with the logic of this film to interpret this shot as expressing Katherine's emerging understanding that her relationship with Petruchio has, up to that point, been childish and immature, and that her seeming submission to Petruchio is intended as an invitation to enter into a mature relationship in which they are partners rather than combatants. This reading is supported by the recognition that Katherine's gesture of submission at the conclusion of her speech, kneeling before Petruchio and extending her hand to him, mirrors Petruchio's extension of his hand to her after his initial domination of her. In that scene, after he has held the stick that she was hitting him with to her throat and she has indicated submission, he offers his hand to her, in order to pull her up out of the wool bin. Katherine refuses to take his hand, so he twists her arm behind her back in order to force her to appear before Baptista with him. During their wedding night, when they initially enter the bedroom, Petruchio attempts to be tender with her, gently kissing her on the shoulder and reaching out to her in bed, only to be hit very hard on the crown of his head with a bed-warmer. In this context, Katherine, in kneeling and extending her hand to Petruchio, is not necessarily expressing submission as much as she may be expressing regret for her part in their former childish relationship.

Marjorie Garber has identified the Christopher Sly induction as crucial to understanding Shakespeare's play, as it "introduces and mirrors all the major issues that will preoccupy the actors in the main drama to come" (59). Among the issues that Garber identifies are the impersonation of nobles and commoners: Sly is "a tinker wrongly convinced that he is a nobleman" (*ibid.*), and the lord is "an actor playing the part of a nobleman" (*ibid.*), and Bartholomew the page masquerades as a "lady" whom Sly wishes to have sex with. Although Zeffirelli omits the induction and approximately 70 percent of Shakespeare's play (according to Pilkington's estimate), the crucial theme of inversion is amply demonstrated by Zeffirelli using visual means. The reaction of Petruchio's household staff to his extreme behavior on his wedding night, and the enthusiasm with which they participate in Kate's restoration of order to his house certainly suggest Petruchio may be a nobleman in terms of birth, but in terms of behavior is "wrongly convinced" of his nobility.[9] A similar dichotomy is visually represented by Zeffirelli between Katherine and Bianca: although Katherine is volatile and violent, she ultimately easily assumes the matriarchal role and puts the house in order. In the opening scenes of the film Bianca is portrayed as a flirt who actively enjoys the attention of many men, who later has no qualms about publicly humiliating her husband at his own wedding feast. Which is the Shrew, and which is the virtuous wife? These observations indicate that Zeffirelli's approach, in representing Shakespeare's plays on film, is not the reductive approach that Pilkington, Grossberger, and Kaufmann suggest it is. Rather, Zeffirelli utilizes an approach to Shakespeare's plays that distinguishes between their narrative and thematic elements. Narrative elements are expressed utilizing those portions of the play-text that directly advance it; thematic elements are rendered visually. Zeffirelli utilizes Shakespeare's dialogue in a minimalist manner which effectively relates the exposition, crisis, climax, and denouement of the play to the audience, while the thematic concerns of the play are related to the audience through the use of visual analogues. The function of the Sly induction in Shakespeare's play is fulfilled by the carnival explosion that begins Zeffirelli's film, in which we see nobles acting like commoners and commoners taking on the roles of nobles. Carnival inversion is at the heart of the visual strategy of this film.

Zeffirelli's approach to dialogue and theme remains consistent throughout his three filmed adaptations of Shakespeare's plays. Roger Ebert, in his "Great Movies" review, notes that Zeffirelli's 1968 film of *Romeo and Juliet* is "focused on love, while Baz Luhrmann's popular version of 1996 focused on violence." In representing *Romeo and Juliet*, Zeffirelli again eschews the idealized spectacular sets of Cukor's film and grounds his film in a realistic depiction of a Renaissance town by shooting his film entirely on location in Italy. This setting, coupled with costumes used in the film, will be shown to facilitate a reading of the film's Verona as deeply corrupted.

In addition to casting teenagers to play the eponymous roles, Zeffirelli conspicuously foregrounds the inner dynamics of the Capulet family in his film. Early in the film, as Capulet tells Paris, "the earth has swallowed up all my hopes," we see Lady Capulet glaring at her husband through a window; it is obvious that she dislikes him. Any claim that Capulet himself might make to benevolence of character is certainly compromised by his later action of breaking down the door of Juliet's room and throwing her to the floor when she refuses to marry Paris. The Nurse proves herself a hypocrite by first enthusiastically participating in Juliet's marriage to Romeo, and later just as enthusiastically suggesting that Juliet ignore her marriage vows and marry Paris.

Zeffirelli's emphasis on the Capulet family in his film serves to amplify critical responses to the play which suggest that the love between "the star-crossed lovers" is an incorruptible love in a corrupted world, and that Romeo and Juliet form the anima and animus components of a "shared soul": a scourge figure sacrificed to purge the world of corruption. Jungian criticism was certainly in widespread use at the time of the film's production, and Zeffirelli seems to have taken a great deal of effort to associate the Capulet home with corruption. Juliet's costume at the Capulets' ball is virtually identical to the costume depicted in the portrait of Lucrezia Borgia at the Musée des Beaux-Arts, and Tybalt's costume is very similar to that worn by Cesare Borgia in Melone's portrait. If Zeffirelli intends the Capulet family to represent in microcosm the state of society in his vision of the renaissance, Zeffirelli's alignment of the Capulets with the Borgias indicate that the audience is to view this society as deeply corrupted.

Where Zeffirelli used carnival inversions as the structural principle by which he represented the thematic elements of *The Taming of the Shrew*, he uses a dichotomy between the artificial and the organic to visually represent the themes of *Romeo and Juliet*. The social world of the film is depicted as in Zeffirelli's earlier representation of Shakespeare on film, utilizing colorful costumes against the grey background of stones used in constructing buildings. As The Prince rides into the square to restore order after the civil brawl that opens the film, the noise of his horse's hooves on the paving stones is accentuated on the sound track. This is the artificial world, and he is at the apex of its hierarchy. Yet, *Romeo and Juliet*, like *The Taming of the Shrew*, also begins with a sequence showing public life in the open square. Here, however, it is not a procession into a church yard that is depicted; rather, the camera tracks through an open marketplace in which people are depicted buying and selling vegetables, as the soundtrack is punctuated by people calling "fresh peas and greens."

Zeffirelli uses the organic in this film to characterize the love between Romeo and Juliet. The Capulets' garden, where the two first declare their love for one another, is depicted by Zeffirelli as a place of unrestrained, lush growth of foliage. The visual sense of unrestrained growth is reinforced through Whiting's and Hussey's acting choices; as Romeo and Juliet embrace they kiss impulsively, unable to control their passion as Juliet's eyes roll over because of the intensity of what she is feeling. Wind blows through the trees as they embrace on the balcony, and as Romeo leaves the Capulet home he is depicted as running through a forest while laughing and happily grabbing at leaves. Friar Laurence is introduced to us as he crawls through wild plants in order to find ingredients for his potions; Zeffirelli utilizes a close-up shot to introduce him in which he literally seems to emerge out of a bush. This close-up shot is followed by a long shot which clearly establishes that he is outside of city walls, gathering flowers.

Zeffirelli is consistent in his association of Romeo and Juliet with organic imagery up until Juliet's funeral. Flowers are placed on her body before she is taken into the vault, but once she is in the vault, it is depicted as a barren environment in which Juliet is completely surrounded by stone and decaying corpses. Blue spotlights are used in the exterior shot depicting Friar Laurence's approach to the crypt, making the trees surrounding the cemetery appear to be barren of leaves as he hurries, only to find Juliet awakening to discover Romeo's dead body. The final image shown in the film is of the mourners entering the church in which Romeo and Juliet's bodies have been laid in state; the audience sees a city wall in the background through the stone entrance way to the church. Romeo and Juliet have been engulfed by the corrupted world of the artificial, in which their incorruptible love is unable to survive.

Just as Zeffirelli substitutes roughly 65 percent of Shakespeare's play of *Romeo and Juliet* (according to Pilkington's calculation) with visual material that directly supports core themes of this play, he utilizes several strategies in representing *Hamlet* to foreground that play's core themes (as identified by Marjorie Garber) of acting, action, and boundaries (470). The play's discourse on acting as represented in Act III, scene ii by Hamlet's directions to the players, and in the Player's monologue as given in Act II, scene ii are cut from Zeffirelli's script. However, this film of *Hamlet* establishes a discourse on acting practices from its outset, in its depiction of a scene not found in Shakespeare's play: the funeral of Old Hamlet. Establishing shots used in the scene clearly show the corpse of Old Hamlet, lying in his coffin; Claudius, presiding over the funeral; and Polonius, comforting Gertrude. Hamlet approaches Old Hamlet's sarcophagus, and is addressed by Claudius: "think of us/As of a father: for let the world take note,/You are the most immediate to our throne;/And with no less nobility of love/Than that which dearest father bears his son,/Do I impart toward you." Zeffirelli thereby depicts a tableau in which an actor who is best known for his performances in Hollywood action films (Mel Gibson) now plays Hamlet surrounded by actors who had each played Hamlet in notable stage productions: Alan Bates plays Claudius, Ian Holm plays Polonius, and Paul Scofield plays Old Hamlet. It is interesting that Claudius first addresses Hamlet with the line "Think of *us* as a father." Gibson's performance as Hamlet is here aligned with a theatrical tradition of Shakespearean performance. The scene also introduces us to Glenn Close's Gertrude. Close would have been familiar to Zeffirelli's contemporary audience through films such as *Fatal Attraction* (in which she played a psychotic and sexually transgressive woman), *The Big Chill* and *The Natural* (in which she played characters who embodied nurturance and mothering). This scene shows Zeffirelli at his most reflexive; Hamlet/Gibson is silent throughout this scene, contemplating what Claudius/Bates says to him with his eyes lowered. This is a Hamlet who has many choices, including performance choices, ahead of him. Unlike previous canonized performances of *Hamlet* on film, Gibson's delivery of the famous soliloquy from Act III, scene i ("To be or not to be") occurs after Polonius and Claudius have "loosed" Ophelia to him while hiding behind an arras, is set in the castle's crypt, and is delivered to his father's sarcophagus. Unique acting choices are not confined to Gibson, but rather pervade this film. John McEnery's Osric seems defiant rather than deferential; this Osric continues to fan himself with his hat regardless of whether Hamlet tells him it is hot or cold, and leaves the scene smirking at Hamlet's acceptance of the wager. This Osric clearly knows what is to come, and seems delighted at the prospect.

Although this Hamlet does not speak in this opening scene, he does pick up a handful of dirt which he spreads over his father's corpse. This Hamlet is presented to us in terms of action from the outset of this film. This earlier action is mirrored by his later violent smashing of his sword against the castle ramparts after first meeting the ghost, and in a later action of kicking a pile of scrolls off of a table as he is brought into the throne room to be questioned by Claudius as to the whereabouts of Polonius. A later scene depicts Hamlet forging and sealing the letter which will lead to the deaths of Rosencrantz and Guildenstern; the latter of which Hamlet had shoved up against a wall when Hamlet had felt that Guildenstern would "play upon" him like "a pipe." This Hamlet is clearly a robust man of action, and revels in his physicality. During the final fencing match between Hamlet and Laertes, Hamlet is clearly enjoying the bout, still maintaining his "antic disposition" by acting comically on the fencing stage and winking broadly at Gertrude.

Zeffirelli is also acutely aware of the importance of the theme of boundaries to Shakespeare's play. Zeffirelli's treatment of this theme in his production of this film suggests that he perceives these boundaries as far less discrete than commonly thought. Paul Scofield's ghost wears no supernatural armor and is depicted as sitting on a bench on the castle ramparts, wearing a common shift or robe instead of the extravagant armor and capes that characterize Olivier's, Kozintsev's, and Branagh's ghosts. Scofield's ghost appears to be an ordinary man come back from the dead, and his performance seems all the more frightening because of this. The boundary between madness and sanity is depicted by Zeffirelli through his treatment of Ophelia as she wanders through the halls of Elsinore attempting to seduce any man who comes her way. As Ophelia hands "Rosemaries for rememberance" and "Pansies for thoughts" to Laertes, Claudius and Gertrude, she actually hands dried bones to Laertes and sprigs of dead wheat to the others. In her insanity, she symbolically communicates a truth that is not allowed to be spoken: Laertes' father is dead, and Claudius and Gertrude's marriage is barren. Zeffirelli utilizes a convention in filmmaking seen in Hitchcock's *North by Northwest* and in Olivier's *Hamlet* to depict a further crossing of boundaries. Glenn Close was only nine years older than Mel Gibson and is therefore, like Cary Grant's "mother" or Olivier's Gertrude, far too young to be his mother and therefore could be a viable sexual partner for him.[10] Zeffirelli utilizes this convention to suggest the possible crossing of another boundary, that of incest. During what Mary Z. Maher has referred to, in "The Un-Hamlet," as the "Ghostus Interruptus" scene in this film, Hamlet, while showing the portraits of Claudius and Old Hamlet to Gertrude, throws Gertrude down upon the bed, lies on top of her, and passionately kisses her. The ghost then appears nominally to "whet his blunted purpose," but it seems far more consistent with the logic of the scene that the ghost "blunts his whetted purpose." The degree to which the ghost has succeeded at this seems unclear; as Hamlet leaves Elsinore with Rosencrantz and Guildenstern, Gertrude gives Hamlet a deep kiss on the mouth, indicating that the ghost may have merely postponed an encounter between them.

6. Zeffirelli

Despite a critical tendency to consider Zeffirelli's adaptations of Shakespeare's plays as the work of a "popularizer," Zeffirelli's three films of Shakespeare's plays show him to be an intelligent filmmaker who actively engages with the plays he represents in order to find visual analogues for the themes he finds presented in the works of Shakespeare. Although this approach has left his work open to the objection that he is merely "flattering the young," the analogues Zeffirelli utilizes in representing Shakespeare's themes demonstrate that he understands and seeks to maintain their importance to their seminal work. Zeffirelli's approach is not the reductive approach employed by Luhrmann, in which Shakespeare's play is almost exclusively mediated through contemporary popular culture; rather, Zeffirelli approaches each of these films as a unique project. The decision to employ "the battling Burtons" in his first representation of Shakespeare in order to draw on their star images is answered by the decision to employ unknown teenagers to portray the lovers in his second, and both decisions are again refuted by the casting strategy he utilizes in his third. Zeffirelli's approach is ultimately concerned with the uniqueness of each play he encounters, and with presenting that uniqueness in a manner which most effectively exploits the abilities of cinema to do so. Like Olivier and Welles before him, Zeffirelli does not merely film Shakespeare; he attempts to find a uniquely filmic vocabulary for representing Shakespeare, and deserves acclaim for his efforts. Finally, Zeffirelli's approach represents his solution to the problem of representing Shakespeare's plays on film in a socio-historical context which was increasingly privileging the visual over the word. His method of creating visual analogues to Shakespeare's play proved, as demonstrated by the financial success of his films, to be an appropriate choice in the socio-historical context for which his films were created.

Chapter 7

Kott, Brook, Richardson and Polanski

From the beginning of the Second World War to the late 1960s, films of Shakespeare's plays in mainstream English language American and European cinema showed many consistent tendencies. Firstly, predominantly acclaimed films tended to be the work of an acclaimed "auteur" of Shakespearean films with connections to stage productions (Olivier, Welles and Zeffirelli were all acclaimed theatre or opera directors). Secondly, although strategies of adaptation occasionally differed (Olivier and Welles favored a strategy of juxtaposing the play against countertexts, whereas Zeffirelli favored a strategy of creating visual analogues for the thematic elements of the play) the works of each "auteur" were invariably focused on character, with a clearly identifiable "star-part." The tragedy of Olivier's *Hamlet* is a personal tragedy that elicits our sympathy but has social implications mainly within the diegesis of the film. *Chimes at Midnight* certainly examines the disparity between the "official" record, the "popular" record, and "personal" histories, but the film's focus on the relationship between Hal and Falstaff directs us to perceive the film's denouement as personally catastrophic to both of them but lacking in further social implications. Because of its association with the often tempestuous and very public relationship of Richard Burton and Elizabeth Taylor, *The Taming of the Shrew* engages its popular audience through a strategy of recognition, without making any claim regarding the treatment of women in our society.

In the late 1960s and early 1970s a wave of what might be considered to be nihilistic representations of Shakespeare in the cinema appeared. Heavily influenced by Kott's *Shakespeare: Our Contemporary*, this group of films retained consistency with the tradition of connecting filmed adaptations of Shakespeare to the stage established by Olivier and Welles, but eschewed the tendency to focus around a "star-part" by employing actors who were not easily recognizable to popular film audiences. These films also depicted the tragic results of dramatic action as applicable to the entire social context represented by the diegesis of the film—as opposed to only the central character.

Few would disagree that *King Lear* is intended by Shakespeare to represent a nihilistic vision. Many critics agree that the play exemplifies several characteristics associated with a vision of the end of the world. Kott writes "The exposition of *King Lear* shows a world that is to be destroyed" (103), and summarizes the irretrievable devastation and loss depicted in the play: "The theme of *King Lear* is the decay and fall of the world ... the world is not healed again ... there is no young and resolute Fortinbras to ascend the throne of Denmark ... there will be no coronation.... Everybody has died or been murdered ... this is a morality play in which everyone will be destroyed: noble characters along with the base ones, the persecutors with the persecuted, the torturers with the tortured" (120–121).

The challenge faced by Peter Brook, in adapting King Lear to the cinema, was to dramatize the play in a manner that would engage the sensibilities of a mainstream North American or European cinema audience. In his preface to Kott's *Shakespeare: Our Contemporary*, Brook notes that he had met Kott and remained in contact with him (ix). There is a critical consensus regarding the degree to which Brook's 1971 film of *King Lear* is influenced by Kott (Buhler 138; Kennedy 175). Kott had argued that, in 20th-century drama, tragedy had been displaced by the notion of the grotesque, which he explores in the following passage: "This new grotesque ... deals with problems, conflicts and themes of tragedy, such as: human fate, the meaning of existence, freedom and inevitability, the discrepancy between the absolute and the fragile human order. Grotesque means tragedy rewritten in different terms.... The downfall of the tragic hero is a confirmation and recognition of the absolute; whereas the downfall of the grotesque actor means mockery of the absolute and its desecration ... tragedy brings *catharsis*, while grotesque offers no consolation whatsoever" (104).

In *Filming Shakespeare's Plays*, Anthony Davies states that Brook's "film makes Shakespeare's play a revelation of the grotesque rather than a tragedy, and there is some justification for the suggestion that in this film Beckett and the critic Jan Kott come dangerously close to displacing Shakespeare" (143). Many critics agree that Brook's use of costume and mise-en-scène are central elements in this film. Stephen Buhler reads the film's landscape as "pitilessly bleak" (139). Davies similarly observes, "The animal-skin costumes ... indicate the relationship and the distinction between man and beast" (144). The map of England used in the opening throne room sequence is drawn not on parchment or paper but rather on an animal skin. As Lear rises from his throne in anger to pronounce banishment on Cordelia and Kent the combination of his hunched back with a bear-skin draped over it gives the audience an image of Lear as a great hulking bear—an image which Brook's camera lingers over for several seconds, firmly seating this animalistic impression of Lear in the minds of the audience. Goneril's castle appears in exterior shots to be constructed of stone, and in interior shots appears to be constructed of a mixture of stone, mud, and thatch. These elements of costume and mise-en-scène interact to produce a vision of a world that has just barely become civilized, its characters just perceptibly removed from their animal origins. Costume and mise-en-scène here affirm Kott's assertion of the absence of the absolute.

There is further critical consensus regarding Brook's heavily stylized use of cinematography, editing, and sound. Buhler finds that "Brook employs several distancing and disorienting techniques throughout the film" (139), which Kenneth Rothwell summarizes in "Representing 'King Lear' on Screen": "This film ... exploits meta-cinematic rhetoric ... it ... flaunts its identity ... its black-and-white starkness shows a winter world of ironic despair in grainy shots and deliberate out-of-focus frames ... discontinuities, zoom-fades, accelerated motion, rapid editing, complex reverse angle and over-the-shoulder shots, montage, jump cuts, overhead shots, silent-screen titles, eyes-only close-ups, and hand-held cameras as well as stationary, immobile ones" (217–219). Rothwell believes that Brook's overdetermined use of style in this film is part of an attempt to "declare independence from the constraints of page and stage and to make a genuine effort at converting the Shakespearean experience into a cinematic idiom" (217).

The cinematic idiom created by Brook gives the audience a view of a reality which is fragmented and fractured from itself. Three sequences in the film which indicate a change of setting in the plot[1] are photographed and edited in order that the transitions between exterior shots showing the travelling caravans and interior shots showing characters conversing in the carriages seem abrupt and unnatural, setting a tone of disconnection—rather than continuity—between the interior and exterior shots. An unnerving shot begins the film with the camera panning right to left, and then left to right, across a static crowd of people who appear jammed together in the frame. They stand motionless and frozen in place and expression, however their facial tics, breathing, and blinking demonstrate that this is not a freeze frame shot. The shot is disrupted by inter-titles which show the opening credits. After the second interruption, the camera adopts a pattern of highly random tracking motions across the faces in this crowd. During Lear's speech from the heath, in-focus shots of Lear's full face timed to coincide with the flashes of lightning that light the heath are inter-cut with out-of-focus shots of Lear's face timed to coincide with the absence of the lightning. As the scene progresses, images are increasingly divorced from dialogue, and the cinematic convention of the axis of action is violated by shots of Lear's right profile inter-cut with shots of Lear's left profile. As Edgar relates the history of Poor Tom as a serving man who "did the deed of darkness with his mistress" to Lear, shots of Edgar from two angles are inter-cut—a main close shot of Edgar which is out-of-focus, with a low-angle in-focus mid-shot timed to coincide with the booming of the thunder. These two shots are further inter-cut with extremely tight out-of-focus shots of fragments of Lear's face. During the mock trial scene, shots of Goneril and Regan are inter-cut with shots of Lear denouncing them, suggesting that he is hallucinating. As he finishes denouncing them, an inter-cut shot of Cordelia suggests a further hallucination.

Brook employs juxtaposition of contradictory images consistently throughout the film to suggest a disparity between the perceptions of the characters and the realities that they perceive. Audaciously violating the codes of illusionist continuity editing and cinematography, Brook creates a cinematic idiom which represents both the outer appearances and the individual psychological states of his characters. Regan's statement, "yet he hath ever but slenderly known himself," can be applied to the majority of the characters that populate this fractured and fragmented world. Just as the heath scene represents the most famous storm in the history of English drama because of its depiction of the outer storm as a representation of Lear's inner psychological state, the cinematic and editing techniques of this film allow the audience to experience the world of this film as the characters experience the world of this film. In "Two-Dimensional Shakespeare: *King Lear* on Film," Peter Holland writes:

> At the start of the reconciliation scene between Lear and Cordelia.... Brook never shows Lear and Cordelia in the same shot, never allows them to appear on screen together until Lear identifies his daughter.... Brook introduces a new shot, showing Lear in profile and now sharing the screen with Cordelia who is unexpectedly shown to be very close to him. The reunion is accomplished, father and daughter are reconciled, by the combination of her verifying of his act of naming her and the camera's act of showing them so physically close together. It is moving and powerful, the language of the scene and the work of the camera perfectly married to chart the coming together of the characters, the translation from text to film performance fully accomplished [64–65].

Although Davies suggests, "For the most part, the camera is held still" (145), *King Lear* should not be classified either as a montage or as a mise-en-scène film. Rather, Brook uses montage techniques to emphasize the psychological isolation of characters, and uses mise-en-scène techniques to establish psychological connections between characters. In the opening throne room sequence, as Goneril, Regan, and Cordelia give their declarations to Lear, and as Lear banishes Kent and Cordelia, Goneril's declaration is filmed in shallow focus with Cordelia visible over her left shoulder, emphasizing the disparity of the realities which they experience. A shallow-focus over the shoulder shot of Cordelia's back with Lear visible in the distance accompanies his utterance that "nothing will come of nothing," and Brook pans from a shot of Lear and Kent together in the frame to a shot of Kent isolated in the frame as Kent is banished. Similarly, a long tracking shot around the exterior of Goneril's castle follows Lear and Kent together in the frame as Kent—in his guise as Caius the servant—re-establishes his relationship with Lear, just as a long tracking shot follows Edmund through Gloucester's castle as he visits the dying Cornwall. Voiceover narration is also used by Brook to establish connections between characters. Edgar's "World world oh world" voiceover is answered by Gloucester's "As flies to wanton boys" voiceover, signifying a renewed relationship between these characters as they reunite to facilitate their escape.

The central dynamic of Brook's *King Lear* is founded on a dichotomy between people in narcissistic isolation versus people in altruistic connection. After the blinding of Gloucester, Cornwall is stabbed by a servant who is then bludgeoned to death by Regan. Brook depicts the bludgeoning by showing only Regan in the frame, her face twisted with rage as she flails the off-screen servant. By placing only Regan in the frame, Brook reveals her egocentrism and narcissism to us. At that moment in the film the only reality that Regan is aware of is of her impulse to kill the servant, and of her need to gratify that impulse. Regan's actions are here divorced from any concerns outside of her own ego—they do not stem from a motivation to preserve the integrity of the state that Gloucester has threatened, or to avenge the attack on her husband, or to ensure that the servant is brought to any kind of justice for his action. The only factor that motivates Regan is that her fight-or-flight response has been activated, as the only reality she perceives is that of her own emotional state. Brook inter-cuts this sequence with an image of another servant who watches this dual murder and mutilation with a blank expression on his face, suggesting that he feels no emotional connection between himself and the events that he is witnessing. Emotionally unaffected by two murders and the mutilation of a helpless old man occurring within 15 feet of him in less than three minutes, he maintains his posture of isolation from the events that he is immersed in as there is "nothing in it for him." Conversely, at the conclusion of the film, we are presented with a series of images of the dying Lear dropping out of the frame inter-cut with images of Albany, Kent, and Edgar giving their final utterances. Brook here presents one shot which pans from a close up of Albany giving his final statement, to a close-up of Kent giving his final statement, to a close-up of Edgar giving his final statement, inter-cut with a static shot of the dying Lear as he drops out of the frame. Albany, Kent, and Edgar are here united in their reaction to Lear's demise by the panning motion of the camera inter-cut with images of the dying Lear. This final inter-cutting of two stylistically disparate shots serves to temper Brook's nihilistic vision with a hope of people having overcome their narcissistic impulses and formed genuine connections with one another.

As Brook and Tony Richardson were contemporaries at the Royal Shakespeare Company, Richardson would certainly have been aware of Brook's famous 1962 stage production of *King Lear*, of Kott, and of the influence Kott's work was having on the theatrical community. Richardson's 1969 film of *Hamlet* offers a challenge both to the conventions of mainstream cinema and the conventions of the theatre. Stephen Buhler notes, "From the outset, Richardson developed the production for both theatrical and cinematic presentation. He was drawn toward the Roundhouse Theatre in London (which was built as a switching station and repair depot in Victorian times) because of its challenge to conventional theatrical spaces" (41).

Richardson's production seems defined not by what it is attempting to do, but by what it is attempting not to do. Having won an Academy Award for best director six years before this production, Richardson was certainly aware of mainstream cinema conventions, just as his experience with the BBC and the English Stage Company would certainly have made him aware of current theatrical conventions. Richardson seems to have chosen the deliberate contradiction of other productions as his primary approach to this production.[2] In the context of this discussion Richardson's approach seems to be the ultimate expression of the grotesque. If "mockery and desecration of the absolute" (Kott 104) are chief characteristics of the grotesque, a carnivalesque approach to Hamlet in which virtually everything is presented in a manner inverse to what literary, cinematic and stage tradition might prompt its audience to expect from what is called "the most celebrated drama in the English language" would certainly preclude the audience from reading the production as classically tragic.

The film has many interesting effects. Buhler notes, "At times we are completely nowhere, as the dark recesses of the space leave the actors alone in a 'black void.' ... No attempt is made to represent the Ghost of Hamlet's father; only blinding light and near-deafening sound briefly fill the void and highlight the reactions of those who indeed 'see' the specter" (42). The nunnery scene is presented as a delightful flirtation between Hamlet and Ophelia, its mood changing from affection to anger only when Hamlet realizes that Polonius is listening. Nicol Williamson's remarkable performance as Hamlet gives this production its clear center. Buhler writes: "Nicol Williamson's ... snarling delivery of the character's indictments of the corruption that surrounds him impressively reflects the spirit of the student movements of 1968.... This Hamlet is an eternal and eternally world-weary graduate student, impatient with pretense yet naively hopeful that some ringing truth can be heard amid the hypocritical lies that pass for 'sensible' discourse (42).

Buhler's assertion that Williamson's performance encourages a "contemporary" reading of the film is supported by Robert Shaughnessy, who notes in "Stage, Screen, and Nation" that the mise-en-scène of this film performs a similar function, stating that the brickwork of the Roundhouse recalls "the rain-streaked tenements and industrial wastelands of early 1960s British working-class realist cinema" (72). The use of Renaissance properties and costumes reinforce the relevance of the production's depiction of a dysfunctional and carnivalesque Renaissance court to the audience for which the production is mounted. In *1956 And All That: The Making of Modern British Drama,* Dan Rebellato notes that the goal of Richardson's school of directing and Williamson's school of acting was "to restore sincere, authentic unity to the voices of the national culture" (99). In aligning his film with contemporary concerns in terms of performance and mise-en-scène, while simultaneously eschewing the techniques of mainstream cinema and theatre in his production, Richardson implies a critique of mainstream popular culture by inverting its aesthetics. It is this sense of inversion and dysfunction that permeates Richardson's film. The incestuous relationship of Laertes and Ophelia; the disparity in ages between Hamlet and Ophelia, Gertrude and Claudius, and Gertrude and Hamlet; the casting of Marianne Faithfull as Ophelia; and the invasion of the throne room by the bedroom ensure that no catharsis will be experienced by, and no consolation will be offered to, the audience at this film's conclusion. In line with Kott's concept of the grotesque, there is no tragic fall to confirm the absolute, nor is there any absolute worth confirming in Richardson's film.

In a conference presentation entitled "The Nightmare of History:

World War II's Effect on Jan Kott, and Jan Kott's Effect on Postwar British Theatre," John Hugh Cameron notes that "Roman Polanski's film version of *Macbeth* [was] heavily influenced by Kott." As a product of mainstream Hollywood cinema, Polanski's film is constructed to appeal to several segments of its potential marketplace. In maintaining a high degree of fidelity to the play[3] and in utilizing obscure classically trained actors (as opposed to Hollywood stars) Polanski attempts to appeal to that segment of the potential audience that would expect Polanski to present a traditional, conservative reading of the text in which "misgovernment enters the community not because of defects in the system of monarchy, but at the behest of agents of darkness. The kingdom has prospered under Duncan and will again see good days under Malcolm. The reign of Macbeth is foul but aberrant. In the end Scotland regains its good health and the play ends on an optimistic note" (Pearlman 251).

Yet Polanski subverts the viability of such a reading (thereby appealing to the liberal sentiments of another potential segment of the film's popular audience) through the use of countertexts which suggest that the source of Macbeth's corruption is to be found not in the interventions of malign agents, but rather is embedded in the social system presented in the film. The thrust of Polanski's interpretation of the play is to realize "a vision of a world in which Macbeth's actions are the unacknowledged norm" (Buhler 84). Far from being a naïve innocent corrupted by the forces of evil, Macbeth is presented as capable of deceit at his first encounter with the witches, lying to Banquo that the witches have vanished "into the air" when in fact they have simply shut the door to their cavern in Macbeth's line of sight, but out of the range of Banquo's. E. Pearlman further notes that "these witches are not fantastical; they are exactly as they seem. They do not disappear 'into the air' as do Shakespeare's fiends, but into an underground cavern" (254). Polanski is most audacious in his use of the countertexts in his presentation of the character of Ross. In "The Very Painting of Your Fear: Roman Polanski's *Macbeth* and Akira Kurosawa's *Kumonosu djô*," Yong Li Lan writes:

> The slightness of Ross' textual character in particular is adroitly used to make him an ubiquitous silent presence whose pleasant face and expression contradict and block the reading of his callous instrumentality in Macbeth's crimes, including his startling betrayal of his 'dearest coz' Lady MacDuff and her children by opening the castle gates to their assassins as he leaves.[4] He performs this last atrocity as easily as he tells MacDuff his family are slain and shifts allegiance to Malcolm, and it is the very absence of speech and the banal conventionality of what little there is that Polanski uses to convert Ross from a presumably decent character into a much more sinister figure than Macbeth himself, whose inner torments are revealed in his soliloquies. Hence, when it is (of course) Ross who crowns Malcolm at the end with "Hail, King of Scotland!," the

apparent happy unity between the close-up of his smiling face and his words is a deeply subversive image of justice reinstated [116].

Polanski's apparent fidelity to the text is also called into question by the degree of irony with which he imbues the text. Although Polanski "tries to translate the richness of Shakespeare's words more directly into images and techniques" (Buhler 84) by coupling the verbal images of the play directly with visual images given in the film, these couplings frequently demonstrate an interpretive function. While observing the arrival of Duncan from her castle, Lady Macbeth "sees and becomes a bird of prey hovering before its attack; in voiceover she identifies herself with the raven 'That croaks the fatal entrance of Duncan/Under my battlements'" (Buhler 86). Her later descent into madness suggests, however, that the raven may have in fact been croaking a warning, either to herself or to Duncan. During the vision brought on by the witches' potion, Macbeth hears, "Beware MacDuff ... none of woman born shall harm Macbeth" while seeing an image of a caesarian birth, and also hears, "Macbeth shall never vanquished be until Great Birnam Wood to high Dunsinane Hill shall come against him," spoken to him by hideously cackling apparitions of Malcolm and Donalbaine. This presentation suggests that in Polanski's vision the witches may be trying to warn Macbeth of the danger he faces. As Buhler notes, "While appearances may indeed be deceiving, some visions are false only by nature of the interpretations placed upon them" (87). The fallibility of Macbeth's interpretive faculty is demonstrated in the disparate presentations of Banquo's ghost. Although Banquo is murdered with an axe in his spine, Macbeth's hallucination of Banquo's ghost corresponds not to the reality of Banquo's murder, but instead to the embellishments of the first murderer, whose fumbling delivery when reporting the murder to Macbeth should indicate that he's inventing at least part of his story. Although Macbeth is later provided with an accurate representation of Banquo's murder during the vision sequence, he still does not question the disparities between the differing versions of events that he has been given.

In Polanski's vision, Macbeth murders Duncan in reaction to the knowledge that Malcolm will ascend the throne. The final image in Polanski's film is of Donalbain approaching the witch's cavern, thereby reinforcing our sense that the existence of tyranny is due to a systemic problem rather than an aberrant intervention, and that the cycle of violence that tyranny precipitates will continue to escalate until the systemic problem is resolved. Macbeth's rise and ultimate fall belies the tragic in that his trajectory is commonplace in the world presented by Polanski. Although the events of his life and death have great personal importance to him, in the world in which he exists they are merely representative of "business as usual." It is Macbeth's delusion that his commonplace ambition is indicative of personal superiority that relegates him to the grotesque, yet one of the results of this delusion of grandeur is his consistent misreading of the attempts of the witches to warn him. Polanski's vision is equally as nihilistic as Brook's and Richardson's. Macbeth is neither fated nor manipulated in Polanski's vision, but rather makes poor choices through the use of his personal agency.

Brook's depiction of the psychological states of egocentrism and narcissism, Richardson's dislocation of the text of Hamlet from its traditional readings to a carnivalesque reading and Polanski's depiction of the fall of Macbeth initiated by the misapplication of his exercise of agency express the grotesque as defined by Kott. Through openly confronting the issues they perceive as crucial to their immediate socio-historical contexts, these films express a bleak critique of those contexts. Ironically, despite the potential for subversive and effective social critique indicated by these films, the release of Polanski's *Macbeth* initiated the "18-year gap," a period during which television would become the primary site of direct Shakespearean media representation. There would be no direct adaptation of Shakespeare's plays using Shakespeare's language in mainstream American or European cinema released until 1989.

CHAPTER 8

The 1970s and 1980s

The period from the release of Polanski's *Macbeth* to Branagh's *Henry V* has been described as "the 18-year gap"—during this period no significant films of Shakespeare's plays were produced in mainstream cinema and "it looked as if television had displaced cinema as the photographic medium for bringing Shakespeare to the modern audience" (Davies xi). Although it was believed that Hollywood had rejected Shakespeare in this time period, the predominant strategy utilized in mainstream cinema to dramatize Shakespeare's plays had merely changed. Many specifics of the plays (names, places, situations, thematic functions, narrative functions) remained; however, the use of Early Modern English was displaced by contemporary English, and the use of Early Modern settings were displaced by contemporary and futuristic settings. Films constructed by use of this strategy conspicuously reference elements of the seminal Shakespearean play, but follow narrative trajectories never anticipated in the seminal play to the extent that "Shakespeare" becomes conspicuous by "his" absence. The resultant work often does not usually strike the audience as an intentional representation of Shakespeare's plays as much as it appears a separate work in its own right; even if one that is reminiscent of Shakespeare's play. This strategy of adaptation had been frequently used in mainstream cinema prior to the 1970s and 1980s: 1955's *Joe Macbeth* displaced *Macbeth* to a contemporary cinema-noir setting, and 1956's *Jubal* displaced *Othello* to a "western" setting. The Academy Award for best picture of 1961 was won by the musical *West Side Story*, intentionally based on *Romeo and Juliet*, but updated to reflect an urban gang setting contemporary to 1961.

Representations of Shakespeare's plays produced during the "18-year gap" were distinguished in their engagement with their seminal plays on a thematic level: analogues were often dramatized which represented meditations on and re-workings of the central meaning effects of the seminal plays. An important precursor to the adaptations of Shakespeare's plays released in the 1970s and 1980s is Wilcox's *Forbidden Planet*, released in 1956. *Forbidden Planet* is frequently posited as an adaptation of *The Tempest*, although Metro-Goldwyn-Mayer has claimed no intentional relationship between this film and the play. Despite this claim, in a review of *Forbidden Planet* Damian Cannon notes that *Forbidden Planet* "updat[es] Shakespeare's *The Tempest* to a science-fiction setting." Chris Steinbrunner and Burt Goldblatt, in *Cinema of the Fantastic*, have identified several elements of the play that are represented in the film. Altair IV functions as *Forbidden Planet*'s island; Morbius, with his command of Krell technology, is the equivalent of the necromancer Prospero; Robbie is his obedient Ariel. Altaira, in her initial naivety and formation of a love relationship with Adams that reintroduces her to society, re-imagines Miranda and the development of her relationship with Ferdinand; and the destructive monster that springs from Morbius' subconscious mind represents Caliban (265–7). The screenplay obliquely re-imagines Prospero's command of and preoccupation with magic as Morbius' command of and preoccupation with language. It is Morbius' skill as a philologist that enables him to decipher the Krell code. His superior command of language is evidenced in the screenplay via his sardonic wit[1] and also in his frequently poetic use of language.[2] Although *Forbidden Planet* utilizes many elements of *The Tempest*, it also completely rejects Shakespeare's political satire and the reconciliation of the play's conclusion in favor of a nihilistic view of mankind. Whereas the conspirators on the island are presented as ludicrous and are ultimately forgiven, the monster from the id is presented as deadly and—as we are assured at the film's conclusion—the guarantor of the inevitable future failure of humankind (which will repeat the failure of the Krell). Prospero's famous utterance, "This thing of darkness I acknowledge mine," is here supplanted with Morbius' frantic "I deny you" in response to Adams' assertion, "That thing is you." Judith Buchanan writes, in *Shakespeare on Film*, "The partial identification between Prospero and Caliban implied in the play, however, becomes in the film a complete identification between their equivalent characters. This identification is rendered explicit since master and creature become in this telling of the tale two conflicting expressions of the same person, id and super-ego of the same troubled psyche" (154).

Although *Forbidden Planet* acknowledges Shakespeare as part of the cultural heritage it belongs to, it is far more expressive of Freudian pessimism at the onset of the nuclear age than it is of Elizabethan Romance drama. Buchanan further notes that "The central concern with a huge, and potentially hugely destructive, source of power in the film must also have had an obvious resonance for 1950s audiences living in a "post–Hiroshima world" (*Shakespeare on Film* 152).

The examination of *Forbidden Planet* shows that *The Tempest* here has thoroughly undergone a process that Linda Hutcheon calls "Indigenization" (158). This process requires the performance of three types of transformations upon the seminal work. The first is Historicizing/Dehistoricizing, in which the work is dislocated from the setting specified by the original author to a setting specified by the adaptor. In the second, Racializing/Deracializing, analogues are found to approximate class and social dynamics inherent in the seminal work. The Third, Embodyings/Disembodyings, has characters physically represented by different physical types of actors in different socio-historical periods. In *Forbidden Planet*, *The Tempest* has been Dehistoricized from its setting of an island in the Mediterranean during the Renaissance and Rehistorized to a setting of the planet Altair IV in the early 2200s. Caliban is Deracialized from his existence as the son of Sycorax and Racialized as a monster from the Id, and Ariel is Disembodied as a spirit to be Embodied as Robbie the Robot. Prospero the wizard is represented as Morbius the philologist, and Ferdinand the crown prince is represented as Adams the Commander. Where *Forbidden Planet* departs from *The Tempest* is that where Prospero is completely in control of his magic and Ferdinand is submissive to him, Morbius is not in control of his Id, and it is left to Adams to force the realization upon him. In *Danse Macabre*, Stephen King suggests that the American popular culture of the 1950s often reflected a distrust of science and an idealization of the military, as science had recently produced the real possibility of extinguishing all life from the planet, but the military had effectively protected the world from the threat of Nazism (94). The depiction of Morbius as the scientist who loses control over his experiment and of Adams as the military Commander who saves the day is consistent with the aforementioned distrust and idealization.

Representations of Shakespeare's plays in the mainstream Hollywood cinema of the 1970s and 1980s were equally aligned with the assumptions of the American popular culture of their socio-historical period, which had recently undergone a massive shift in attitudes. The two top grossing American films of 1965 were *The Sound of Music* and *Doctor Zhivago*. These films featured classically trained actors, opulent production values, and espoused conservative social values (the von Trapp family escapes Nazism, and Yevgrav ultimately finds his niece); whereas five of top ten grossing American films of 1970 were *MASH*, *Woodstock*, *Little Big Man*, *Joe*, and *Five Easy Pieces*. Those films featured social criticism, breakdowns in traditional relationships, distrust of institutions, and (in the case of the latter two films) realistic production values. In a decade during which mainstream American cinema was very deliberately breaking with what had been considered its "classical Hollywood" past, direct adaptations of Shakespeare's plays were not considered financially viable. During this decade "method acting" was in vogue—this was the decade in which Clint Eastwood and Jack Nicholson were among the top international stars, while Peter O'Toole, Richard Harris, and Richard Burton were increasingly considered as "has-beens." The aesthetics of Renaissance drama and classical acting styles were perceived as utterly in conflict with the aesthetics of 1970s Hollywood.

Coppola's *The Godfather* and *The Godfather: Part II* currently occupy the number three and number 37 positions on the American Film Institute's list of the 100 greatest American films, and were considered among the most influential and commercially successful American films of the 1970s. Connections between *The Godfather* films and Shakespeare's plays have been made: albeit infrequently and anecdotally. In his review of *The Godfather*, Tim Dirks states, "It was filmed as a modern version of Shakespeare's *King Lear* (featuring a king and three sons: Sonny, Michael, and Fredo)." In "The Godfather: The Coppola Restoration," Dave Kehr argues that the "films remain the 20th-century answer to Shakespeare's plays of royal succession, with the twist that here Prince Hal grows up, not into Henry V, but Richard III." The interesting point that Kehr misses here is that the Henry IV plays do not portray Prince Hal as growing up as much as they portray Prince Hal portraying Prince Hal growing up. Hal is creating a "star image" of himself as the prodigal son returned in order to consolidate political power. Michael's loss of his own humanity is the real tragedy of the first film, and can appropriately be described as tragic because his lack of self-insight prevents him from realizing that this is happening to him.

If "humanity must perforce prey upon itself like monsters of the deep," the first *Godfather* film differs from Shakespeare by presenting these monsters as a product of nurture rather than nature. In the opening wedding sequence, care is taken to distinguish Michael from his family. Whereas the rest of the family are dressed opulently, Michael is dressed in a military uniform. Michael further distances himself from his family by stating, "That's my family, Kay, that's not me," when relating how his father and Luca Brasi had intimidated a bandleader into terminating Johnny's contract. Michael also seems distanced from his family in terms of his emotional affect. Sonny's rages at Carmine's treatment of Connie, Fredo's tears at the attempt on Vito's life, and Vito's tears when learning of Sonny's death demonstrate that although this is a community of gangsters, it is also a community of vitality and warmth. Although sincere and well-spoken, Michael clearly lacks this vitality and sense of connectedness. Although he is shown enjoying a date with Kay immediately before learning of the attempt on Don Vito's life, Michael is unable to express his feelings toward her, which precipitates Clemenza's reproach: "Mikey, why don't you tell that nice girl you love her? I love you with all-a my heart, if I don't see-a you again soon, I'm-a gonna die."

According to a National Center for PTSD fact sheet entitled "PTSD and Older Veterans," emotional numbness is considered a normal reaction of human beings to war (1). At the onset of the film Michael is a decorated veteran who has fought in the Pacific theatre and has had his picture on the cover of *Life Magazine*. "Most war heroes don't feel brave or heroic at the time, but they do their duty, despite often feeling overwhelmed and horrified, in order to protect others" (*ibid.*). Michael's decision to kill McCluskey and Sollozzo is not, in his conscious mind, inconsistent with his previous refusal to join the family business—he believes he is acting as a soldier in protection of his father. The later murder of Apollonia completes Michael's traumatization: when he reappears after Sonny's murder to reestablish his relationship with Kay, his manner is completely devoid of warmth or spontaneity of expression. Throughout the scene detailing Michael's reestablishment of his relationship with Kay, every word he speaks and gesture he makes is now calculated and stylized, as he is now constructing an image of himself—and by extension the Corleone family—as a respected leader of business and industry. The emotional subtext of the scene makes it obvious that he is not deeply in love with Kay, but wishes to marry her in order to cultivate an image of himself as a loving family man. Like Richard of Gloucester, Michael may very well have muttered, "Was ever woman in this manner wooed?" at the conclusion of this scene. By the conclusion of the first film Michael has directly threatened Fredo and murdered Carmine; his brother and brother-in-law, respectively. Although Michael believes that he is engaged in the process of legitimizing the family business, he has undertaken courses of action that would have been anathema to Don Vito's belief system. Like Lear, Michael "hath ever but slenderly known himself"; Shakespeare's Richard III intentionally pursues villainy believing himself to be by nature "subtle, false and treacherous" whereas the first film documents a process by which Michael becomes a villain by denial.

Marjorie Garber has identified Shakespeare's play of *Richard II* as employing a chiastic structure: the play begins with Richard in power and Bolingbroke in exile, and ends with Bolingbroke in power and Richard in exile/murdered (238–269). Interestingly, Coppola also utilizes a chiastic structure in his presentation of the relationship between Michael and Vito. The film begins with Vito in control and at the center of "the family business," whereas Michael still wears his military uniform and disavows any interest in the operations of the Corleone crime family. By the conclusion of the film, Michael is in control and at the center of "the family business," and Vito has retired/died.

If *The Godfather* can be considered the *Richard II* of the series, *The Godfather: Part II* is the *Macbeth* of the series as the seminal play and the resultant film are both heavily concerned with the issue of futility. Macbeth's efforts to consolidate his power and security are mirrored by Michael's efforts to consolidate his power and his family's security. Macbeth's efforts are destined to fail because he does not understand he is being manipulated; Michael's efforts are destined to fail because he does not understand that he has only replaced his father in title, not in esteem. Whereas Don Vito was respected, Michael is feared and resented. Kay has her third pregnancy terminated and leaves Michael because she believes their marriage is "unholy and evil." Fredo participates in the attempt to assassinate Michael because he has been "stepped over" and belittled by Michael's ascension to power. Macbeth's isolation at Dunsinane after the flight of his thanes is mirrored by Michael's isolation on the dock of his estate after the flight of his wife and the murder of Fredo. As Michael sits in silence, completely alienated from his family and friends, the mood of the scene is consistent with Macbeth's musing, "I have lived long enough: my way of life/Is fall'n into the sere, the yellow leaf;/And that which should accompany old age,/As honor, love, obedience, troops of friends, I must not look to have; but in their stead/Curses, not loud but deep, mouth-honor, breath,/Which the poor heart would fain deny, and dare not."

The Godfather: Part II also utilizes the technique of reporting significant events. The execution of the first thane of Cawdor, the murder of Duncan, and the suicide of Lady Macbeth in *Macbeth*; and the abortion, Fredo's first trip to Cuba, and Fredo's murder in *The Godfather: Part II*; are never presented directly. In a film series that is notorious for its depiction of graphic violence, Coppola could easily have supplied a scene directly depicting Fredo's murder, just as Shakespeare—who had Gloucester's eye put out on stage—could easily have supplied a scene directly depicting the murder of Duncan. Reported events serve similar purposes in both instances: dramatic emphasis is maintained on the effect of the event on the protagonist rather than on the characters directly involved in the event. It is not as important to know that Duncan has died as it is to know that

Macbeth has done the deed, and it is not as important to know that Fredo has died as it is to know that Michael has ordered the deed done. Garber has argued that, like *Richard II*, *Macbeth* also utilizes a chiastic structure in which at the play's onset, Macbeth is horrified at the prospect of murdering Duncan whereas Lady Macbeth is emotionally impervious to the potential act's implications. By the play's conclusion Macbeth has "almost forgot the taste of fears" and is "supp'd full with horrors" whereas Lady Macbeth has been driven insane by her guilt (695–723). Interestingly, Coppola also establishes a chiastic structure in *The Godfather: Part II*, intercutting between two parallel narratives. The first begins with a completely isolated Vito as a young man, and traces his gradual establishment of his eventually large family; and the second begins with Michael surrounded by his large family, and traces his gradual alienation of his family to his eventual isolation.

Released in 1990, *The Godfather: Part III* is the *King Lear* of this series. Here, the central issue that Coppola is taking up is that of the abdication of responsibility for one's actions. Just as Lear wishes to resign the throne but retain all of "the addition to a king," Michael has finally managed to make the family business "completely legitimate" yet still covertly travels in mob circles, never directly engaged in mob activity but always influencing it. Michael's quest for redemption in this film is uncharacteristically naïve: he believes that he can undo the wrong he has done by literally buying indulgences, only to find "just when I thought I was out ... they pull me back in." In "Shakespeare's Cinematic Offshoots," Tony Howard notes that Coppola leaves the question of Vincent's loyalty unanswered[3] (307), and further notes that "*Lear* gave Coppola three structural high points: the opening, the storm—Michael goes into hiding and is struck down not by madness but a diabetes attack ... and the catastrophe" (*ibid*.). Michael's final "howl" at Mary's death provides the film with its finest moment. Although this film is by far the weakest of the series, this final direct visual reference to Shakespeare's play has an emotional impact unparalleled at any other moment in the series.

Where Coppola attempts to recast Shakespeare in the image of an Italian-American experience in *The Godfather* and *The Godfather: Part II*, Paul Mazursky attempts to recast Shakespeare in the image of a disaffected contemporary urbanite in his 1982 film, *Tempest*. Where Shakespearean influences remain unstated in Coppola's films, Mazursky calls attention to them in a manner which Vincent Canby believes to be mistaken. In "'Tempest' Opens With Nod to Shakespeare," Canby writes, "It's ... depressing to suspect that the film maker sees the Prosperos of our time as being nothing much more than overachieving, middle-class neurotics." Unfortunately, there is little in Mazursky's film that serves to contradict this reading. Phillip Demetrius (Mazursky's Prospero) seems unable to reconcile himself to two facts: he and his daughter are aging, and affluence does not—in and of itself—guarantee satisfaction.

This is borne out by the troubled relationship depicted between Phillip and Miranda, as portrayed in this film by Molly Ringwald. Miranda's resentment toward her father is manifested whenever he refers to her as "Kid" (she angrily replies, "Kids are goats") and when he attempts to dance with her on the island. As part of his middle-life crisis, Phillip is having difficulty conceiving that Miranda is now of an age when she wishes to seek her own dance partner rather than dance with her father. Interestingly, it is Raul Julia's Kalibanos who becomes Phillip's teacher in this regard: when Phillip confronts Kalibanos over the attempt to seduce Miranda, Kalibanos insists, "She is woman, boss, soon she will want a Bonnie Johnnie inside her." Phillip's final acceptance of Miranda's womanhood, and by extension his own mortality is indicated when he responds to Kalibanos' statement "You are god, boss" by simply stating, "I'm not a god, I'm a monkey, just like you."

Regarding the relationship between Phillip and Kalibanos, Judith Buchanan argues that its portrayal updates Shakespeare's depiction of Renaissance colonial politics with a contemporary depiction of 20th-century colonial politics: "[Kalibanos] is the developing world's impoverished, uneducated local who, paradoxically, attempts to reclaim some personal power through opportunistic sycophancy to the tourists and travelers from the First World. His efforts to exploit his American visitors through touristic selling and sycophantic flattery are small-scale, crudely expressed and honest in their transparency. By contrast, the Americans' exploitation of him for expert knowledge of the area and for manual labour is of a subtler order" (*Shakespeare on Film* 170).

Mazursky's *Tempest* was released 13 and a half months prior to *The Big Chill* and exudes a similar zeitgeist; comfort and affluence produce a sense of meaninglessness in the lives of their protagonists. Phillip's crusade against his own mortality seems linked to his association of New York City as a place of death and sterility. For instance, at a New Year's Eve party, he describes his fellow party-goers as "all dead," and feels that his life lacks significance. Far from being cast adrift, this Prospero leaves Manhattan for a barren island on the Aegean, and attempts to recapture some sense of magic in his life. There are two types of magic presented in the film: Phillip's magic, which produces the tempest that will bring all of the characters to the island for the final reconciliation, and Kalibanos' magic as performed with his chorus of dancing sheep. Like The Fool in *King Lear*, Kalibanos is portrayed as a buffoon who nevertheless has great wisdom to offer. An example of this occurs during the storm scene when it becomes apparent that Philip is no longer in control of the Tempest that he has conjured, prompting Kalibanos' rebuke: "You are not god, boss." The wisdom offered by Kalibanos and confirmed by the concluding "We'll Take Manhattan" number is that Phillip is simply wrong and that New York is a great place; it is again Phillip's perceptions that are problematic.

In "A Hamlet You Can Drink To: Surveillance, Technology, and the Bard in Strange Brew," Melissa Croteau argues that Rick Moranis' and Dave Thomas' film of *Strange Brew*, released in 1983, posits *Hamlet* not as an icon of Western high culture, but rather as a generic cultural product. Croteau argues that *Strange Brew* takes many elements of *Hamlet*'s plot and themes to produce a work of mass entertainment—in the film the Elsinore Brewery conveniently has an insane asylum just up the road, representing the play's setting and theme of madness. Croteau further notes that although trapped in the brewery's computer system, the ghost of Pamela's father emerges at the film's climax with the comment "cool special effects, eh," representing the play's ruminations on the nature of the dramatic illusion, while the use of multiple frames for the films' action represents the play within the play. In addition to the presence of Bob and Doug as "comic buffoons" (Croteau) representing Rosencrantz and Guildenstern, the film also includes two teams of hockey players dressed in uniforms similar to those worn by the storm troopers in the first Star Wars trilogy, and there are numerous product-placements in the film. The cumulative effect of all of this is a suggestion that hockey, KFC, beer, donuts, Star Wars, and Shakespeare are equally generic cultural products which can be consumed together as they are merely part of a greater whole. Toronto is further relegated to the status of a generic city—an important composite establishing shot features Casa Loma, the Molson Brewery, and the Kew Beach Water Works together on the edge of Bluffer's Park. In reality none of these places are within two miles of each other. At the conclusion of *Strange Brew*, Pamela (representing Hamlet) regains control of the brewery and marries Jean (a former hockey player and representative of Ophelia), and Bob and Doug are awarded a load of beer to drink for their assistance. *Strange Brew*'s orientation to *Hamlet* is carnivalesque; like Stoppard's *Rosencrantz and Guildenstern Are Dead*, the minor characters are given center stage, but unlike Stoppard's play, they represent lords of misrule rather than mere functionaries, and it is their ability to exercise their free will (however ineptly), that leads to the comic resolution.

Godard's 1987 film entitled *King Lear*, incorporates some preliminary footage shot in anticipation of an abortive production financed by the Cannon group, directed by Godard, and written by Norman Mailer. The film was to depict Lear as an aging mob boss named Don Leano, but Mailer decided to leave the project after his first meeting with Godard. Godard's film begins with some footage of Mailer working on the script, followed by a title card proclaiming, "KING LEAR: A FILM SHOT IN THE BACK." The little of the film that is comprehensible seems to depict a plot in which one of Shakespeare's descendants attempts to reclaim Shakespeare's plays, which were supposedly lost at Chernobyl, by following two people around and recording what they say. In his *Washington Post* review of the film, Desson Howe notes: "The veteran of the French New Wave is—if anything—at war with the bard. If Shakespeare cuts a crystalline line, Godard splash-paints with the camera. Where the playwright values clarity and poetry, Godard seems to go for obfuscation and banality. Shakespeare aims for universality, while Godard seeks to devalue everything. His work is intensely personal, specifically closed to objective interpretation— and resistant to explication." Seen in this light, Godard's *King Lear* can be viewed as an extreme case of the rejection of Classical Hollywood values that inaugurated the 18-year gap. The film rejects previous notions of aesthetics to the extreme that it is utterly incomprehensible. The rebellious spirit which prompts the famous "white toast" diatribe in *Five Easy Pieces* here assaults the audience with the same vigor and bitterness with which Robert Dupea assaults the waitress in Rafaelson's film.

After the 18-year gap, and throughout the "Branagh era" (as Crowl describes it), the strategy of retaining many specifics of the plays[4] but displacing the use of Early Modern English with contemporary English, and displacing the use of Early Modern settings by contemporary and futuristic settings, was consistently employed in mainstream cinema. The most popular example of this strategy to date is Disney's 1994 release of *The Lion King*, with which the Disney corporation appropriates the narrative functions of *Hamlet* to expound the virtues of an arbitrary and regimented hierarchy that recalls the medieval doctrine of "divine right of kings." The "circle of life" in *The Lion King* replicates the corporate culture that the film is a product of. In the *The Lion King* there is no option other than accepting your place in the "circle of life" which serves to establish social rank and delineate otherness—Simba's villainous uncle is voiced with a British accent, his chief henchman is visually represented as a hyena and is voiced by Whoopi Goldberg, just as the ape/witch doctor speaks with an African accent. In the film, Timon and Pumbaa sing of the "Hakuna Matata" "problem-free philosophy" that promises "no worries for the rest of your days," and also ensures that you will not ask questions or question authority. The central conflict again is precipitated by the villain's flawed moral character, again representing the occasional bad person who rises to eminence in an otherwise good system. As an animated film *The Lion King* is completely reliant on the audience's willingness to accept manufactured images as an illusion of reality without question in order to willingly suspend its disbelief. Here Shakespeare is not only noticeable by his absence, he is completely subverted. Whereas *Hamlet* is concerned with the depiction of a dysfunctional political system which replicates itself and all of its problems into perpetuity, the Disney corporation suggests that virtue is to be found by taking your place in the system without ever questioning it.

From the beginning of the millennium, the strategy of retaining many specifics of the plays but using contemporary English, and contemporary and futuristic settings was consistently employed in mainstream cinema in teen movies. In *Collaborations with the Past*, Diana Henderson notes that the teen comedy *10 Things I Hate About You* (1999) is intentionally positioned as an adaptation of *The Taming of the Shrew* (194). However, this film also subverts the play. Kat's designation as a shrew is here precipitated by her being the one girl in her high school who refuses to conform to normative gender roles, as evidenced by her utter lack of interest in the prom. Far from being tamed, Kat—after rejecting the initial advances of Patrick Verona—is shown to have been correct in her refusal to participate in the activity around the prom, which largely serves to reduce teenage girls to sex objects. Kat's difficult behavior is shown to have resulted from bitter experience, and is further shown to have been intended to protect Bianca from finding herself in a similar situation. Similarly, *She's the Man* (2006), although deliberately constructed as and described as an "homage" to *Twelfth Night* by director Andy Fickman, deliberately recalls yet subverts Shakespeare's handling of gender. The plot involves Viola's attempt to prove herself as skilled a soccer player as her former boyfriend by posing as a boy in a private school in order to join the soccer team. Although Coach Dinklage frequently berates the members of the team for behaving like "girls," it is revealed at the climax of the film—when Viola's real gender is revealed—that his construct of "girlishness" is independent of biological gender, and that he sees Viola as a valued and respected member of his team regardless of the fact that she is biologically female. Whereas Shakespeare's Viola is married by the Duke of Orsino at the conclusion of *Twelfth*

Night, the Viola of *She's the Man* chooses Duke Orsino—who is portrayed in the film as her social peer—as her partner at the conclusion of Fickman's film.

The utilization of themes and motifs frequently ascribed to Shakespeare by Coppola, Mazursky, Godard, and Moranis and Thomas indicate that the 18-year gap was a period in which the strategy utilized in mainstream cinema to represent Shakespeare had changed, although the influence that Shakespeare's plays had in mainstream popular culture had remained constant. The predominant strategy used to represent Shakespeare's plays in mainstream American cinema during this period was already a widely used mode of representation at the beginning of the 18-year gap, and continues to be widespread in its current use. This suggests that interest in representing elements of Shakespeare's plays remains constant; however, differing strategies in representing Shakespeare in the cinema achieve prominence over others at different points in time. Representing Shakespeare's plays has remained a consistent practice in mainstream cinema. The notion of "the 18-year gap" results from a tendency to privilege films which approach a seminal play as a gestalt over films which approach a seminal play as a resource containing disparate elements. Zeffirelli's tendency to privilege the visual over word precipitates a devaluing of his works by critics who posit a "canon of Shakespeare on film," despite the fact that his approach is consistent with his contemporary mainstream cinema. Films of the 1970s and 1980s which conspicuously reference elements of Shakespearean plays, but follow narrative trajectories never anticipated in the seminal plays, have also been devalued by critics who posit a "canon of Shakespeare on film," despite the fact that the approaches utilized in their production are—like Zeffirelli's—also consistent with their contemporary mainstream cinema.

CHAPTER 9

Branagh

According to Samuel Crowl, in *Shakespeare at the Cineplex,* prior to 1989, filmed adaptations of Shakespeare's plays were chiefly consumed by "the elite art-house audience" (12). This would have rendered them a highly unreliable source of return on investment at the box office. The simultaneous financial and critical success of Kenneth Branagh's *Henry V* demonstrated that the cultural capital of Shakespeare's plays could be transformed into a viable source of financial capital at the box office, and thereby inaugurated the 1990s wave of mainstream Shakespearean film adaptations.

As mainstream cinema conventionally demarcates all moral lines clearly, the moral ambivalences presented in Shakespeare's play of *Henry V* would have violated a mainstream cinema audience's expectations of a protagonist. Branagh's film of *Henry V* is targeted at a mainstream cinema audience, prompting Branagh to address the issue of mainstream cinema audience expectations while dramatizing the film. The protagonist of Shakespeare's play, who is simultaneously "the mirror of all Christian Kings" and one of the most ruthless, cold, and manipulative characters to be found in the Shakespeare canon, is presented in Branagh's film in a manner consistent with a mainstream cinema audience's expectations of a protagonist in 1989.

A brief survey of three mainstream blockbuster films released in 1989 reveals the extent to which Branagh's King Henry assumes many of the common characteristics of a mainstream action hero. Tim Burton's *Batman,* Richard Donner's *Lethal Weapon 2,* and John Glen's *License to Kill* present protagonists who are mourning the loss of a loved one, pursuing a vigilante campaign to redress injustices, and who act according to an individual moral code which supersedes the ineffective normative moral codes of the protagonist's social context. (Batman, in pursuit of his independent vigilante campaign, avoids due process by attempting to murder Jack Napier; Martin

Riggs throws his badge away to deal with drug dealers who are diplomatically immune from prosecution; James Bond resigns his commission to pursue a vendetta against the drug dealers who have attacked his friend.)

Branagh's use of flash-back sequences that depict King Henry's earlier days at the Boar's Head tavern, contextualizes King Henry's relationships with Falstaff, Bardolph, Nym, the Page, Pistol, and Mistress Quickly, suggesting that King Henry is mourning the loss of these relationships. King Henry's expression seems to be one of shame at the rejection of Falstaff, and is definitely one of shock at the execution of Bardolph. Near the film's conclusion, as King Henry and the French King discuss the destruction caused by the war, a lap dissolve reveals that King Henry is thinking of the friends that he betrayed,[1] and of his friend[2] who betrayed him. The importance of these relationships to King Henry is further demonstrated by his choice to carry the body of the Page to burial during the famous five-minute-long tracking shot.

Like Batman, Martin Riggs, and James Bond, King Henry's goal can also be seen as seeking redress for various injustices, namely the reclamation of lands he believes usurped by France, the purgation of traitors from his own court, and the redress of insult from the Dauphin. Also like them, King Henry is possessed of a personal moral system that supersedes the normative system of his immediate social context, as demonstrated by the emphasis Branagh places on King Henry's frequent personal commitment and public calls for subservience to God. Although all of King Henry's religious utterances are extant in Shakespeare's play, they are presented in Branagh's film in a completely sincere manner, with no hint of irony or cynicism. Our acceptance of King Henry as a highly moral character subservient to the will of God is further reinforced by the omission of any material in Shakespeare's play that reveals King Henry's manipulative and sometimes malicious nature. The incident in Act IV, scenes vii and viii where Fluellen and Williams are manipulated to a near brawl by King Henry simply for his amusement is completely cut. The conflict which precipitated King Henry's whim to play them for fools—wherein Williams offers King Henry his gage—is altered by the omission of several lines to appear here as a sobering lesson given Williams by King Henry on the subject of the integrity of the King. King Henry and Fluellen appear to be near confidantes, as Fluellen is embraced by a King Henry who proclaims Fluellen his countryman in the aftermath of Agincourt. This omission of any material in Shakespeare's play which would compromise the viability of King Henry as a moral character permeates the film through to the final scenes which depict him as sincere and warm in his love suit to Catherine.

All reference to his verbal subjugation of her as it appears in the play is simply omitted.

With a morally infallible protagonist who precipitates and is at the center of a nexus of violence and destruction, Branagh's film of *Henry V* possesses the same logical contradiction as do *Lethal Weapon 2*, *Batman*, and *License to Kill*. Branagh's film also deals with that contradiction in the same manner as those films: by avoiding it and instead structuring the narrative progression of the film around the protagonist's interpersonal relationships. For example, Burton's *Batman* is concerned with Batman's troubled relationships with Vicki Vale and Alfred; Donner's *Lethal Weapon 2* is concerned with Riggs' connection to Murtagh's family and loyalty to his dead wife; Glen's *License to Kill* is concerned with Bond's loyalty to Felix, his emerging relationship with Pam, and his affection for "Q." Branagh also presents King Henry's character in terms of interpersonal relationships—every action and speech of King Henry's is presented in terms of its relation to another character in the film. As he addresses his soldiers before Harfleur, the scene is edited in such a way that King Henry appears to be personally addressing specific characters. The line "lend the eye a terrible aspect" appears, through the use of eyeline matches, to be directed at Exeter, who complies. King Henry then looks at Williams, brandishes his sword, and says "dishonour not your mothers," causing Williams to draws his own sword wearing an enthusiastic expression in response.

The rejection of Falstaff is treated as an intimate and private moment that takes place between two friends, and emphasizes the strength of their emotional bond. As Falstaff carouses he sees King Henry entering the room from the off-screen space and becomes very animated and happy, greeting King Henry enthusiastically. The two friends embrace and warmly beam at one another. As Falstaff speaks to King Henry, ending with the line "Banish plump Jack and banish all the world," King Henry's face drops in shame, and we hear his thoughts in a voiceover narration—"I do, I will." Falstaff realizes this and is stunned, disbelievingly saying, "We have heard the chimes at midnight, Master Harry, Jesus, such days we have seen." King Henry's face has by this point dropped completely. He glances embarrassedly at the floor while thinking, "I know thee not, old man."

Branagh's use of the voiceover here serves a dual purpose. Paired with the image of King Henry's face dropping, it establishes the King's reluctance to hurt someone to whom he is obviously very attached. Simultaneously, Falstaff's understanding of what King Henry is thinking at this moment, despite the fact that it remains unspoken, establishes the emotional depth of their relationship. As our attention is focused on Falstaff's pain and

King Henry's regret and embarrassment, the fact that King Henry is undertaking a morally questionable act to consolidate his power is never allowed to occur to us.

Branagh achieves this same effect in the scene depicting the execution of Bardolph, which is arguably King Henry's most morally questionable act. In Shakespeare's play, Bardolph is not present as King Henry orders his execution on the pretext that the French must be treated well, in order that they will settle down quietly and willingly under English rule. King Henry here is far more concerned with the consolidation of his power than he is with the welfare of his own troops, or of his former close friend.

In Branagh's film Bardolph is executed in front and at the command of King Henry. As the sequence opens, Fluellen greets King Henry and tells him that Bardolph is to be executed for a petty theft. Through editing, Fluellen's utterance of the name, "Bardolph," coincides with the entrance of Bardolph, accompanied by a dissonant chord on the soundtrack. We are then presented with a close-up shot of a stunned King Henry, whose position and expression do not change for the rest of the sequence. King Henry, in shock, is barely able to nod the execution order. We are presented with an ironic flashback sequence in which King Henry tells Bardolph that he shall likely "hang a thief." The execution takes place, after which King Henry tearfully delivers his rationalization for this action. Shakespeare's opportunistic and morally ambivalent King Henry is here transformed by Branagh into a King Henry so morally infallible that he justly punishes crime even at the expense of great personal pain.

Branagh provides the omniscient point of view only to the Chorus and the audience, establishing a sense that—as members of the audience—we are his true intimates and confidantes. During the introductory throne room scene King Henry enunciates, "We'll bend it to our awe" clearly, in order that the clergy and nobles present should hear it. The next line, "Or break it all to pieces" is spoken in a voice so soft that no one within the diegesis of the film could have heard it, and is accompanied by a sudden close up shot showing an uncertain expression on King Henry's face, which is directed at the audience alone. To everyone within the diegesis of the film King Henry appears strong, determined and resolved to conquer France. Only the audience and the Chorus are aware that the young King is deeply uncertain of the legitimacy of this course of action. This motif recurs throughout the film. King Henry's threat of murder and rape to the governor of Harfleur is staged in such a way as that both the governor and representatives of Harfleur, and King Henry's forces, would not be able to see his facial expression. King Henry's sigh of relief at the governor's surrender is for the information of the audience only, making us aware that—despite his display of brazen confidence to his soldiers and the governor—he has used the threat of rape and murder as a bluff to trick the governor into surrendering, and had no real intention of pillaging and sacking Harfleur. In both instances, actions on King Henry's part that appear in the play and in the diegesis of the film as morally objectionable are made palatable for a mainstream audience by Branagh's decision to privilege the audience with information the characters in the diegesis of the film would not have access to.

As Branagh intended *Henry V* for a mass audience, his chief concern was to present a film that would conform to mainstream expectations of what a protagonist is supposed to be and do. To accomplish this, Branagh constructed his character and his narrative in order that a mainstream audience could identify his King Henry as the type of protagonist current in the mainstream blockbuster films of 1989. However, in many ways Branagh deliberately invites comparisons between his film and Olivier's *Henry V*. Branagh's *Henry V* clearly responds to Olivier's. The action of Olivier's film is encompassed by a frame which indicates that the audience is intended to understand what they are seeing initially as a re-creation of a performance of *Henry V* at the Globe, and later as a filmic analogue to a theatrical performance. Branagh's film aligns itself clearly with cinema from its outset, as Derek Jacobi delivers the first soliloquy of the Chorus while walking through a sound stage within which lights, props, sets, and camera equipment are strewn. Both films are concerned with the artifice an individual must assume to project an ideal of kingship. In Olivier's film, we see the actor portraying Henry V nervously coughing backstage, before proceeding onstage to project the full grandeur of his role. In Branagh's film, when we first see King Henry he is introduced in his full grandeur as he enters the throne room, dramatically backlit in a wide angle long shot, to the accompaniment of awe inspiring music on the soundtrack; however, throughout Branagh's film close shots are used to depict Henry V in moments of private uncertainty and doubt. Olivier's Agincourt is pristine and bloodless; the skies are blue, no blood is seen on-screen, and costumes are unstained at the conclusion of the battle. Branagh's Agincourt is staged as a muddy, grimy pit; black blood spews out of a soldier's mouth as he is surrounded and stabbed to death by three armored men, and water splashes ubiquitously as King Henry and his soldiers frantically redeploy their positions. Judith Buchanan, in *Shakespeare on Film*, notes that "whereas for the battle of Agincourt Olivier stopped shooting whenever the sun went behind a cloud, Branagh stopped shooting whenever the sun came out" (195). The most famous shot in Olivier's film, which was referred to by Robert White in an unpublished lecture as one of the "three great rides in film history," represents the mounted French forces approaching Agincourt. The French forces gallop toward the field wearing colorful uniforms and bearing colorful pennants, moving from screen right to screen left. The most famous shot in Branagh's film depicts the English forces leaving Agincourt on foot, covered in mud and led by King Henry bearing the body of the page, moving from left to right as they stagger towards the funeral pyre. Where Olivier's film is intended to inspire his audience to the cause of war, Branagh's film asks his audience to consider the cost of war. Although Branagh's *Henry V* finds its genesis in Adrian Noble's 1985 Royal Shakespeare Company stage production, the resultant film embodies a dialogic encounter between Branagh and Olivier on the subject of the meaning of Shakespeare's play.

The pattern wherein Branagh transforms a stage production he was involved in into a film that confronts the work of another director was repeated with the release of *Much Ado About Nothing* in 1993. Having played the role of Benedick in Judi Dench's 1988 Renaissance Theatre Company production, Branagh once again chose to create a film in which the relationship of his work to cinema, rather than the stage, is foregrounded. In *Shakespeare at the Cineplex,* Samuel Crowl notes that the critical tendency to proclaim Branagh as the heir to Olivier and Welles has led to a critical tendency to underestimate and completely ignore the impact that the films of Franco Zeffirelli have had on Branagh (5). The strategy of referencing and rejecting Olivier's approach utilized by Branagh in *Henry V* is recalled by a similar strategy of referencing and rejecting Zeffirelli's approach utilized by Branagh in *Much Ado About Nothing*.

Whereas *Henry V*[3] is clearly intended for the portion of the mass audience interested in a "prestige production," *Much Ado About Nothing*, with its use of established Hollywood stars and sumptuous location shooting, was intended for the summer movie-going portion of the mass audience. Up to that point in time, in terms of box office receipts, Zeffirelli had been the clear champion of Shakespeare in the cinema. *The Taming of the Shrew* was a box-office success which relied on the star images of the two principal players to facilitate the act of reading by the audience. *Romeo and Juliet* is, to date, the most financially successful adaptation produced of Shakespeare's work in the cinema. Just as Branagh in many ways aligned *Henry V* with Olivier's film, he also did not resist the opportunity to "have a go" at Zeffirelli.

Branagh's casting decisions for *Much Ado About Nothing* certainly seem to echo those made by Zeffirelli. *Henry V* and *Dead Again* had established both Branagh and Emma Thompson as international stars by the time of the film's release. (As mentioned above, Branagh was widely considered the heir to Olivier and Welles whereas Thompson had won the Academy Award for Best Actress that year for her performance in *Howard's End*, and was also appearing that same year in two Academy Award nominated films: *The Remains of the Day* and *In The Name of the Father*). Although many of the prominent roles in *Much Ado About Nothing* are played by established stars,[4] Branagh's decision to cast the relatively unknown Kate Beckinsale as Hero and Robert Sean Leonard as Claudio mirrors Zeffirelli's decision to cast Olivia Hussey as Juliet and Leonard Whiting as Romeo. In both cases the casting decisions are age-appropriate; Zeffirelli uses teenagers to play teenagers whereas Branagh uses a 19-year-old to play Hero, and a 24-year-old to play Claudio—ages consistent with Samuel Crowl's speculation that Claudio and Hero would have been in their early 20s (68).

The Taming of the Shrew and *Romeo and Juliet* both open with a gaze over a cityscape; in the case of the former we see Lucentio's gaze and hear his voice as he reacts with wonder when he first sees Padua; in the case of the latter we see a cityscape of Verona obscured by fog as we hear the disembodied voice of the chorus assure us of the fate of the "star-crossed" lovers. Conversely, *Much Ado About Nothing* opens with Beatrice's disembodied voice accompanying a "sing-along" presentation of Balthazar's song against a black background. The image fades to a painting of the Tuscan countryside, and the camera then pans left to reveal the actual countryside that the painter is representing, continuing until Beatrice is framed in a close-up as she finishes her recitation. Branagh is "having a go" at Zeffirelli in multiple ways here. The vision of Padua that Lucentio gazes upon in *The Taming of the Shrew* is very obviously a huge landscape painting; Branagh begins *Much Ado About Nothing* with a landscape painting and then pans to reveal a real landscape. In *Romeo and Juliet* Zeffirelli's camera pans right to eventually focus on a close image of the setting sun while the disembodied male chorus speaks; Branagh's camera pans right to a close shot of Beatrice accompanied by her female voice. Branagh's film aligns and contrasts itself with Zeffirelli's from the outset.

Branagh references many of the elements of Zeffirelli's films, but frequently uses them in a contradictory manner. One of the most striking moments in *Romeo and Juliet* occurs at the masked ball when the "star-crossed" lovers first meet. In an often emulated shot, Romeo and Juliet dance as part of a group of people who hold hands while dancing in a circle; they face each other as the tempo of the dance increases; the camera focused on their smiling faces in close-up as the background whirls around them. At the conclusion of the dance a lone troubadour sings "What Is a Youth" which foreshadows the tragedy to follow at the onset of their relationship. In Branagh's film, "Sigh no more" is reprised twice. Firstly, in the garden scene Balthazar performs the song as Branagh's camera circles around the performers, Claudio, Don Pedro, and Leonato in an elaborate manner that recalls and reverses the dynamic of Zeffirelli's famous dance shot. Secondly, in the final dance of joy the entire cast sings while many of the players form small groups in which they join hands and dance in circles as the camera tracks out to a high crane shot. Branagh appropriates Zeffirelli's pairing of the circular dance and the song, but uses them to depict the joyous couplings at the conclusion of the plot rather than to foreshadow the tragedy to come at the onset of the plot.

Similar to the challenge he faced in *Henry V*, Branagh needed to formulate a strategy of dramatization that would facilitate his intended audience's reading of *Much Ado About Nothing*. In 1993, films dealing with "women's issues" were becoming prevalent in Hollywood cinema. In 1989, Jodie Foster won the Academy Award for Best Actress for her performance in *The Accused*, a film concerned with deconstructing the social tendency to perceive rape victims as having initiated the assault. In 1991, Foster again won this award for *The Silence of the Lambs*, in which she portrayed a novice FBI agent pursuing a serial rapist and murderer while dealing with the sexist attitudes of her superiors, the witnesses and experts she consults during her pursuit of the murderer, and Dr. Hannibal Lector, an imprisoned serial murderer she interrogates for insight into his thought processes. Released in 1991, *Thelma and Louise* depicted two women as ultimately resorting to suicide in order to escape the entrapment they faced within a society in which they were repeatedly marginalized and disenfranchised. Also released in 1991, *Fried Green Tomatoes* depicted the story of the friendship between a socially transgressive woman in depression-era Georgia, and her best friend, a physically abused housewife who comes to live with her after being rescued from the relationship. The Depression-era story in this film is further framed with a narrative concerning the empowerment of a neglected housewife in a contemporary setting. Many critics of Shakespeare's play (and Branagh's film) find Hero's decision to forgive Claudio as something of a non-sequitur. This can be explained and justified by reference to the way that *Much Ado About Nothing* uses the treatment of Hero and the depiction of male violence as a subtext that aligns Branagh's film with its contemporary Hollywood cinema.

Beginning the film with Beatrice's monologue delivery of Balthazar's song establishes at the film's onset that the dominant perspective of this film is a female perspective, and further establishes that this perspective is critical of men, albeit in a good natured fashion. Crowl has noted that Branagh deliberately presents Claudio as naïve and emotionally immature (68) in order to allow the audience to react to his behavior with some sympathy; what Crowl hasn't noted is that the majority of the men in this film can be seen in this light. Don Pedro's proposal to Beatrice seems to come out of nowhere, and provides the film with an early uncomfortable moment. Thompson's facial expression and nuance of voice when she responds indicate confusion followed by the soft yet firm tone of rejection she might utilize when refusing a child, which is unsurprising as there has been no interaction between them that might suggest the proposal would be appropriate or welcome. The deception of Benedick is overplayed to hilarious comic effect by Richard Briers, Robert Sean Leonard, and Denzel Washington, yet beneath the comic effect there is an issue of Benedick's naivety—surely the overstated voices these men are using in a private conversation should indicate the possibility of falsehood to a listener. Benedick's weak attempts at flirtation with Beatrice, and his outrageous preening of himself in front of the mirror also indicate an element of narcissism in his character. Although these scenes are played to comic effect, they do indicate a subtext in Branagh's film that is critical toward the notion of masculinity.

The narcissism, naivety, and immaturity that are played to comic effect prior to the first wedding ceremony also provide the dramatic underpinnings for that ceremony and the sequences to follow. One element of Branagh's portrayal of Claudio and Benedick is their tendency toward play violence. Benedick first shoves Claudio when he learns that he is in love with Hero, and later Benedick and Claudio cuff one another when having a disagreement. Although funny to watch, this play violence in response to a perceived slight represents a latent form of real violence in response to a perceived slight that erupts at the wedding scene. It is crucial to Branagh's depiction of the slander of Hero that the dialogue from the play depicting Margaret's conversation with Borachio is cut from the film, and displaced with a scene depicting Margaret copulating with Borachio, which Don Pedro, Don John, and Claudio view from behind, thereby obscuring Margaret's features. Although this would predispose a viewer to be sympathetic to Claudio—he believes he has just seen his betrothed having sex with another man—the violence with which the wedding scene is depicted seems excessive despite this. Claudio knocks down standards and benches, grabs Hero, spins her around, and throws her to the ground. While she is on the ground he attempts to slap her again, but is blocked by Beatrice. Leonato then grabs Hero, drags her by the hair and throws her to the ground. Once she is on the ground Leonato again strikes her hard.

Although Claudio's violence here might seem explained by immaturity and a legitimate sense of betrayal, Leonato's seems completely out of proportion as he has been given no direct evidence to support the claims of Claudio and Don Pedro, and, as Hero's father, he should be aware that her character would not allow this behavior. At this point it should be remembered that, in Branagh's dramatization, the dialogue between Margaret and Borachio is never represented; however, Don Pedro exclaims that he heard Hero "confess the vile encounters they have had a thousand times in secret." As this confession never occurred in Branagh's film, Don Pedro is clearly embellishing upon what he has seen in order to justify an expression of the violence that is always latent. Hero's slander provides an excuse for the men to express their latent violence, which they convince themselves to be a legitimate reason. Judith Buchanan writes that "the latent misogyny of the community as a whole is horribly exposed" (*Shakespeare on Film* 204).

Although Benedick advises Leonato to "be patient" and attempts to get to the bottom of the slander, he does nothing to restrain Leonato or Claudio from their physical attacks on Hero, but later physically restrains Beatrice from pursuing revenge against them. Crowl notes that the scene between Benedick and Beatrice in the chapel is filmed in order to depict the shift in Benedick's imaginative vision when declaring his love to Beatrice (74–75); her wish that Claudio be killed is now his mission. (Incidentally, the play violence which previously characterized the relationship between Benedick and Claudio is now displaced by real violence when Benedick challenges Claudio; Benedick grabs Claudio's jaw so forcefully while shoving him up against the wall that Claudio rubs his jaw for several minutes afterward.) The later wooing scene further confirms that it is now Beatrice who is firmly in control of their relationship; Benedick attempts to flirt with her while she keeps him focused on his promise to kill Claudio.

Branagh's final inversion of Zeffirelli occurs when Benedick and Beatrice agree to marry. Although Benedick seems to have the "last word,"5 Benedick's final imperative that Don Pedro "never flout at [him] for what [he] ha[s] said against [marriage]; for man is a giddy thing" here serves as confirmation that the female perspective established at the film's onset now dominates his imaginative vision. Zeffirelli's *The Taming of the Shrew* concludes on a similar note: Kate gives her famous speech demanding that women submit to their husbands, yet sneaks off on Petruchio to the obvious amusement of the wedding guests before he can complete bidding them good night, thereby rendering his displayed dominance of her problematic. Similarly, although Branagh allows Benedick a similar "show" of victory, it is obvious that, in adopting the female perspective represented by Beatrice, his displays of naivety, narcissism, and dominance are behind him.

The success of *Henry V* can be attributed to Branagh's anticipation of his contemporary audience's expectations of the behavior of a protagonist, and the success of *Much Ado About Nothing* can be attributed to Branagh's alignment of his film with contemporary "women's films." In his 1996 film of *Hamlet* Branagh attempts to align Shakespeare's play with his contemporary audience's expectations of the epic film. Branagh's decision to use a "complete" text compiled from all of the existing quarto and folio versions certainly satisfies the unacknowledged criterion that epic films should be of greater than normal length. Branagh's use of a plethora of Hollywood stars to portray not only major but also many minor parts satisfies the unacknowledged criterion that epic films should feature an ensemble cast of star players. Branagh's use of the 70mm format traditionally reserved for epics, coupled with his decision to use Blenheim Palace as his setting of Elsinore, certainly satisfy the criterion of the grandiose scope and feel that are associated with the epic. At the time of *Hamlet*'s release, two subgenres of the epic were prevalent in mainstream film culture: the historical epic and the romantic epic. The popularity of the historical epic in the 1990s is easily demonstrated: *Dances with Wolves* won the Academy Award for Best Picture in 1991; *Gettysburg*—a 261-minute cinematic recreation of the eponymous battle—was released in 1993, in 1994 *Schindler's List* won the Academy Award for Best Picture; *Braveheart* won the Academy Award for Best Picture in 1996. The popularity of the romantic epic is equally easily demonstrated: released just seven weeks prior to Branagh's *Hamlet*, *The English Patient* won the Academy Award for Best Picture in 1997; *Titanic* won the Academy Award for Best Picture in 1998; *Sense and Sensibility*[6] was nominated for the Academy Award for Best Picture in the same year as *Braveheart*. Where Branagh's mise-en-scène and costumes (his Prince, for example, wears a black 19th-century British military uniform) align his *Hamlet* with the then popular historical epic, his decision to cast Julie Christie (who played Lara in *Doctor Zhivago*) as Gertrude and Kate Winslet (who played Marianne in *Sense and Sensibility* and Rose in *Titanic*) as Ophelia align his *Hamlet* with the then popular romantic epic. In "Shakespeare and the Movie Genre: The Case of Hamlet," Harry Keyishian also suggests that Branagh's *Hamlet* is constructed to conform to the criterion of an epic (78), and J. Lawrence Guntner agrees, in "Hamlet, Macbeth, and

King Lear on Film," that the presence of Julie Christie reminds the audience viewing Branagh's *Hamlet* of *Dr. Zhivago*'s Lara (126). Crowl agrees that Branagh's *Hamlet* "follows the model of David Lean's intelligent epics, from *Lawrence of Arabia* (1962) and *Doctor Zhivago* (1965) to *A Passage to India* (1984)" (135). Branagh's epic, however, is constructed to appeal to as many segments of his marketplace as possible: Stephen Buhler writes, "certainly Branagh's own Hamlet, with its assertive and sexually active hero, attempts to do better than Olivier's version in holding the attention of audience members who prefer Schwarzenegger to Shakespeare" (114). In addition, the mise-en-scène of this film seems designed to appeal to that segment of the marketplace cultivated by the Royal Shakespeare Company, which operated under Peter Hall's edict that productions of Shakespeare should always be "relevant"—according to Alan Sinfield, in "Royal Shakespeare: Theatre and the Making of Ideology" (183). In *Shakespeare on the Screen: Kenneth Branagh's Adaptations of Henry V, Much Ado About Nothing, and Hamlet*, Tanja Weiss states: "The 19th century ... production design shows up a later Victorian era plus/minus a decade. The exact time cannot be identified, or specified, ... In fact, the time remains as vague as to refer to nothing other than is absolutely necessary.... Since the audience (or at least part of the audience) would know that the great European empires had to face their decline in that century, there is also the film's notion of an empire at its close, the story of Hamlet and his family is also a story about a declining empire" (144–145).

As in the cases of *Henry V* and *Much Ado About Nothing*, Branagh had played the role of Hamlet on stage (in a 1988 Renaissance Theatre Company production which was directed by Derek Jacobi), but situated his film firmly in the world of cinema rather than the theatre. The cinematic techniques employed by Branagh in this production recall the cinema of Orson Welles (the repeated use of long takes and circular tracking shots which frequently violate the axis of action), as does the mirrored hall.[7] Judith Buchanan notes that both Kozintsev's and Branagh's films of *Hamlet* begin with an image of the name "Hamlet" chiseled in stone (*Shakespeare on Film* 207). The cutaways inserted into the film by Branagh represent a technique specific to film which foregrounds the presence of the medium; however, they are used by Branagh "for the sake of clarity, characterization and additional information" (Weiss 127).

Branagh utilizes the traditional mainstream Hollywood motif of the doppel in his presentation of the disparity between Hamlet and Fortinbras. Where Branagh's Hamlet is fair, blonde, uniformed, and delivers his most famous soliloquy to a mirror, his Fortinbras (who has Hamlet's "dying voice") is ruddy, dark-haired, wears battle armor, and is presented as a military commander giving orders during the capture of Elsinore. Old Hamlet is presented as Hamlet's idealized and patriarchal figure, as Weiss notes "the Prince has idealized his father, and more generally, it suggests that Hamlet's perspective is subjective and easily distorted whenever the memory of his father is concerned" (181). Hamlet's idealization of his father seems to be shared by the Danish Court in Branagh's realization. The statue of Old Hamlet, erected to mythologize his reign, presents him in a suit of medieval amour despite the fact that he is always depicted in the flashbacks of his lifetime in a 19th-century military uniform. The exaggeration of this presentation suggests that the Danish court mythologizes Old Hamlet to this degree in order to obliterate the memory of Old Fortinbras. According to Buhler, "Young Fortinbras revenges his father's death and defeat at old Hamlet's hand…. Branagh suggests that Hamlet is a faithful son to a possibly faithless father" (120).

Branagh's 1996 film reinstates every line of dialogue and character cut from previous films of *Hamlet*, and brings the issue of imperialism to the foreground. The male characters in Branagh's Elsinore wear military uniforms, and short visual sequences superimposed over dialogue reinforce the sense of Denmark as one node of a larger imperial network. The use of mythologization to legitimate the imperial network is also examined—every one of the flashback sequences involving Old Hamlet shows him in a military uniform, however his ghost appears to Hamlet not as an apparition but as a statue that has come to life. As the historical setting for Branagh's film is the early 19th century, Old Hamlet would only have worn medieval armor when he was posing for the construction of the statue. Is the apparition that confronts Hamlet the ghost of his father, or is it the ghost of the myth constructed to politically legitimate his fathers' reign? The film further highlights the use of mythologization to legitimate the imperial network at its conclusion. The superfluous murder of Osric suggests that Fortinbras' soldiers have instructions to kill everyone. However, Horatio's offer to tell Hamlet's tale of "casual slaughters" provides Fortinbras with a legitimization of his invasion; therefore, Horatio is spared to fulfill this function. The funeral rites accorded to Hamlet further support Fortinbras' agenda—with Hamlet mythologized as sacrificing his life to purge Denmark of corruption, Fortinbras reinforces his legitimacy as a candidate for Denmark's throne by aligning himself with the now deified Hamlet's condemnation of Denmark's polity prior to *their* intervention. The Fortinbras line assumes eminence once again, the official history of the Hamlet line is re-written to support the Fortinbras claim to the throne, and the larger imperial network remains intact.

Branagh's utilization of the doppel motif to establish the difference between the Hamlet and Fortinbras lines, however, suggests that the change of personnel experienced by the larger imperial network is a change of kind, not of degree. The final image of Branagh's film, which depicts the destruction of the statue of Old Hamlet, immediately recalls the toppling of statues of Stalin and Lenin that accompanied the collapse of the U.S.S.R. Hamlet is portrayed by Branagh as having the blonde hair, blue eyes and fair complexion associated with "classic northern European features," and the scene in which Hamlet is confronted by his father's spirit emphasizes extreme close-up shots of their blue eyes. Fortinbras, has deep brown eyes, a dark complexion, and is portrayed throughout the film as indifferent to the power sharing arrangements of the established imperial network. An early cutaway sequence shows Fortinbras reprimanded by Old Norway for his intended invasion of Denmark; Fortinbras placates his Uncle by agreeing to a "promised march over" Claudius' "kingdom," but uses this new agreement as a ruse to entrench his soldiers in order to invade Denmark. Whereas threats in the imperial network are depicted as traditionally dealt with through the unspoken agreements, secret conspiracies, and covert murders favored by Polonius[8] and Claudius,[9] Fortinbras establishes himself through direct military confrontation and blatant, decisive violence. In Branagh's film, the decadent, fair skinned Hamlet line is usurped by the dark complexioned and violent Fortinbras, leaving the viewer with an impression that the dysfunctional social order of Claudius' rule has now been displaced by an even more ruthless and amoral polity.

Although critically acclaimed, *Hamlet* recouped only 26 percent of its production budget at the box office, which represented Branagh's first commercial failure. This was largely due to the marketing strategy behind the film's release. The film was released in only one theatre in each of New York, Toronto, and Los Angeles on December 25, 1996. On January 24, 1997, the film opened to a limited North American release of fewer than 100 screens. It was rumored at the time of these releases that a shorter version of the film was to be offered in a general release during the summer of 1997; however, that release never materialized. Branagh's next representation of Shakespeare in the cinema, *Love's Labour's Lost*, recouped 2 percent of its production budget. The consensus among critics was that Branagh's decision to fuse the tropes of a 1930s mainstream musical (including several popular Broadway songs of the 1930s) with a heavily cut version of one of Shakespeare's most opaque plays, was, according to Roger Ebert's *Chicago*

Sun-Times review of the film, an "awkward join." In recent years, although Branagh has not attempted a mainstream cinematic adaptation of Shakespeare (although *As You Like It* was released theatrically in Europe, it was shown only on Home Box Office and then went straight to video in North America) the 2011 release of *Thor* indicates that Branagh has returned to the mainstream of international cinema directors. Branagh's approach to Shakespeare in the cinema seems increasingly preoccupied with the attempt to represent seminal plays within the confines of established cinematic genres. *Henry V* and *Much Ado About Nothing* reflect their contemporary cinema in terms of popular expectations of a protagonist in the case of the former, and in terms of association with popular issues in the terms of the latter. Conversely, *Hamlet* and *Love's Labour's Lost* are almost completely dramatized in a manner that places them well within the confines of an established genre in their contemporary cinemas. Although the failure of *Hamlet* is more likely a result of an ill-conceived marketing strategy, the failure of *Love's Labour's Lost* indicates that Branagh's audacity may have overstepped his commercial sense. Not only, as Ebert observed, was the cinematic genre utilized by Branagh incompatible with the seminal play, it was also considered a largely defunct genre at the time of the film's release. Branagh's career as a director of cinematic representations of Shakespeare's plays certainly demonstrates the necessity of successfully mediating the seminal play with the expectations of a contemporary mainstream audience; Branagh's successes and failures seem to directly correlate to the degree to which he has achieved this.

Chapter 10

Millennial Shakespeare

In *A History of Shakespeare on Screen*, Kenneth Rothwell's use of the phrase "the Age of Branagh" (246) to describe the resurgence of filmed adaptations of Shakespeare's plays in the 1990s can be simultaneously seen as deeply astute yet deeply inaccurate. The phrase is astute because it is the commercial success of Branagh's *Much Ado About Nothing* (precipitated by Branagh's strategy of reflecting many of the thematic concerns that were prevalent in mainstream cinema in this film) that paved the way for the filmed representations of Shakespeare that were released in the second half of the decade. However, the phrase is inaccurate because these films do not merely reflect the prevalent concerns of their contemporary mainstream cinema, they wholeheartedly embrace them. Where Branagh's success can be seen as a final validation of the cinematic "actor-manager" (Buhler 120) tradition that Welles and Olivier attempted to establish, Loncraine's, Luhrmann's, Taymor's and Almereyda's films belong far more to a then emergent subgenre in mainstream cinema than they do to previous traditions of filming Shakespeare's plays.

Coining the phrase "millennial cinema" as a descriptor of contemporary cinema in the year 2000, in "Tomorrow Is My Birthday: Placing Apocalypse in Millennial Cinema" Dianne Sippl identifies five films that she believes to exemplify "apocalyptic" (5) motifs that characterize the cultural zeitgeist of the "millennial moment" (7). Sippl here defines apocalypse as characterized by "irretrievability ... the personal and social incapacity to regain what has been lost, even if afforded the ground for beginning again" (5). Among the five films that Sippl includes in her analysis is Paul Thomas Anderson's *Magnolia*; with an Oscar-nominated director (for his previous film, *Boogie Nights*) and a stellar ensemble cast including Tom Cruise, Jason Robards, Julianne Moore, Melinda Dillon and William H. Macy, *Magnolia* is certainly situated within mainstream cinema. Among themes and motifs that Sippl identifies as operant in *Magnolia* are a society or culture that undermines or consumes its children (9), reflexive contemplation of the function of media (10), an apocalyptic moment that is depicted with religious or mystical overtones (9), and the possibility of a new beginning precipitated by the apocalyptic moment (10).

Sippl confines her analysis to films released between 1997 and 2000; however, several major studio films released much earlier in the 1990s also share the characteristics of millennial cinema that Sippl identifies with *Magnolia*. Released in 1991, Michael Tolkin's *The Rapture* depicts the trajectory of an alienated woman from a sexual libertine to a devout born again Christian who is forced by God to test her faith by murdering her own daughter. Once the test is passed, the apocalypse ensues and the protagonist is offered eternal bliss in exchange for a declaration of love for God; appalled at the arbitrariness of the creator's nature, the protagonist opts for eternity in purgatory over submission to a capricious deity. Clint Eastwood's *Unforgiven*, released in 1992, tells the story of a former gunslinger who briefly abandons his children in order to pursue a bounty. While doing this, the gunslinger experiences an illness in which he sees visions of the angel of death, and by the film's conclusion he literally embodies the persona of the angel of death, riding into town on a pale horse in order to slaughter the personnel who administer the town's establishment. David Fincher's *Alien 3*, also released in 1992, begins with its protagonist crash-landing onto a planet occupied by former prisoners who have established a millenarian religious cult. Early in the film the protagonist must preside over the autopsy of her ersatz daughter who was killed in the crash, and the bulk of the film details the protagonist's efforts to destroy the alien before a major corporation can capture it in order to use it as a weapon. At the film's conclusion the alien is destroyed by being doused with molten lead and then water (baptism by fire and water) and the protagonist commits suicide by allowing herself to fall backward into the vat of lead, while assuming a cruciform pose.

At the release of *The Rapture*, Mimi Rogers (who earned an Academy Award nomination for Best Actress for her performance in this film) was an established actress who had been cast in leading roles by high profile directors such as Ridley Scott, Ron Howard and Michael Cimino. Eastwood was clearly an established "star" and icon at the release of *Unforgiven*, which won four Academy Awards, including the Oscar for Best Picture and another for Eastwood as Best Director. *Alien 3* was the third installment in a highly successful horror/science fiction franchise and starred Sigourney Weaver, who at that point in her career was an established star with three academy award nominations to her credit, the first of which was for her performance in the second installment in the *Alien* franchise. Although Sippl is correct in her observation that millennial cinema was an operating subgenre of cinema at the time of the turn of the century, this subgenre was clearly established in mainstream cinema far earlier than Sippl's analysis indicates.

According to *Shakespeare at the Cineplex*, "the Age of Branagh" (as Kenneth Rothwell calls it) encompasses the period from the years 1989 to 2001 (Crowl 1). Yet the bulk of Branagh's output, in terms of adaptations of Shakespeare on film, was released in the first half of this time period, ending approximately at the mid-point, in 1996 (with *Love's Labours Lost* being released near the end of this period, in 2000). The films of Loncraine, Luhrmann, Taymor and Almereyda were released in 1995, 1996, 1999 and 2000 (respectively), in the latter half of this time period. As argued in the previous chapter, Branagh's approach to filmed representations of Shakespeare is to create a film that aligns its seminal play with contemporary popular expectations of a protagonist (in the case of *Henry V*), or a film that aligns its seminal play with contemporary conceptualizations of the position of women in society (in the case of *Much Ado About Nothing*). Although an argument can be ventured that *Hamlet* can be read as incorporating many of the elements of millennial cinema, Branagh's decision to dramatize *Hamlet* utilizing the romantic and historical epic subgenres, and his commitment to a full-text version of the play are radically divergent from the approaches employed by Loncraine, Luhrmann, Taymor and Almereyda. In "Hawke Ascending," Robin Wood posits that Branagh's decision to employ a full-text version of the play may have been influenced by a desire to avoid accusations of "infidelity" (11) to Shakespeare's play. If Wood is correct, the integrity of Shakespeare's play remains a central concern for Branagh. Wood also writes, "It would be misleading to describe Almereyda's film as a version of 'Hamlet.' More accurately, he uses Shakespeare's text for his own purposes, of which Shakespeare could never have dreamed: it must be seen not as Shakespeare's 'Hamlet' but as the Almereyda/Hawke *Hamlet*" (11). This final divergence from Branagh on the part of Almereyda can also be seen in the films of Loncraine, Luhrmann, and Taymor. Whereas Branagh's adaptations of Shakespeare attempt to utilize contemporary conventions to facilitate their audiences' reading of Shakespeare, the films of Loncraine, Luhrmann, Taymor, and Almereyda utilize Shakespeare in order to produce a work of millennial cinema. In this respect, it can be viably argued that the period that Rothwell refers to as "the Age of Branagh" ended in 1996 with the release of *Hamlet*, and that the latter half of the decade was characterized by works more accurately described as "Millennial Shakespeare."

A further disparity between Branagh's films in the first half of the decade and the films of Loncraine, Luhrmann, Taymor and Almereyda can be seen in the cinematic traditions they access. Branagh's films are the work of an auteur who clearly seeks to compare and contrast his work with the work of other auteurs. As mentioned in the previous chapter, Branagh's *Henry V* can clearly be seen as a response to the work of Olivier, and *Much Ado About Nothing* clearly reflects Zeffirelli's use of casting and scenography in *The Taming of the Shrew* and *Romeo and Juliet*. Branagh's *Hamlet* clearly echoes the work of Welles,[1] contrasts with the spatial strategy of Olivier,[2] and utilizes the scope of David Lean.[3] The works of Loncraine, Luhrmann, Taymor, and Almereyda also include motifs and tropes from other established auteurs or films; however, where Branagh references the works of others to establish his own identity as an auteur, Millennial Shakespearean films tend to be reflexive of media as a part of the films' larger meditation on the state of contemporary culture.

In *Richard III*, for example, Loncraine's depiction of media is as ubiquitous as it is inconsistent in the way various media are represented. The film begins with a pre-credit sequence in which, after some titles which set the context for the action of the film, we see an extreme close-up shot of a teletypewriter ribbon printing the message "RICHARD GLOUCESTER IS AT HAND HE HOLDS HIS COURSE TOWARD TEWKSBURY." After the pre-credit sequence, we are presented with a sequence depicting a ball in which the York faction celebrates their victory. Richard Gloucester ascends the orchestra stage and addresses the revelers with the first 11 lines of his famous soliloquy from Act I, scene i of the play. The scene shifts via an abrupt cut from the public address to private musings given in a restroom, as Richard recites lines 12 through 27 of the soliloquy to himself while using the urinal and checking his appearance in the mirror. At line 27, Richard looks slightly beside his image in the mirror, and, seeming to see the camera/audience behind himself, then turns around and addresses lines 28 through 32 directly to the camera/audience. As he leaves the washroom, he gestures for the camera/audience to follow him, and continues to address the camera/audience directly through the next scene. Media, as represented by the teletype, conveys the military information of Richard's attack; as represented by the public address system, conveys Yorkist propaganda to the revelers; and, as represented by the camera/audience, conveys a voyeuristic depiction of Richard in the washroom, followed by an invitation for the audience to be Richard's confidante. These early scenes show the variability of media both in function[4] and in perspective.[5] The function of media is never stable in this film. In a later scene, Richard listens to a gramophone that is playing jazz music as he peruses photographs of his dead victims while wearing a smug expression on his face. The camera/audience objectively views Richard's equivocation of murder with the pleasurable aesthetic experience of jazz, both conveyed to him by disparate media.

Loncraine's splitting of the first soliloquy into public/objective, private/objective and private/subjective moments is repeated at several points during the film. As Richard initially woos Lady Anne, his suggestion that "your bed-chamber" is another place he might be fit for is addressed directly to the camera/audience in the style of a bawdy aside which Lady Anne does not hear. This bawdy aside, and the later unrestrained glee with which McKellen's Richard addresses the audience after his successful wooing of Anne represent the chief departure of McKellen's portrayal from Olivier's. Where Olivier's Richard constantly addresses his camera/audience with a detached irony over which he constantly maintains control, McKellen's Richard addresses his camera/audience with a full range of emotional responses which he apparently cannot contain. Whereas power is a goal which Olivier's Richard achieves through careful strategy, to McKellen's Richard, power seems more like an addiction which must constantly be fed. Where Olivier's Richard is content to realize his ambitions through scheming and manipulation, McKellen's Richard engages in direct acts of violence. Interestingly, Loncraine's film, unlike Olivier's, associates Richard with the wild boar, the historical Richard III's personal device, in two scenes. Firstly, as Richard negotiates the murder of Clarence with Tyrell he tosses apples toward a caged wild boar, throwing one apple with such force that the boar squeals in pain to Richard's obvious great amusement. Secondly, at a later point in the film Stanley's dream of being attacked by Richard (who has metamorphosed into a wild boar) is immediately followed by a scene in which Richmond states (in a line not found in Shakespeare's play) "the boar hath shown its tusks." In medieval mythology, which Shakespeare's audience would have been familiar with, the boar would have represented bravery, intelligence, and perseverance. In Loncraine's film, however, the boar is aligned with gluttony and aggression, in concert with a contemporary audience's notion of a boar simply as a wild pig. The gluttony and aggression of the wild pig are interchangeable with Richard's in the logic of Loncraine's film.

Loncraine's film also departs from Olivier's in its treatment and foregrounding of Lady Anne, Queen Margaret, Queen Elizabeth and Princess

Elizabeth, who collectively, in this film, seem to perform a similar function to the chorus of servants in Kurosawa's *Kumonosu djo*. The four women are often portrayed as a collective body that comments on the decline on the polity under Richard's rule, and attempts to protect the young princes and one of its own members, Princess Elizabeth. Interestingly, Princess Elizabeth, who does not appear in Shakespeare's play, is presented in Loncraine's film as a pale, meek, and silent teenager who is very much under the protection of Queen Elizabeth. (Kate Steavenson-Payne, the actress who portrays her, was 18 or 19 years old at the time of filming.) Queen Elizabeth's response to Richard's proposal that he marry the princess is responded to with the immediate marriage of the princess and Richmond, as depicted in another scene which is not found in Shakespeare's play. As Richard is haunted by ghosts on the eve of the battle of Bosworth Field, another interesting departure from Shakespeare's play occurs as the first and last voices that haunt Richard are the voices of the women. Catesby responds to Richard's terror by rocking Richard like a baby; whereas Richard was formerly the persecutor of children, this scene reveals that Richard himself has been an impulsive child all along; his previous seemingly performed and perfunctory appearance of being upset by Queen Margaret's curse now appears to have possibly been genuine.

Richard's death is portrayed in a manner that is strikingly similar to Fincher's portrayal of Ripley's death in *Alien 3*, the only significant difference being that, where Ripley's suicide by leaping into a vat of molten lead is intended to save humankind,[6] Richard's suicide by leaping into fire seems almost a realization of an effort to bring hell into existence on earth. As Richard and Richmond climb up the superstructure of the abandoned power-station at the film's finale, the bare girders of the superstructure suggest that the world they are fighting over is barren and devoid of fertility. Richard and Richmond stare at each other as they stand on the precipice, and Richard says (in a line displaced from Act V, scene iii of the play), "let us to't pell-mell/If not to heaven, then hand in hand to hell" to Richmond, and then falls backward (as Ripley had) into the flames. We are shown a medium shot of Richard falling into the flames (as Fincher had shown us with Ripley); however, as Richard falls he grins and waves at the camera/audience, with the jazz song "I'm Sitting on Top of the World" playing on the soundtrack. We are then shown Richmond, staring downwards to camera left as Richard falls. Richmond then stares directly at the camera/audience and grins at us with exactly the same leer as Richard had at the wooing of Lady Anne. Although Richard is physically dead, the implication here is that his legacy will continue under the leadership of

Richmond, as Richmond has become Richard's spiritual, as well as physical, successor.

Although Baz Luhrmann's film of *Romeo + Juliet*, released the next year, is ostensibly designed to appeal to a teenaged audience, the energy of the film conceals a nihilism equal in its profundity to the various nihilisms that Loncraine, Taymor and Almereyda express in their films. The thematic structure of Luhrmann's film is similar to Almereyda's in that both films are concerned with what Wood refers to in "Hawke Ascending" as "life within (and under) contemporary capitalism" (11). However, where the thematic structure of Almereyda's film emphasizes the displacement of the real by simulacra, the thematic structure of Luhrmann's film emphasizes the displacement of the connotative symbol by the denotative sign. Luhrmann utilizes a strategy of symbols (which are associated with the film's religious or apocalyptic tones) juxtaposed with signs (which are associated with the social world of Verona beach).

The film begins with an image of a television, which is seemingly hovering in space toward the camera. The television's screen initially displays white noise, but then presents some of the opening credits followed by the image of a typical news anchorwoman reciting the prologue using the traditional "objective voice" of a news reporter. We are then presented with a montage that establishes the Capulet and Montague corporate towers, which are each topped with huge eponymous billboards displaying the owner's name. Here, the film establishes its logic of signs as directly tied to corporate practices. This logic will remain consistent throughout the film, most notably through the practice of displacing terms that would seem anachronistic in the film's contemporary setting from their original context to a new function as corporate logos. For example, Capulet calls for his "long sword" in the film, and reaches for a shotgun which sits on a rack that displays the embossed logo "LONGSWORD"; the courier company that fails to deliver Friar Laurence's letter on time is called "Post Haste Dispatch"; and the theatre that Romeo walks into is called "The Globe."

However, the same shot that establishes the film's logic of signs also establishes its logic of symbols. Located directly between the Capulet and Montague towers, stands a huge statue of Christ with its arms and palms open. Christ and cruciform imagery are as equally ubiquitous in this film as are corporate logos, suggesting a philosophical dichotomy between the materialism and violence of the corporate and the unconditional, redemptive love of the divine. Juliet's bier is conspicuously decorated with neon crosses and she has a small shrine which she prays to in her room, Friar

Laurence has a large cross tattooed on his back, and Juliet's gift of "love's faithful vow" is accompanied by her physical gift to Romeo of her rosary. The consistent utilization of this religious imagery throughout the film suggests that the redemptive love of the divine provides possibilities that are thwarted by the materialistic and violent nature of the society that the film depicts. Tybalt's murder of Mercutio immediately precedes a severe storm that seems to materialize without warning; Romeo shoots Tybalt at the base of the Christ statue, and shouts, "I am fortune's fool" to the statue under a deluge of rain, suggesting that the rain represents the tears of Christ at Romeo's sin.

Other symbolic imagery is used to characterize Romeo and Juliet; when we are first introduced to Romeo he is sitting on a carousel in a children's playground—this composition is slightly overexposed, suggesting that Romeo is in a state of grace and innocence. His later vision of Juliet's bier, as he says, "but he that hath the steerage of my course direct my sail," suggests that Romeo and Juliet are enacting a preordained plan. When they meet at the Capulet's ball, Luhrmann again juxtaposes signs with symbols to great effect. In this film, "Queen Mab" is literally a metaphor for an ecstasy pill, which Romeo swallows before entering. The ball is a gaudy and decadent affair; Mercutio is in drag wearing a feather boa on the Capulet's grand staircase singing the disco hit, "Young Hearts Run Free," Tybalt hungrily French-kisses Lady Capulet, and Capulet wears a Roman toga. The decadence and Capulet's costume (coupled with the later images of the pseudo-Roman statuary in Capulet's garden) align this society with ancient Rome, another social order which was undermined and consumed through its own decadence. In Luhrmann's vision, Romeo and Juliet first meet only after Romeo, completely overwhelmed by the combination of an ecstasy pill and the debauchery he witnesses, dunks his head in a sink full of water in order to neutralize the effects of the drug. It is in the subsequent moment of clarity—after he has rejected the party and, by extension, the debauchery of this society—that he sees Juliet through a huge aquarium. Romeo and Juliet view each other through the glass at length as beautiful tropical fish swim between them. The ethereal nature of this scene is reinforced by the symbolic imagery that Luhrmann deploys here: Romeo is dressed as a medieval knight, whereas Juliet is dressed as an angel; these costumes both symbolize purity and a connection to the divine (Galahad, Bors and Perceval achieved the Holy Grail in medieval legend); symbols which contrast their relationship sharply with the signs that Luhrmann uses to depict the secular.

Luhrmann's use of signs and symbols occasionally lacks clarity, however.

The initial brawl between the Capulets and Montagues at Verona Beach very obviously references the musical scores composed by Ennio Morricone for Sergio Leone's spaghetti westerns. The conflation of Tybalt with the villains of Leone's mythic west is not revisited at any other point in the film, however, rendering it as little more than a reference to popular culture designed to attract the attention of a contemporary audience, rather than a strategy for furthering the thematic structure of the film. Similarly, one of the film's strongest uses of a sign comes when we first see an exterior shot of the Capulet mansion. Long, red banners are unfurled from every window, visually aligning the Capulet's wealthy lifestyle with fascism. The scene which follows this shot—featuring an overstated performance by Diane Venora punctuated by slow cranking of the camera—comically represents the vanity and spiritual shallowness of Lady Capulet, and thereby diminishes the impact of Luhrmann's alignment of the Capulet's wealth with the sense of fascism established by the preceding exterior shot. Prior to their mutual suicide, Romeo drives his car through the streets of Verona Beach at high speed, with several police cars and a helicopter—which highlights Romeo's car with its searchlight—in pursuit. The scene culminates with Romeo briefly taking a priest hostage before he enters the church. Although Luhrmann does use the helicopter's searchlight to highlight the statue of Christ in this scene, no attempt is made to explain to the audience *how* the police found out that Romeo had come back to Verona Beach. Again, the sequence seems deliberately contrived to satisfy a younger audience's expectation of the action of a car chase rather than fulfill any narrative or thematic function, thereby weakening the structure of Luhrmann's film. *Romeo + Juliet* is at its best when it remains faithful to the thematic structures that Luhrmann establishes in his system of signs and symbols. The film's conclusion presents a montage of Romeo and Juliet's happiest moments immediately followed by images of Capulet, Montague, and Captain Prince in a state of utter despair over their loss, effectively suggesting that the divine in human nature and hopes for the next generation have been completely eradicated by the violence and materialism of the corporate world.

Although in many ways far more nihilistic than Luhrmann's *Romeo + Juliet* is, Julie Taymor's *Titus*, released in 1999, manages to end on a note of optimism. Sippl's description of Anderson's *Magnolia* as "the most brazenly apocalyptic film of the millennial moment, both literally and figuratively" (7) could have been applied to Taymor's film. Sippl supports her statement by citing *Magnolia*'s December 17, 1999, release date, and its "overall form and content," which are structured around the convergence of the life trajectories of several individuals during a day in the San Fernando Valley, and the redemption and possibilities of a new beginning that this convergence brings. Taymor's *Titus*, released eight days after Anderson's film, presents Shakespeare's dramatization of the collapse of the Roman Empire, yet deviates from Shakespeare's play in its mise-en-scène which conflates the historical setting of ancient Rome with a contemporary urban setting. Titus is first presented to us marching in full Roman armor, whereas young Lucius is initially presented to us wearing a contemporary t-shirt while playing with toy soldiers. This mise-en-scène seems to suggest that what we witness on the screen not only has great relevance for us, but directly involves us.

Taymor certainly opens the film not only by radically crossing the 1400-year gap between the Fall of Rome and the millennial moment, but also by informing us that children will be a central concern in her film. The contemporary opening depicts Young Lucius' play as increasingly frenzied and violent: Young Lucius throws his toy soldiers around a kitchen table making sounds of explosions with his mouth, and eventually begins to spray ketchup on his soldiers in a parody of bloodshed. Sounds of distant explosions are heard on the soundtrack; the sounds become louder, and the kitchen begins to disintegrate: walls crack, plaster dust flies everywhere, glass breaks, and Young Lucius cowers under the kitchen table. A soldier runs into the room, scoops the terrified child up in his arms, and frantically carries Lucius out of the building as it disintegrates around them. The soldier runs from the contemporary setting of the building, through a mist which leads into a deserted ancient arena, and hoists the child into the air to the sound of cheers from an invisible audience.

The film also concludes in this arena; at the center of the arena there is a now a tableau featuring the dining room table from Act V, scene iii of the play, surrounded and covered with the murdered bodies of Lavinia, Tamora, Titus and Saturninus. The audience is comprised of people in contemporary dress who stare mutely at the display in front of them, wearing expressions that register shock and horror. Young Lucius, the previous innocent who needed to be rescued, now releases Aaron's baby from his cage. As Young Lucius does this, the screaming of a single baby on the sound track multiplies into the screaming of dozens of babies; the sounds of the babies crying are then displaced by the sounds of birds calling and bells ringing on the soundtrack, which in turn are displaced by swelling music on the soundtrack as Young Lucius carries the baby into the sunrise. Miranda Johnson-Haddad notes, in "A Time for Titus: An Interview with Julie Taymor," that when asked why she had conceived these opening and closing scenes which have no equivalent in Shakespeare's play, Taymor responded, "The development of the child from innocence through knowledge to compassion is, to me, the essentially most important theme" (Johnson-Haddad 35). The innocent child who plays at toy soldiers becomes, in Taymor's film, the compassionate child who promises a new beginning.

Taymor's treatment of the common theme of children in millennial cinema is much more complex than Loncraine's or Luhrmann's. Where Loncraine's children are portrayed as victims entirely at the whim of powerful adults to protect or harm them, and Luhrmann's children are seen as possessing an incorruptible love which cannot be allowed to survive in a corrupted world, Taymor 's film demonstrates that children will emulate the behavior that they see demonstrated in the world around them. In *Shakespeare at the Cineplex* Samuel Crowl describes Alan Cumming's Saturninus as "an insipid brat who strikes poses" (208) and is "limp" (209), without noting that this portrayal of Saturninus is entirely consistent with Taymor's treatment of children in the film. Saturninus is portrayed by Taymor as emblematic of the polity of Rome in its entirety: the country is populated by people who have not developed from innocence through knowledge to compassion; rather, they have developed from innocence through ignorance to cruelty. Taymor repeatedly insists, in the mise-en-scène of her film, on portraying Saturninus as a child. When Saturninus sits on the throne, he is completely dwarfed by its outsized dimensions, as well as those of the wolf, the emblem of Rome that sits over the throne. As Saturninus addresses the Senate in Taymor's dramatization of Act IV, scene iv of the play, the tantrum of screaming and crying with which Saturninus addresses the Senate is far more consistent with the behavior of an out of control child than it is with a leader of the most powerful state on the planet. Tamora's attempt to placate him by gently "shushing" him and stroking his hair is far more consistent with the behavior of a mother attempting to control a tantrum than it is with a wife and empress communicating with her husband. The portrayal of Saturninus as a child even characterizes his death; whereas Lavinia's neck is broken by Titus, Tamora is stabbed through the throat by Titus, and Titus is impaled with a candelabra by Saturninus, Lucius kills Saturninus first by ramming a serving spoon down his throat, and then administering a coup-de-grace with a pistol. Saturninus is a child at his death, choking on a spoon too large for his mouth.

Where Saturninus, as a narcissistic, whiny, and ineffectual persona represents one possible result of failure to develop from innocence through knowledge to compassion, the cruelty of Titus, Demetrius and Chiron represents another. Crowl has noted that Taymor's camera, in her depiction of the taunting of Lavinia after her ravishing, "pivots to catch her tormentors as they scamper away. Taymor has each actor pull down his pants to moon his victim. The crime is horrendous; the response infantile" (212). In Taymor's depiction of Act IV, scene ii of the play, the room in the palace where Demetrius and Chiron meet Aaron is a game room, replete with noisy pinball machines and arcade games. The implication is that Demetrius and Chiron have been desensitized to violence by a culture that celebrates pseudo-violence. Their infantile response to their ravishing of Lavinia is entirely consistent with a lack of understanding of the enormity of their acts. Although Lavinia hallucinates that she is between two tigers when she scrawls Demetrius' and Chiron's names in the sand, this hallucination indicates her subjective state of mind. To Lavinia, Demetrius and Chiron are tigers; however, to Taymor, Demetrius and Chiron are overgrown children who act entirely out of impulse with no understanding of the implications of their behavior. Interestingly, Taymor also presents Titus in an infantilized manner when he is in the bathtub. Tamora's declaration at Titus' execution of Alarbus—"O cruel, irreligious piety"—is again consistent with a characterization of Titus as a child: children often follow rules without question or understanding of any moral principle that underlies rules. Titus is pious here in his adherence to the ritual, but irreligious in that he fails to understand that the ritual signifies larger principles. Like Demetrius and Chiron, Titus is also connected to the celebration of pseudo-violence by our culture; when he hoists Demetrius and Chiron to be slaughtered, Titus' facial expression and tone of voice explicitly recall the expressions and tone utilized by Anthony Hopkins in the role for which he is most famous: that of Dr. Hannibal Lector.[7] Like that of Demetrius and Chiron, the violence of Titus is directly linked to a larger contemporary celebration of violence. Although Crowl, in the title of his chapter, characterizes Taymor's Rome as "A Wilderness of Tigers" (203), it seems equally appropriate to consider Taymor's Rome as a demonstration of Freud's axiom that a child, if given the power, would destroy the world. Taymor's Rome is almost exclusively populated with children, and destroys itself in the conclusion of Taymor's film.

Where Taymor's Rome empowers its children to either cruelty or compassion, Almereyda's Manhattan seems to disempower its children by conflicting them with an ambivalent existence. Almereyda not only displaces *Hamlet* from early-modern Elsinore to contemporary Manhattan, but also radically revises it in a manner consistent with that utilized by Welles in *Chimes at Midnight*. Like Welles, Almereyda also relies on the disparity between the seminal play and inter-texts which he inserts in order to establish the central thematic structure of his film. In "To Be or Inter-Be: Almereyda's End-of-Millenium *Hamlet*," Alessandro Abbate states that the film demonstrates "a shift from reality to simulacrum" (85), and notes that "as Hamlet sits staring at digital footage of Ophelia on his palm monitor, Thich Nhat Hanh ... philosophizes ... from the TV set in Hamlet's room" (*ibid.*). Hanh, according to Abate, is "a celebrated Buddhist teacher-monk" (*ibid.*), and from the TV set delivers the film's sole utilization of monologue and dialogue not found in Shakespeare's play, in the following passage transcribed from Almereyda's screenplay: "We have the word 'to be,' but what I propose is the word 'to inter-be.' Because it's not possible to be alone, to be by yourself. You need other people in order to be.... Not only do you need mother, father, but also uncle, brother, sister, society. But you also need sunshine, river, air, trees, birds, elephants and so on.... So it is impossible to be alone. You have to inter-be with everyone and everything else" (37).

In Almereyda's vision, corporate culture is in the process of displacing reality and real relationships with the manufactured image. Almereyda's film bombards us with billboards, posters, signs, and the various insignia of urban corporate culture, suggesting the degree to which the manufactured image obfuscates reality. As a filmmaking student and as a photographer Hamlet and Ophelia share the vested interest in constructing manufactured images with the corporate culture they are immersed in. Hamlet spends an equal amount of time watching a digital movie of himself delivering fragments of the fourth soliloquy to the amount of time he spends delivering it; this he does in the action section of a Blockbuster video store in an attempt to stir himself to action that here is conflated with his construction of another artificial image. Similarly, Ophelia drowns herself in a simulacrum of a waterfall located in the lobby of an office tower (Almereyda used the fountain at the Guggenheim museum as his location for this shot), suggesting that simulacra are not only displacing real life, they are displacing death as well.

Visual countertexts suggest that Ethan Hawke's Hamlet is destroyed not because he is outsmarted by Claudius, but rather because he is hopelessly conflicted. Robin Wood suggests that "if Hamlet senior (a deliberately unimposing Sam Shephard) was preferable to his younger usurper and murderer, it was not by that much, and a matter of degree rather than essence. (Nor is Fortinbras ... going to be any improvement on Claudius)" (11). One of the film's most discussed shots depicts the ghost of "Hamlet senior"[8] dematerializing into a Pepsi machine—a shot which utilizes an icon of contemporary corporate culture as a visual emblem of the film's theme of the dissolution of the individual that globalization precipitates. When we first meet Hamlet and Ophelia, they have already sustained significant emotional damage due to this process. Although Ophelia has reached physical maturity and is obviously involved in a sexual relationship with Hamlet, she rides a bicycle (whereas the other characters in the film use motorized means of transportation), has her sneakers tied on for her by Polonius, and cries but does not resist when Claudius and Polonius tape a recording device onto her. All of this suggests that Ophelia's emotional development has become fixated at a far earlier stage than her physical development. Hamlet is *literally* mad for much of this film; the majority of his great speeches are depicted by Almereyda through scenes in which Hamlet sits in front of his editing station silently watching himself deliver "What a piece of work is a man!" (Act II, scene ii), "So of it chances in particular men" (Act I, scene iv) and "To be or not to be" (Act III, scene i). In *Shakespeare at the Cineplex*, Crowl discusses Almereyda's film, and refers to "the tormented and fractured state of Hamlet's soul and imagination" (194). Wood further describes Hamlet as "a confused and neurotic dropout" (11), and Abate states that Hamlet is "an alienated young man" (83) whose "major problem is that he does not seem to understand that he simply cannot stop life; you cannot push the 'still' button, and rewind the passage of time" (84). This Hamlet seems to spend much of this film in a dissociated state in which he obsessively views himself on video in order to convince himself that he exists. This fails, and Hamlet is destroyed because, as Hanh suggests, one requires relationships with others—*real* people—in order to exist: "to be." During the "nunnery" (Act II, scene ii) scene Ophelia runs away at the mid-point of Hamlet's tirade, which prompts him to call her answering machine and leave several messages completing the speech. Later, as Hamlet recites, "How all occasions do inform against me" (Act IV, scene v) in the washroom of an airplane, he repeatedly stares at himself in the mirror. The final montage of moments which concludes Almereyda's film is contextualized by Hamlet's obsessive need to record and observe himself in order to exist, suggesting the conclusion of a process by which individual identity is subsumed by manufactured images that are devoid of personal meaning.

Each of the four films discussed conspicuously references the visual iconography of 20th-century fascism. Loncraine's Richard Gloucester is frequently dressed in uniforms identical to those that Hitler wore when posing for photographs. The red banners outside of the Capulet home in Luhrmann's film recall the swastika banners immediately behind the stage in Riefenstahl's *Triumph des Willens*, and are also identical in shape and length to the red banners that Taymor uses to decorate the exterior of Mussolini's EUR building, which figures prominently in her film, as does 1930s Italian fascism (Buchanan, *Shakespeare on Film*, 250). The overwhelming tall, narrow skyscrapers (which recall the proportions of Riefenstahl's, Taymor's and Luhrmann's banners) that are introduced in the first scene of Alymereyda's film are consistently recalled in Alymereyda's visual imagery throughout the film. Shots of the Manhattan skyline emphasize the uniformity of the city's architecture, in the tall, narrow framework of the window behind Polonius and Ophelia in Alymereyda's representation of Act I, Scene iii of the play, in the uniform shelves of videocassettes that Hamlet walks through in the blockbuster video store, and in numerous other shots. (Interestingly, Anderson's *Magnolia*, in its depiction of the presence of a television set in every major scene in the film, and in its depiction of Frank's attempts to indoctrinate men into a cult founded on hatred of women, also engages fascism as a motif.) Fascism, in Loncraine's vision, is characterized by militarism and an absolute male leader, but is resisted by a chorus of females. Loncraine's statement is ultimately nihilistic; the Princess Elizabeth is not saved from the fascist Richard by her marriage to Richmond, but instead is bonded in marriage to Richard's acolyte. Luhrmann, through his presentation of the swastika-like banners that adorn the Capulet home, represents fascism as associated with the corporate globalization and the decadence of the Capulets and Montagues, and contrasts it with the unrealized possibility of the redemptive love of the divine. Taymor sees fascism as a function of cruelty, and sees the compassion that Young Lucius ultimately develops as an antidote to fascism. Finally, Almereyda, like Luhrmann, associates fascism with the age of corporate globalization, and, also like Luhrmann, suggests that it may be impossible to resist contemporary corporate fascism. Like *Magnolia*, each of these films anticipates the millennial moment as a final realization of the repercussions of the 20th-century's legacy of military and corporate violence. Although Loncraine, Luhrmann and Almereyda seem to suggest that redemption or renewal is not possible as there will always be a Richmond ready to fill the shoes of a Richard, the flock may simply be unwilling and/or unable to comprehend the message of the savior, or it is too late to find a solution, Taymor, whose vision is the most relentlessly bleak of the filmmakers discussed here, finds a possibility of a new beginning and a better life through the fostering of compassion in individuals.

Conclusion

Reviewing the titles of monographs devoted to the study of Shakespeare in the cinema reveals a tendency to conceive of Shakespeare, the corpus of Shakespeare's plays, and the corpus of representations of Shakespeare in the cinema as discrete and holistic entities, each of which forms an individual discrete entirety. Typical titles read *Shakespeare on Film*, *Apocalyptic Shakespeare*, *Shakespeare at the Cineplex*, *Filming Shakespeare's Plays*, *Shakespeare, Cinema & Society*, *A Concise Companion to Shakespeare On Screen*, *Shakespeare and the Moving Image*, and *Shakespeare in the Cinema: Ocular Proof*. In each title, Shakespeare is described as a specific personage. Collectively, his plays seem to represent a specific body of work, and individually his plays seem to represent specific self contained entireties. For instance, even Diana Henderson begins her introduction to *Collaborations with the Past* with the heading "Shakespeare, Mon Amour" (1). Similarly, in *Political Shakespeare* Jonathan Dollimore and Alan Sinfield reveal this tendency to conceive of Shakespeare as an entirety:

> Almost like a religious relic, he [Shakespeare] constitutes a powerful cultural token. Shakespeare's plays are one site of cultural production in our society—they are one of the places where our understanding of ourselves is worked out and, indeed, fought out. A culture is a signifying system through which ... a social order is communicated, reproduced, and explored. This signifying system has continually to be produced—social orders and cultural orders must be seen as being actively made: actively and continuously, or they may quite quickly break down.... Shakespeare's plays constitute an influential medium through which certain ways of thinking about the world may be promoted and others impeded, they are a site of cultural struggle and change [154–155].

"Shakespeare" is here always referred to in the singular, as an entity which each element of the heteroglossia in our society attempts to appropriate as speaking for itself. However, Diana Henderson contends that adapting Shakespeare instead fragments his work to create new patterns. For Henderson, "Shakespeare" seems to be an infinite collection of resources capable of producing an infinite number of results rather than a unified corpus. Henderson's analysis focuses on Sir Walter Scott's *Kenilworth* as an adaptation of *Othello* (39–103), Woolf's *Mrs. Dalloway* as an adaptation of *Cymbeline* (104–154), and Andy Fickman's *10 Things I Hate About You* as an adaptation of *The Taming of the Shrew* (194–199). Henderson's analyses here presuppose that adaptors (or "bearers of Shakespeare" (1) as she calls them) focus on specific elements of a play rather than on the play as an entirety. Henderson also asserts the importance of the socio-historical context of a work's production in her focus on adaptations produced not only in disparate media, but in widely differing contexts.

When approaching films[1] of Shakespeare's plays by placing as equal an emphasis on Linda Hutcheon's "How?" and "Where/When?" parameters as would normally be placed on her "Who/Why?" parameter[2] it becomes apparent that the socio-historical context within which an adaptation is produced exerts a high degree of influence. Virtually all of the films discussed in the preceding chapters have been shown to be deeply influenced by the conventions of their contemporary cinema. This finding applies equally to films made by recognized "auteurs" of Shakespeare in the cinema, and to films made by directors who are not normally given "auteur" status. Despite their presumed rivalry, the approaches utilized by Olivier and Welles bear startling similarities in the manner they both employ visual, aural, and/or verbal countertexts to query their seminal plays, which suggests their approaches are mutually influenced by their socio-historical context, and are not simply a matter of personal inspiration. Kurosawa and Kozintsev are considered to be vastly superior filmmakers to Andy Fickman or Rick Moranis/Dave Thomas, yet this study has shown that all of their films are a direct response to their contemporary socio-historical context. Cinematic approaches to representing Shakespeare's plays, then, shift not only as a function of historical place, but also of historical time.

The approach used here also challenges many of the orthodoxies currently reflected in the critical literature dealing with representations of Shakespeare's plays in the cinema. Crowl's conception of an "international phase" (1) of Shakespeare in the cinema that was inaugurated by the works of Olivier and Welles, is challenged here by showing how widespread through Europe film adaptations of Shakespeare were in the silent era. Similarly, noting the similarities in Olivier's and Welles' approach to Shakespeare's plays, as well as the equal sophistication of their cinematic technique, challenges the orthodoxy by which Olivier is thought to "[look] back at theatre" (Buhler 96) whereas Welles exploits the properties of film.

The notion of the "18-year gap" is challenged when similar criteria are applied to representations of Shakespeare's plays in mainstream cinema released in the 1970s and 1980s as are applied to Kurosawa's works. Kurosawa is proclaimed a genius for displacing *Macbeth* to a feudal samurai setting and dramatizing it in contemporary Japanese; by contrast, Coppola's displacement of *Richard II* and *Macbeth* to the United States of the 1940s and 1950s is not acknowledged by reviewers at the time of the release of *The Godfather* and *The Godfather: Part II*. Finally, the widely accepted notion of "the Branagh Era" is challenged by recognizing the disparities between Branagh's first three cinematic adaptations of Shakespeare's plays and films released by other directors in the same decade. Although Branagh's financial success certainly paved the way for other filmmakers to receive funding for their projects, the films of Loncraine, Luhrmann, Taymor and Almereyda are far more aligned with millennial cinema than they are with the films of Branagh.

This suggests that the phrase "Shakespeare in the cinema" is something of a misnomer, and that further study needs to focus on the many disparate "Shakespeares" we find in the cinema. If the result of mainstream cinematic practices in representing Shakespeare's plays are to indeed "remake him in our own image" (2), as Henderson suggests, studies of this practice should consider representations of Shakespeare's plays in the cinema as a subset of contemporary cinematic practice, rather than as a discrete object of study in its own right.

For example, the discussion of films made prior to the introduction of sound recording technology shows that filmmakers not only use their contemporary cinematic techniques when adapting a play, but also impose contemporary tropes and motifs onto the play-text. Stow's *The Tempest* uses a linear narrative to dramatize a plot that Shakespeare dramatized using embedded recounted narratives, and reflects the European cultural trope of "the wild man." Kent's *A Midsummer Night's Dream* focuses on the most familiar elements of Shakespeare's play with a sophisticated use of pantomime, and in its costuming strategy, reflects the European cultural tendency to associate a virginal feminine state with one of spiritual purity. Lo Savio's *Re Lear* uses hand tinted color to depict changes in the emotional state of its protagonist, and in Lo Savio's *Il Mercante di Venezia*, Shylock is associated with the stock villain of Victorian melodrama. Kent's film of *Twelfth Night* is focused around one incident from Shakespeare's play, but his use of a mise-en-scène and deep space composition to place Malvolio in the foreground and Olivia's entourage in the background finds a filmic solution to a problem of representing this scene without sound. Benson's *Richard III* contrasts contemporary stagecraft with the realism afforded by cinema to suggest a disparity between public manipulation and private murder in the absence of recorded soliloquys.

Similarly, Dimitri Buchowetzki's 1923 film of *Othello* employs the crowd as a form of chorus which punctuates both Othello's fortunes and his decline. Othello is clearly idealized by the citizenry of Venice and Cyprus, and large crowds follow him wherever he goes.

One crowd scene depicts a public outcry over Othello's arrest for having married Desdemona. His arrival in Cyprus is accompanied by a similar gathering of a large crowd bearing beating drums to honor his arrival. During the night of liberty decreed by Othello to celebrate his wedding, the celebrations of the crowd again are depicted. Othello's decline is also related through depictions of the crown; its members observe that Othello is not being sent to save them from the Turks. A final crowd scene depicts Cassio relating the news of Othello's death to the citizens of Cyprus, accompanied by a final prayer requesting mercy for Othello's soul.

All of the silent films discussed conform to contemporary conventions concerning the length of films. A length of one reel was considered the standard for distribution between 1908 and 1911, the years between which Stow's, Kent's, Lo Savio's and Benson's one-reel films were released. By the 1920s, a length of two to three reels for "feature" films had become conventional: Buchowetzki's *Othello* clearly follows this convention. The films also conspicuously feature changes in the narrative structure of the play, and the addition of contemporary tropes in order to facilitate their audiences' understanding of the material.

Sound adaptations of Shakespeare's play-texts prior to World War II also demonstrate the characteristics of their contemporary cinema, which included the frequent utilization of carefully cultivated "star images" and spectacular sets which provided a sense of exotic, grand scope. For example, the opening credits of Taylor's *The Taming of the Shrew* give top billing to Mary Pickford who was known as "America's sweetheart" and "the world's sweetheart" at the time. Taylor presented Pickford as a representation of the contemporary ideal of "the New Woman," and happiness in marriage is only found after Petruchio submits to Katherine's taming. This would have directly contradicted a contemporary audience's expectations of Mary Pickford; conversely, Fairbanks' Petruchio is very much within the confines of his star image, wearing a cap with an enormous feather just as Fairbanks' *Robin Hood* wore, and a bandana just as Fairbanks' *Black Pirate* wore. His Petruchio also seems to be impervious to physical pain, which reflects Fairbanks' star image as an icon of masculine strength.

Taylor's film has also been noted for its elaborate exterior and interior sets and costumes, a quality which it shares in common with Dieterle and Reinhardt's 1935 film of *A Midsummer Night's Dream*, Cukor's 1936 film of *Romeo and Juliet*, and Czinner's 1936 film of *As You Like It*. Casting by star image is another quality shared in common by these films. In Dieterle and Reinhardt's film, the established screen "heavy" Victor Jory was cast as Oberon, the immensely popular James Cagney was cast against type as Bottom, a star comedian, Joe E. Brown, was cast as Flute, and Mickey Rooney, a child star, was cast as Puck. Cukor followed a similar strategy when casting his film. Romeo was played by Leslie Howard, a well-known romantic lead; Juliet was played by Norma Shearer, who was well known for playing women who resisted sexual mores; Tybalt was played by Basil Rathbone, who was established as a sinister, sword-wielding villain' and Mercutio was played by John Barrymore, who was recognized as the patriarch of the Barrymore family. Czinner cast Elizabeth Bergner in the role of Rosalind, which she had been acclaimed for portraying on stage more than 600 times.

These films also provide additions to Shakespeare's play-texts in order to facilitate their audience's understanding. Dieterle and Reinhardt's film depicts an early "waving" contest between Lysander and Demetrius as they compete for Hermia's attention; later in the same sequence, Helena attempts to place a garland on Demetrius' head to his obvious annoyance. As the crowd in the opening sequence collectively sings a love song, close-up shots of Lysander and Hermia, as members or the crowd, are intercut to provide the sense that they are singing the song to one another establish their bond; whereas, shots of Lysander and Demetrius are inter-cut when the crowd begins to sing a battle song. Cukor's film features an extended dance scene in which Romeo first meets Juliet, during which she avoids Paris and obviously gravitates toward Romeo. Czinner's film presents Rosalind marching through a gate that swings closed behind her to reveal the legend "Epilogue," and uses a series of dissolves that presents Rosalind's costume as transforming from that of Rosalind to that of Ganymede and back again, to signify that Rosalind is providing a final soliloquy that is directed solely at the audience, and is distinct from the narrative of the film.

Working as each other's contemporaries during and after the Second World War, Olivier and Welles both rejected mainstream cinema's emphasis on realism/illusionism and made films that constructed meaning through the audience's recognition that the film is relating a narrative. Olivier's *Henry V* and Welles' *Macbeth* are films that both reveal the apparatus of the dramatic illusion: the action of *Henry V* is framed by a narrative of an early modern stage performance, and Welles' *Macbeth* is created and manipulated by the Weird Sisters throughout the film. Olivier's *Hamlet* and Welles' *Othello* reflect a theme of entrapment that characterized post Second World War European cinema by presenting their mise-en-scène as a non-negotiable labyrinth through which their protagonists inexorably move toward their fates. Olivier's *Richard III* is depicted as creating a narrative within the main narrative by controlling the vision of the audience; similarly, Welles structures *Chimes at Midnight* around disparate narratives that provide conflicting information about historical events.

Both directors conspicuously use properties unique to cinema to eschew the realism/illusionism of mainstream cinema. Olivier uses zoom lenses in *Henry V* to give a natural landscape the appearance of a theatrical flat. He also uses cameo lighting during Hamlet's instructions to the players to underscore the scene's meditation on dramatic technique, and uses a long tracking shot which depicts Richard III as an ersatz director who addresses the camera directly while, by opening and closing windows, controlling the audience's perspective. Welles allows lightning to cast shadows on a cyclorama that Macbeth is standing in front of, which signals to the audience that Macbeth is a character controlled by a narrative; Welles also frequently frames shots through lattices and bars in order to heighten the audience's sense of entrapment in *Othello*, to the extent of shooting Roderigo's murder from Roderigo's hiding place beneath the floor-boards of a Turkish bath. Finally, *Chimes at Midnight* is entirely structured around a visual disparity between the pre-credit sequence and the credit sequence, which is used to establish three separate, often contradictory, narratives that signify the meaning of the film through their disparity.

Olivier and Welles both find a cinematic language with which to query Shakespeare's plays in an exploration of contemporary issues. *Henry V*, *Richard III* and *Chimes at Midnight* are all concerned with the issue of how the purposes of propaganda are achieved through the careful establishment of a cult of personality, and *Hamlet*, *Macbeth* and *Othello* are all concerned with the inability of their protagonists to escape a labyrinth in which they are entrapped, and an unavoidable tragic destiny. These motifs were common in post–Second World War European cinema and literature, some famous examples being Reed's *The Third Man* and Rosselini's *Stromboli*.

Where Olivier and Welles capture the zeitgeist of post Second Word War Europe, Kurosawa captures the zeitgeist of post Second World War Japan. *Kumonosu djô* and *Warui yatsu hodo yoku nemuru* are clearly responses to their contemporary political climate. Kurosawa uses Shakespeare's plays to explore the rampant corporate and governmental corruption of 1950s and 1960s Japan. A uniquely Japanese Shakespeare tradition had been established in the 19th century, and Kurosawa's adaptations feature many performance paradigms specific to Japanese culture. In *Kumonosu djô*, Washizu's character is presented using the techniques of Kabuki theatre, and Asaji's movements are typical of Noh drama. *Ran*'s Lady Kaede is also initially presented using movements typical of Noh drama, and Hidetora's makeup resembles the mask of actors portraying the aged in Noh drama. The corruption of the Public Corporation in *Warui yatsu hodo yoku nemuru* is made possible through the misapplication of Seppuku, a ritual suicide traditionally employed to prevent the dishonor that would be faced by Samurai who had fallen into enemy hands, which is utilized by Iwabuchi to prevent his corporate officers from reporting their kick-back scheme to the police or press.

Kurosawa's films seem to convey their meaning effects by simultaneously referencing and challenging Shakespeare's plays in order to provoke comparisons and contrasts between the play and his film. Although Kurosawa follows the narrative of *Macbeth* in *Kumonosu djô*, his depiction of feudal Japan as irredeemably corrupt would have served to dissipate his contemporary audience's nostalgia for a mythologized imperial Japan. *Warui yatsu hodo yoku nemuru* ultimately attributes Nishi's defeat being to his physically outnumbered by the corrupt businessmen he wishes to expose at a crucial moment, rather than to any lack of character or resolution on his part, which would have suggested that Japanese society had become so irretrievably corrupted that any attempt to oppose it would have been futile. *Ran* depicts the eradication of Hidetora's line not merely as a result of the foolishness of age, but also of the patriarch's inability to contain the violent society he had spent his life engendering.

Ran was also made at a point in Kurosawa's career when he made films for an international audience, and shows the influence of both Japanese traditions and international traditions. Although Lady Kaede is originally described by Kurogane as conforming to a traditional Japanese myth concerning a shape-shifting fox, she later is depicted as having assumed the traits of the Western myth of the vampire. Although Kurosawa's use of mise-en-scene and costume clearly identifies a historically specific setting for the film (Japan between 1392 and 1508, a time period known as "the Age of the Country at War"), the three part structure of this film, which is centered around a battle scene which drastically alters the fortunes of the film's central characters, recalls Welles' use of a three part structure in *Chimes at Midnight*, and Kurosawa's stylized color palate recalls that favored by Stanley Kubrick in the latter part of his career. Although *Ran* conflates

Shakespeare's text of *King Lear* with a recognizably Japanese film genre ("jidai geki"—period or costume drama), it also demonstrates the influence of international cinema, and that it was intended to be viewed by an international audience. As the film was released at the height of the "second cold war," *Ran* can be seen as Kurosawa's critique of humankind's predilection for violence.

Like Kurosawa, Kozintsev also adapted Shakespeare's plays in a manner which reflected the realities of his unique time and place in history. Unlike Kurosawa, Kozintsev did so in a manner which represented the seminal plays as discrete entireties. Although Kozintsev is an inter-cultural adaptor of Shakespeare's works, he manages to re-read his seminal plays within the context of his own cultural background, while preserving the identity of his films as adaptations of Shakespeare. Also like Kurosawa, Kozintsev re-reads Shakespeare's play-texts in order to provide a critique of his own time and place in history. Unlike Kurosawa, due to the realities of life in the Soviet Union of the 1950s and 1960s, Kozintsev did not have the freedom to be openly socially critical. Kozintsev's critique is delivered indirectly through cinematography, editing and performance.

Kozintsev opens *Gamlet* by first establishing a binary opposition between formless water and barren rock, and then establishing a second binary opposition between barren rock (suggesting statis) and vegetative landscape (suggesting growth). These binary oppositions metaphorically represent the realities of life in the Soviet Union at the time: the access to the vegetative landscape from the castle (which is associated with rock) has been barred, and the only possible escape can be through the sea, which is later associated with death through Ophelia's drowning and Gamlet's return to the shoreline as he dies. Although Kozintsev presents the play as an entirety, his method of presentation contains an implicit critique. The delivery of Gamlet's first soliloquy through a voiceover on the soundtrack, as Gamlet maintains an outward persona that is utterly inconsistent with what he is thinking and feeling, clearly indicates the danger of making private thoughts public in this polity. The portrayal of Claudius' court as a committee, and of Claudius not only as an observer but as an object of observation clearly associates Kozintsev's Elsinore with the Soviet Union's Politburo.

In *Korol Lir*, Kozintsev uses the Cinemascope frame to place the actions of his characters in a broader social context. The frame is used to show his characters in relation to each other, which demonstrates how their actions are interconnected and have implications for everyone. This is demonstrated during a battle sequence in which Regan and Goneril single-mindedly pursue Edmund while utterly oblivious to the carnage and devastation that is occurring around them; their narcissism is evident in the foreground, and the consequences of their narcissism are made evident in the background through the use of the Cinemascope frame. Interestingly, *Korol Lir* also has a two part structure which is demarcated by the storm, rather than a battle scene. Prior to the storm, Lir's behavior is explosive and frequently out of control, and the other characters in the film exercise restraint and civility. After the storm, Lir is humbled and sincere; however, carnage and devastation rages around him. The film's lack of a definitive conclusion or ending suggests that the consequences of Lir's hubris will outlive him, and the final shot's emphasis on the peasants rebuilding their devastated houses suggests that those who are marginalized by the political agendas of others will continue to be those who will have to deal with the consequence of those agendas.

Like Kozintsev's adaptations, Zeffirelli's are also conspicuously influenced by their socio-historical context. Zeffirelli was working in mainstream cinema during a time in which it had become an intensely visual medium. Although critics often dismiss Zeffirelli's films of Shakespeare's plays as the works of a "popularizer," Zeffirelli's three adaptations of Shakespeare's play-texts show him to be an intelligent filmmaker who finds visual analogues for the themes that are presented in the works of Shakespeare. Although this approach leaves his work open to the objection that he was merely catering to the youth audience of his time, the analogues Zeffirelli uses in representing Shakespeare's themes demonstrate that he understands and seeks to maintain their importance to their original play. Zeffirelli approaches each of his films as a unique project. His decision to cast "the battling Burtons" in *The Taming of the Shrew* draws on their star images; his decision to cast unknown teenagers in *Romeo and Juliet* draws on the emotional realism that they would bring to their roles; his decision to cast Hollywood stars and actors who had starred in notable productions of *Hamlet* in his 1990 film brings the play-text's theme of performance to the forefront.

In addition to casting strategies, Zeffirelli employs a unique visual strategy in each of his three adaptations. *The Taming of the Shrew* is structured around a theme of inversion and reversal that is established through Zeffirelli's use of visual material. The enthusiasm of Petruchio's household staff in recognizing Kate as the unofficial head of the household suggests that Petruchio's nobility is a function only of his birth and not of his behavior. Although Katherine initially seems volatile and violent, she ultimately easily assumes the matriarchal role and puts the house in order; whereas, the opening scenes of the film portray Bianca as a flirt who actively enjoys the attention of many men, and who later publicly humiliates her husband at his own wedding feast, despite her reputation as a mild and submissive female. The dilemma faced by Romeo and Juliet is established by Zeffirelli's visual contrast of organic elements with artificial elements; moments depicting the love between the couple are associated with imagery depicting growth and fertility; whereas, the corrupted social world of the film is associated with imagery depicting buildings and streets made of grey stones. Zeffirelli's casting of *Hamlet* brings not only the issue of performance to the foreground, but also reinforces an Oedipal interpretation of the play by presenting Gertrude as being young enough to be a viable sexual partner for Hamlet.

During the late 1960s and early 1970s, a wave of filmed adaptations of Shakespeare were released that, while foregrounding their connections to stage productions and practices, were heavily influenced by the ideas of Jan Kott, and did not use recognizable stars or star images. Brook's *King Lear* utilizes a cinematic strategy that contrasts people in isolation with people in connection, and attempts to convey individual psychological states through cinematic techniques. Viewers of Brook's film are confronted with a reality that is fragmented and fractured. Contradictory images are consistently juxtaposed throughout the film in order to suggest a disparity between the perceptions of the characters and the realities that they perceive. Brook often violates the codes of continuity editing and illusionist cinematography, and establishes a visual idiom which demonstrates both the individual psychological states of his characters and the actual outer appearance of the world they exist in. The audience experiences the world of this film as the characters experience it, but is also aware of the reality of the world of this film; consequently, the audience realizes the disparity between the reality it is presented with and the warped experience of that reality that the characters in the film contend with. The gap between the reality presented and the characters' subjective experience of it affirms Kott's notion of the absence of the absolute.

Tony Richardson's film of *Hamlet* also affirms Kott's notion of the absence of the absolute through its carnivalistic strategy, which presents us with an incestuous relationship between Laertes and Ophelia; a middle-aged, balding Hamlet in love with a 23 year-old Ophelia, who is portrayed by a well-known rock star; a Claudius who is obviously 10 years younger than Gertrude; a Hamlet who is about the same age as Gertrude; and the invasion of the throne room by the bedroom. As in Brooks' film, the world of this film is so deeply dysfunctional that there can be no absolute worth affirming here.

Similarly, Polanski's *Macbeth* uses visual countertexts to suggest that Macbeth's corruption is not due to the interventions of malign agents, but is actually the embedded norm of the social system presented in the film. Polanski's Macbeth is no naïve innocent corrupted by the forces of evil; rather, he is presented as capable of deceit when he first encounters the witches, as demonstrated when he lies to Banquo that the witches have vanished "into the air" when they have actually gone through a doorway that is in Macbeth's line of sight, but not in Banquo's. Polanski's film ends with the image of Donalbain approaching the witch's cavern, suggesting that Macbeth's tyranny was due to a systemic problem instead of a malign intervention, and that the cycle of tyrannical violence will escalate until the systemic problem is resolved. Macbeth's career is a commonplace in the world presented by Polanski, representative of "business-as-usual." Macbeth's delusion that his ambition indicates his personal superiority is consistent with Kott's notion of the grotesque.

The period between the release of Polanski's *Macbeth* and Branagh's *Henry V* is characterized by a change in the predominant strategy of representing Shakespeare in the cinema. A tradition of representing Shakespeare through the utilization of themes, motifs and other specifics of the play-texts (names, places, situations, thematic functions, narrative functions) had been established as early as 1955. The films of Coppola, Mazursky, Godard, and Moranis and Thomas during this period demonstrate that the influence that Shakespeare's plays had in mainstream popular culture had not changed. The predominant strategy used to represent Shakespeare's plays in mainstream American cinema during this period continues to be widespread in its current use, as demonstrated by the examples of *The Lion King*, *10 Things I Hate About You* and *She's the Man*.

Although it was originally intended as an adaptation of *King Lear*, the release version of *The Godfather* bears structural similarities to the play-text of *Richard II*. Both the film and the play feature a chiastic structure: the play begins with Richard in power and Bolingbroke in exile, and ends with Bolingbroke in power and Richard in exile/murdered; whereas the film begins with Vito in control and at the center of "the family business" while Michael still wears his military uniform and disavows any interest in the operations of the Corleone crime family, but ends with Michael in control and at the center of "the family business," while Vito has retired/died. *The Godfather: Part II* shares a chiastic structure with the play-text of *Macbeth*: at the play's onset, Macbeth is horrified at the prospect of murdering Duncan whereas Lady Macbeth is emotionally impervious to the potential act's implications, but by the play's conclusion Macbeth has "almost forgot the taste of fears" and is "supp'd full with horrors" whereas Lady Macbeth has been driven insane by her guilt; the film features two intercut parallel narratives, the first of which begins with a completely isolated Vito as a young man and traces his gradual establishment of his eventually large family, and the second of which begins with Michael surrounded by his large family and traces his gradual alienation of his family to his eventual isolation. *The Godfather: Part II* also represents *Macbeth's* theme of futility: both plots are concerned with the protagonist's failed effort to consolidate his power and security, and the despair experienced by the protagonist at this failure. Coppola would later conclude his trilogy with *The Godfather: Part III*, which is obviously modeled on *King Lear* in its presentation of Michael's effort, late in life, to abdicate responsibility for his actions while maintaining "the addition to a king."

This pattern of representation was utilized throughout the 1980s. Mazursky's *Tempest* features a storm conjured by a middle-aged architect who is confronting his mid-life crisis. *Strange Brew* deliberately reframes many of the thematic preoccupations of *Hamlet* while aligning Shakespeare with other practices of popular culture, such as beer, Kentucky Fried Chicken and the *Star Wars* franchise. Godard's *King Lear* finds it genesis in the director's inability to adapt Shakespeare's play-text into a contemporary film.

Seemingly intuiting this pattern whereby adaptations of Shakespeare's plays into mainstream films reflect the cultural zeitgeist of the context of their release, Branagh constructed his 1989 *Henry V* in order that the characterization of the eponymous king would conform to a popular audience's expectations of a protagonist. There are significant parallels between Branagh's presentation of King Henry V, and the characters of Bruce Wayne, James Bond and Martin Riggs as presented in several contemporary films. Branagh's 1993 *Much Ado About Nothing* repeats this strategy of conforming to a popular audience's expectations by being deliberately aligned with its popular contemporary subgenre of the "woman's film," and his 1996 *Hamlet* is deliberately aligned with its popular contemporary subgenres of the "historical epic" and the "romantic epic." Branagh's success in adapting Shakespeare's plays to the expectations of a mainstream cinema audience inaugurated the 1990s wave of Shakespeare films.

From the mid–1990s to the turn of the century, the cultural zeitgeist again shifted, and several filmed adaptations of Shakespeare's plays were released that reflected apocalyptic motifs that were becoming prevalent in their contemporary cinema. These motifs included a society that undermines its children, reflexive contemplation of the function of media, an apocalyptic moment that is depicted with religious and mystical overtones, and the possibility of a new beginning precipitated by the apocalyptic moment. Loncraine's *Richard III* foregrounds several types of media including teletypes, photographs, and phonograph records; inserts a motif not found in Shakespeare's subtexts where the young Princess Elizabeth is protected from Richard by Queen Elizabeth and Queen Margaret; and at its conclusion implies through imagery that Richard may have inaugurated hell on earth. The imagery of Luhrmann's *Romeo + Juliet* implies that the redemptive love of the divine is an alternative to the feud between the Montagues and Capulets, and that the relationship of Romeo and Juliet—who are both presented as child-like innocents at crucial points in the film—represents a divine love which is destroyed by the corrupted secular world which surrounds them. Taymor's *Titus* features Rome at its fall as populated by vicious overgrown children who lack compassion; at the film's conclusion, however, these children are displaced by Young Lucius, whose compassion for Aaron's child suggests a possibility of a new life. Almereyda's *Hamlet*, like Luhrmann's *Romeo + Juliet*, presents Hamlet and Ophelia as characters who have become fixated at an adolescent stage of development by the barren world that they inhabit, and who are ultimately destroyed by the confusion created by their own partial compliance with the corruption that surrounds them. The mise-en-scene of this film depicts Hamlet and Ophelia as bombarded with simulacra; however, as a filmmaking student and a photographer, respectively, they are complicit in the process that overwhelms them.

    These examples clearly demonstrate that new patterns are constantly formed when Shakespeare's plays are represented in mainstream cinema. Although adaptation studies frequently suggest a process of "mediation" that occurs when a Shakespearean play encounters a unique socio-historical period, "appropriation" is a far more accurate term in discussing the relationship between the seminal play and the resultant adaptation, as filmed adaptations of Shakespeare's plays utilize their seminal plays to speak to contexts that Shakespeare could never have anticipated or dreamed of, and to communicate meanings in those contexts that Shakespeare never could have intended.

    This suggests that interest in representing elements of Shakespeare's plays remains constant; however, differing strategies in representing Shakespeare in the cinema achieve prominence over others at different points in time. Finally, the examples show that filmmakers clearly do not view Shakespeare's play-texts as discrete entireties which must be replicated. Rather, filmmakers perceive the plays as resources containing component elements, some of which are utilized, and some of which are not. Adapting Shakespeare's plays in the cinema can be described as a process by which a filmmaker disassembles a play-text into its component elements, and from those elements assembles a new and distinct work which is intended to resonate with its own socio-historical context, just as Shakespeare's plays were intended to resonate with theirs. Rather than focusing on "Shakespeare" in the cinema, studies need to focus on the many "Shakespeares" we find in the cinema, each of which is reconstructed to conform to the cultural zeitgeist of its socio-historical context.

Chapter Notes

Introduction

1. See the discussion in Chapter 3 regarding the works of Kurosawa.
2. Holland goes on to describe this "world" as "a carefully chosen, imagined and realized reality against which the action is played out" (53).
3. This was his penultimate film appearance and final starring role.
4. This chronology is not intended as comprehensive; rather it is intended to demonstrate the usefulness of Hutcheon's parameter.
5. This is indicated by the film's most notorious line, voiced by the Nazi Colonel Earhardt in reference to Tura: "Oh, yes I saw him in *Hamlet* once. What he did to Shakespeare we are now doing to Poland."
6. Greenberg performs this not for an audience, but rather to delay a squad of Nazi troops who are attempting to arrest Tura and his company.
7. Although Tim Roth is credited as playing Guildenstern, and Gary Oldman is credited as playing Rosencrantz, the film never gives enough information for the audience to distinguish which of the two titular characters is Rosencrantz or Guildenstern.
8. This also demonstrates their ignorance of the fact that they are locked within a world of fixed outcomes.
9. His recognition that objects will fall at the same speed fails to take surface area into account as a variable, causing him not to realize that a juggling pin and a feather will fall at different speeds.
10. His unresolved hostility toward his father is made hilariously explicit at an earlier point in the film.
11. Dana's behavior here implies that performers who interpret Shakespeare project their own neuroses onto Shakespeare's plays, rendering the difference between Dana's performance as Hamlet and those of Olivier or Branagh as a matter of degree rather than kind.
12. Jefferson is played by Burt Reynolds, whose own career mirrors that of his character.
13. Steel is an American action film star; Dewberry is clearly a representative of the classical British Theatre.
14. The credited title of the film is *The Chronicle History of King Henry the Fift with His Battell Fought at Agincourt in France*.
15. North American release title: *Throne of Blood*.
16. North American release title: *The Bad Sleep Well*.
17. I.e., without being considered part of the acknowledged "canon."
18. Prior to 1915, films were normally a single reel in length. In *An Introduction to Film Studies*, Jill Nelmes credits D.W. Griffith with developing the full-length feature through the release of *The Birth of a Nation* (60). Subsequently, film lengths expanded to two, three, and, later, four reels.)
19. Zeffirelli's 1990 film of *Hamlet* employs a similar approach, yet the discussion will also reveal how this film is a uniquely self-reflexive work.
20. Samuel Crowl refers to this period as "a barren wasteland in which Shakespeare almost completely disappeared from film" (*Shakespeare at the Cineplex* 1), whereas

Anthony Davies notes that "it looked as if television had displaced cinema as the photographic medium for bringing Shakespeare to the modern audience" ("Shakespeare on Film and Television: A Retrospect" 1).

Chapter 1

1. For example, in "Representing 'King Lear' on Screen," Kenneth Rothwell discusses Thanhouser's silent 1916 film, and then proceeds to discuss Brook's and Kozintsev's 1970 films, and several television adaptations.
2. From Act I, scene iv of Shakespeare's play.
3. From Act IV, scene ii of Shakespeare's play.
4. Interestingly, 35 years later, Olivier was one of the foremost Shakespearean actor-managers of his time, and structured his film of *Henry V* around a visual disparity between the meticulously reconstructed and realistic set of the Globe Theatre and blatantly theatrical models and flats used to represent buildings in "exterior" shots. Olivier uses the disparity in his visual strategies as a way of cinematically enabling his "unworthy scaffold to bring forth/So great an object."
5. The running time of the *Silent Shakespeare* DVD is nine minutes. In *Shakespeare on Screen*, Kenneth Rothwell and Annabelle Melzer, however, list the film's length as eight minutes, and Robert H. Ball, in *Shakespeare on Silent Film*, states that, at a length of "890 feet" only "two thirds of the original film remain" (122–125).

Chapter 2

1. Although *City Lights* and *Modern Times* both utilize soundtracks, the former film utilizes unintelligible electronic squawks at the unveiling ceremony to parody speeches by public officials, and the latter film utilizes recorded media only in its own representations of electronic media, such as the closed circuit television announcements of the industrialist, and the pre-recorded vinyl disk introducing the eating machine. Chaplin's song at the conclusion of *Modern Times* sounds like it could be Italian, but is in fact gibberish.
2. Interestingly, Ian Hunter's line delivery, in the role of Theseus, consistently employs the trilled "r," which is a technique that is often popularly associated with stage productions.
3. The film was intended to preserve what had come to be considered her canonized performance.
4. This raises the question as to whether this depiction is an ironic "in-joke" of the same sort as in Marvel comics, where none of the characters are able to figure out that Superman looks incredibly like Clark Kent sans spectacles.

Chapter 3

1. Welles self-consciously described himself in this way when receiving a lifetime achievement award from the American Film Institute.
2. Holinshed's *Chronicles*, Shakespeare's play-texts, and a visual countertext established in the film.
3. For example, Olivier's *Hamlet* was released within a year of Carol Reed's *The Third Man*, a film set in the rubble of Vienna in the period immediately following World War II. *The Third Man* features a nihilistic view of the accomplishments of humankind, as demonstrated in Harry Lime's/Orson Welles' famous quote "In Italy for 30 years under the Borgias they had warfare, terror, murder, and bloodshed, but they produced Michelangelo, Leonardo da Vinci, and the Renaissance. In Switzerland they had brotherly love—they had 500 years of democracy and peace, and what did that produce? The cuckoo clock."
4. For example, when the ghost of Old Hamlet visits Gertrude's bed chamber, the frame initially shows Hamlet at screen center, then tracks left to show Hamlet at screen right and the ghost in the background at screen center; the camera then tracks further left to show Gertrude at screen center, and then tracks right to show Gertrude at screen right with the ghost no longer at screen center. The tracking movement in this shot demonstrates to the viewer that the ghost is seen only by Hamlet and not by Gertrude.
5. Characters appear to be shot against a black background with no scenery visible.
6. Welles would certainly have been aware of Rossellini's film due to the notoriety surrounding its production and release.

Chapter 4

1. This theme recurs in *Kumonosu djô*, *Warui yatsu hodo yoku nemuru* and *Ran*.
2. Washizu fulfills the character functions of Macbeth in this film.
3. Kunihara fulfills the character functions of Duncan in this film.
4. The use of reports of crucial events rather than dramatizations of them serves to align the film with the seminal play's use of reports of crucial events.
5. Asaji fulfills the character functions of Lady Macbeth in this film.
6. We later find that Nishi and Itakura (*The Bad Sleep Well*'s Horatio) have switched identities in order to facilitate Nishi's infiltration of his father-in-law's corporation.
7. It is Tatsuo who demonstrates lack of resolution in revenge in this film. At the wedding he threatens Nishi, and later fires a shot at Nishi, but later we are lead to believe that Tatsuo has gone out with a gun to kill Nishi, to discover he has forgotten about the issue entirely and gone duck hunting.
8. *Dersu Uzala*, released in 1975, was financed by Russian investors and won an Academy Award for best foreign film; *Kagemusha*, released in 1980, was co-produced by Kurosawa, Tomoyuki Tanaka, George Lucas, and Francis Ford Coppola; *Ran* was financed by France's Serge Silberman, who had also produced many of Buñuel's films.

Chapter 5

1. The setting of a medieval stone castle is also utilized in Olivier's and Zeffirelli's respective films of *Hamlet*.
2. Interestingly, in Olivier's film, we see his Hamlet at the top of the castle ramparts at crucial moments, but never at the base of the cliff.
3. There is a critical consensus that Treplev's relationships with Arkadina and Tregorin parallel those of Hamlet to Gertrude and Claudius. Arkadina also directly quotes from Shakespeare's play in the first act of *The Seagull*. Kozintsev would certainly have been aware of this.
4. Garber references Act III, scene ii of the play-text: "And thou, all-shaking thunder,/ Smite flat the thick rotundity o' the world!/ Crack nature's moulds, an germens spill at once,/ That make ingrateful man!"

Chapter 6

1. According to Pilkington, approximately 30 percent of *The Taming of the Shrew*, 35 percent of *Romeo and Juliet*, and 37 percent of *Hamlet* remain intact.
2. For example, Shakespeare's text of Laertes' final plea for Hamlet's forgiveness is heavily cut with the remaining lines distributed between the two characters.
3. For example, Petruchio's "'Twas I won the wager, though you hit the white" becomes "I won the battle you have yet to fight."
4. "What Is a Youth" is a song written for the film of *Romeo and Juliet* by Nino Rota and Eugene Wilder, and does not appear in Shakespeare's play.
5. In which lines from as many as three different plays are used, at one point, in one scene.
6. Iago is referred to in the voiceover as Othello's "en-sign," because the audience would not have been familiar with the term "ancient" being used to convey a military rank.
7. Zeffirelli's use of a wide range of intense colors is visually opposed to Welles' use of monochrome film in *Macbeth* and *Othello*; the visual disparity between the two auteurs corresponds to the thematic disparities between their works. For example, Welles' high contrast monochrome in *Macbeth* is used to depict Macbeth as virtually engulfed by his environment after he is persuaded by the witches to murder Macduff's family, whereas Zeffirelli's impressionistic set painting of Padua reinforces Lucentio's sense of wonder in the opening shots of *The Taming of the Shrew*.
8. Interestingly, Kenneth Rothwell, in *A History of Shakespeare on Screen*, describes Welles' approach to Shakespeare in the cinema as "Dionysian" (69); however, this term is used by Rothwell as a metaphor of contrast between Welles and Olivier (whom Rothwell describes as "Apollonian" [ibid.]) and does not seem to be directly substantiated by Rothwell's analysis of Welles' work.
9. Grumio's offer of the feather-duster visually confirms this.
10. This replicates a convention in mainstream cinema in which actresses cast as leading men's mothers are, in reality, much too young. Eileen Herlie was 11 years younger than Olivier when she played Gertrude to his Hamlet.

Chapter 7

1. These are of Goneril and Regan, of Gloucester, Edgar and Edmund, and of Lear and his Fool, traveling in their caravans to disparate destinations.
2. Richardson's film features a balding Hamlet who is obviously approaching middle-age, a Claudius who is visibly younger than his nephew, a king and queen who hold court while having dinner in bed, a Laertes who is having an incestuous affair with Ophelia, and an Ophelia who is played by a contemporary rock star.
3. The only significant cut appears to be the dialogue between Malcolm and MacDuff given in Act IV, scene iii, lines 1–162 of the play.
4. This action on Ross' part does not appear in Shakespeare's play; it is inserted by Polanski to reinforce Ross' duplicitous and Machiavellian character.

Chapter 8

1. Exemplified in the instance when Morbius tells Adams and Doc where to find the jewelry and silver when he finds that they have broken into his office.
2. When dating the accomplishments of the Krell he repeatedly uses the pleasingly ornate phrase "two thousand centuries ago" whereas the ordinary usage would be "two hundred thousand years ago."
3. According to Jackson, the audience is left wondering if Vincent is Edmund or Edgar.
4. Such as names, places, situations, thematic functions and narrative functions.

Chapter 9

1. E.g., Falstaff, Bardolph, Mistress Quickly, The Page and the other denizens of "The Boar's Head."
2. E.g., Scroop.
3. This is due to its utilization of a cast that was largely unknown to mainstream cinema audiences (Paul Scofield being the possible exception) and cinematographic and editing strategies designed to obscure the budgetary restraints Branagh was under.
4. For example, Denzel Washington as Don Pedro, Keanu Reeves as Don John, Michael Keaton as Dogsberry.
5. He completes their final verbal exchange by "stopping up her mouth" with a kiss in much the same manner that Zeffirelli's Petruchio prevents Kate from refusing to marry him.
6. Although Austen's novel is not intended as epic in scope, Lee's 1995 film features sumptuous costumes, relocates the Dashwood family from the cottage of Austen's novel to a mansion, and features a choreographed procession of happily married couples (some of whom do not become married in Austen's novel) at its conclusion.
7. According to Stephen Buhler (73), Fortinbras' soldiers crashing through the mirrors recalls the famous climax of *The Lady from Shanghai*.
8. Polonius conspires with Reynaldo to spy on Laertes, and with Claudius and Ophelia to spy on Hamlet.
9. Claudius murders Old Hamlet, conspires with Rosencrantz and Guildenstern to spy on Hamlet, and conspires with the King of England to murder Hamlet.

Chapter 10

1. According to Stephen Buhler, Branagh's mirrored hall recalls the conclusion of *The Lady from Shanghai* (120).
2. Olivier's *Hamlet* is staged in vertical space, constantly moving up and down to different levels of his Elsinore, whereas Branagh's camera is constantly tracking and trucking through his uni-leveled Elsinore using only lateral and linear planes.
3. In the decision to shoot in 70mm format, the deep focus shots through enormous exteriors, and the dimensions of the sets.
4. From the teletype as source of objective military information, to the public address system as source of propaganda, to the camera/audience as source of the private unintentionally made public, to camera/audience as source of pact of confidentiality.
5. From the objective perspective of the teletype to the subjective perspective of the Yorkist propaganda, and again from the objective perspective of the camera/audience as voyeur to the subjective perspective of the camera/audience as confidante.
6. Ripley achieves this by preventing the corporation from developing the alien embryo as a weapon.
7. Interestingly, in Ridley Scott's *Hannibal*, Lector binds and murders a Florentine detective while whimsically muttering "Okey

dokey" to himself, suggesting a core of childishness in the personality of this ruthless serial killer.

8. In Almereyda's film the ghost forgoes the ramparts and instead haunts the basement of the "Denmark Corporation's" office tower.

Conclusion

1. This finding applies equally to films classified as canonized, un-canonized and non-canonized.

2. With its emphasis on the auteur of the film, this is the normative parameter in the critical literature concerning representations of Shakespeare in the cinema.

Works Cited

Abbate, Alessandro. "'To Be or Inter-Be': Almereyda's End-of-Millenium Hamlet." *Literature/Film Quarterly* 32.2 (2004): 82–89.
The Abominable Dr. Phibes. Dir. Robert Fuest. Perf. Vincent Price, Joseph Cotten and Hugh Griffith. American International Pictures, 1971.
The Accused. Dir. Jonathan Kaplan. Perf. Kelly McGillis, Jodie Foster and Bernie Coulson. Paramount Pictures Corporation (Canada), 1988.
The Adventures of Bob & Doug McKenzie: Strange Brew. Dirs. Rick Moranis and Dave Thomas. Perf. Rick Moranis, Dave Thomas and Max von Sydow. Metro-Goldwyn-Mayer, 1983.
Alexander Nevsky. Dir. Sergei Eisenstein. Perf. Nikolai Cherkasov, Nikolai Okhlopkov and Andrei Abrikosov. Mosfilm, 1938.
Alien 3. Dir. David Fincher. Perf. Sigourney Weaver, Charles S. Dutton and Charles Dance. Brandywine Productions, 1992.
Almereyda, Michael. *William Shakespeare's Hamlet: A Screenplay Adaptation.* New York: Faber, 2000.
American Film Institute. "AFI's 100 Greatest American Films." 1998. *filmsite.org.* 21 February 2011. http://www.filmsite.org/afi100filmsA.html.
Anderegg, Michael. *Cinematic Shakespeare.* Toronto: Rowman & Littlefield, 2004.
As You Like It. Dir. Paul Czinner. Perf. Henry Ainley, Elisabeth Bergner and Felix Aylmer. Inter-Allied, 1936.
As You Like It. Dir. Kenneth Branagh. Perf. Takuya Shimada, Brian Blessed and Richard Clifford. BBC Films, 2006.
Back to the Future. Dir. Robert Zemeckis. Perf. Michael J. Fox, Christopher Lloyd and Lea Thompson. Universal Pictures, 1985.
Ball, Robert Hamilton. *Shakespeare on Silent Film: A Strange Eventful History.* London: George Allen & Unwin, 1968.
Barry, Ann-Marie. *Visual Intelligence: Perception, Image and Manipulation in Visual Communication.* Albany: State University of New York Press, 1997.
Batman. Dir. Tim Burton. Perf. Michael Keaton, Jack Nicholson and Kim Basinger. Warner Bros., 1989.
The Big Chill. Dir. Lawrence Kasdan. Perf. Tom Berenger, Glen Close and Jeff Goldblum. Columbia Pictures Corporation, 1983.
The Birth of a Nation. Dir. D.W. Griffith. Perf. Lillian Gish, Mae Marsh and Henry B. Walthall. Epoch Producing Corporation, 1915.
The Black Pirate. Dir. Albert Parker. Perf. Douglas Fairbanks, Billie Dove and Anders Randolf. Elton Corporation, 1925.

Bluestone, G. *Novels into Film.* Berkeley: University of California Press, 1957.
Boogie Nights. Dir. Paul Thomas Anderson. Perf. Mark Wahlberg, Julianne Moore and Burt Reynolds. Ghoulardi Film Company, 1997.
Braveheart. Dir. Mel Gibson. Perf. Mel Gibson, Sophie Marceau and Patrick McGoohan. Icon Entertainment International, 1995.
Breaking Away. Dir. Peter Yates. Perf. Dennis Christopher, Dennis Quaid and Daniel Stern. Twentieth Century–Fox Film Corporation, 1979.
Brook, Peter. Preface. Kott, Jan. *Shakespeare: Our Contemporary.* London: Methuen, 1965. ix–xi.
Brown, Constance. "Olivier's Richard III: A Reevaluation." *Focus on Shakespearean Film.* Ed. Charles W. Eckert. Englewood Cliffs, NJ: Prentice-Hall, 1972. 131–145.
Buchanan, Judith. *Shakespeare on Film.* Toronto: Pearson, 2005.
_____. *Shakespeare on Silent Film: An Excellent Dumb Discourse.* Cambridge: Cambridge University Press, 2009.
Buhler, Stephen M. *Shakespeare in the Cinema: Ocular Proof.* Albany: State University of New York Press, 2002.
Bullit. Dir. Peter Yates. Perf. Steve McQueen, Jacqueline Bisset and Robert Vaughn. Warner Brothers/Seven Arts, 1968.
A Bunch of Amateurs. Dir. Andy Cadiff. Perf. Burt Reynolds and Derek Jacobi. Isle of Man Film, 2008.
Buruma, Ian. "The Re-Birth of Japanese Democracy." 31 August 2009. *Project Syndicate.* 20 February 2011. http://www.project-syndicate.org/commentary/buruma29/English.
Cameron, John Hugh. "The Nightmare of History: World War II's Effect on Jan Kott, and Jan Kott's Effect on Postwar British Theatre." Wartime Shakespeare in a Global Context Conference. University of Ottawa, Ottawa. 2009.
Canby, Vincent. "Tempest Opens with Nod to Shakespeare." n.d. nytieswww. 21 February 2011. http://movies.nytimes.com/movie/review?res=9B02E4DB103BF930A2575BC0A964948260&scp=1&sq=tempest%201982&st=cse.
Cannon, Damian. "Forbidden Planet (1956)." 1997. *Movie Reviews UK—Criticism from a British Perspective.* 21 February 2011. http://www.film.unet.com/Movies/Reviews/Forbidden_Planet.html.
Cardwell, Sarah. *Adaptation Revisited.* Manchester: Manchester University Press, 2002.
_____. "Present(ing) Tense: Temporality and Tense in Comparative Theories of Literature-Film Adaptation" July 2000. *Scope.* 20 February 2011. http://www.scope.nottingham.ac.uk/article.php?issue=jul2000&id=288&section=article.
Cartmell, Deborah, and Imelda Whehelan. *Screen Adaptation: Impure Cinema.* London: Palgrave Macmillan, 2010.
_____, and _____, eds. *Adaptations: From Text to Screen, Screen to Text.* London: Routledge, 1999.
Cartmell, Deborah, et al., eds. *Pulping Fictions: Consuming Culture Across the Literature/Media Divide.* London: Pluto Press, 1996.
Chekhov, Anton. "The Sea-Gull by Anton Pavlovich Chekhov." 21 February 2006. *Project Gutenberg.* 21 February 2011. http://www.gutenberg.org/catalog/world/readfile?fk_files=1446789.
Chimes at Midnight. Dir. Orson Welles. Perf. Orson Welles, Jeanne Moreau and Margaret Rutherford. Internacional Films Espanola, 1965.
City Lights. Dir. Charles Chaplin. Perf. Charles Chaplin, Virginia Cherrill and Florence Lee. Charles Chaplin Productions, 1931.
Colley, Nigel, ed. "Gareth Jones' 1933 Moscow Interview Notes with a Soviet Offical Denying the Existence of Any Famine?" 2004. *garethjones.org.* 21 February 2011. http://www.garethjones.org/st_patricks/1933_famine_denial.htm.

Works Cited

Collick, John. *Shakespeare, Cinema and Society.* Manchester: Manchester University Press, 1989.
Costanzo Cahir, Linda. *Literature into Film.* Jefferson, NC: McFarland, 2006.
Croteau, Melissa. "A Hamlet You Can Drink To: Surveillance, Technology, and the Bard in Strange Brew." Annual Conference of the PCA/ACA, San Diego, 2005.
Croteau, Melissa, and Carolyn Jess-Cooke, eds. *Apocalyptic Shakespeare: Essays on Visions of Chaos and Revelation in Recent Film Adaptations.* Jefferson, NC: McFarland, 2009.
Crowl, Samuel. *Shakespeare at the Cineplex: The Kenneth Branagh Era.* Athens: Ohio University Press, 2003.
Dances with Wolves. Dir. Kevin Costner. Perf. Kevin Costner, Mary McDonnell and Graham Greene. Tig Productions, 1990.
Davies, Anthony. *Filming Shakespeare's Plays: The Adaptations of Laurence Olivier, Orson Welles, Peter Brook and Akira Kurosawa.* Cambridge: Cambridge University Press, 1988.
_____. "Shakespeare on Film and Television: A Retrospect." *Shakespeare and the Moving Image: The Plays on Film and Television.* Eds. Anthony Davies and Stanley Wells. Cambridge: Cambridge University Press, 1994. 1–17.
Dawson, Anthony. "Reading Kurosawa Reading Shakespeare." *A Concise Companion to Shakespeare on Screen.* Ed. Diana E. Henderson. Malden, MA: Blackwell, 2006.
Dead Again. Dir. Kenneth Branagh. Perf. Kenneth Branagh, Emma Thompson and Andy Garcia. Mirage, 1991.
Dersu Uzala. Dir. Akira Kurosawa. Perf. Maksim Munzuk, Yuri Solomin and Svetlana Danilchenko. Mosfilm Studios, 1975.
DigitalDreamDoor.com. *100 Greatest Silent Movies.* 19 February 2007. 20 February 2011. http://www.digitaldreamdoor.com/pages/movie-pages/movie_silent.php.
Dirks, Tim. "The Godfather (1972)." n.d. *filmsite.org.* 21 February 2011. http://www.filmsite.org/godf.html.
The Divorcee. Dir. Robert Z. Leonard. Perf. Norma Shearer, Robert Montgomery and Chester Morris. Metro-Goldwyn-Mayer, 1930.
Doctor Zhivago. Dir. David Lean. Perf. Omar Sharif, Julie Christie and Geraldine Chaplin. Metro-Goldwyn-Mayer, 1965.
Dolan, Frances E. "The Taming of the Shrew—Listening to Silence." 2008. *Chicago Shakespeare Theatre—Scholar's Perspective.* 20 February 2011. http://www.chicagoshakes.com/main.taf?p=2,19,3,23,3,14.
Donaldson, Peter S. "Olivier, Hamlet and Freud." *Shakespeare on Film.* Ed. Robert Shaughnessy. London: Palgrave, 1998. 103–125.
The Dresser. Dir. Peter Yates. Perf. Albert Finney, Tom Courtenay and Edward Fox. Columbia Pictures Corporation, 1982.
E.T.: The Extra-Terrestrial. Dir. Steven Spielberg. Perf. Henry Thomas, Drew Barrymore and Peter Coyote. Universal Pictures, 1982.
Ebert, Roger. "'Great Movies' Review of Ran." 1 October 2004. rogerebertwww. 20 February 2011. http://rogerebert.suntimes.com/apps/pbcs.dll/article?AID=/20001001/REVIEWS08/10010301/1023.
_____. "'Great Movies' Review of Romeo and Juliet." 1 October 2004. rogerebertwww. 21 February 2011. http://rogerebert.suntimes.com/apps/pbcs.dll/article?AID=/20000917/REVIEWS08/9170301/1023.
_____. "Review of Hamlet." 1 October 2004. rogerebertwww. 21 February 2011. http://rogerebert.suntimes.com/apps/pbcs.dll/article?AID=/19910118/REVIEWS/101180303/1023.
_____. "Review of Love's Labours Lost." 1 October 2004. rogerebertwww. 21 February 2011 http://rogerebert.suntimes.com/apps/pbcs.dll/article?AID=/20000619/REVIEWS/6190301.

_____. "Review of Romeo and Juliet." 1 October 2004. rogerebertwww. 21 February 2011. http://rogerebert.suntimes.com/apps/pbcs.dll/article?AID=/19681015/REVIEWS/810150301/1023.

_____. "Review of The Dresser." 1 October 2004. rogerebertwww. 20 February 2011 http://rogerebert.suntimes.com/apps/pbcs.dll/article?AID=/19830101/REVIEWS/301010303/1023.

Elliott, Kamilla. *Rethinking the Novel/Film Debate.* Cambridge: Cambridge University Press, 2003.

The English Patient. Dir. Anthony Minghella. Perf. Ralph Fiennes, Juliette Binoche and Willem Dafoe. Miramax Films, 1996.

Farooqi, Nooruddin. "Out of Sight and the Self-Reflexive Cinema of the 90's." 2010. Scribdwww. 20 February 2011. http://www.scribd.com/doc/32526556/Out-of-Sight-and-the-Self-Reflexive-90-s-Cinema.

Fatal Attraction. Dir. Adrian Lyne. Perf. Michael Douglas, Glenn Close and Anne Archer. Paramount Pictures, 1987.

filmsite.org. "All-Time Top Box-Office Films By Decade." 2011. 20 February 2011. http://www.filmsite.org/boxoffice2.html.

Finch, R.D. "Contemporary Kurosawa: The Bad Sleep Well and High and Low." 17 August 2009. *The Movie Projector.* 20 February 2011. http://themovieprojector.blogspot.com/2009/08/contemporary-kurosawa-bad-sleep-well.html.

Five Easy Pieces. Dir. Bob Rafelson. Perf. Jack Nicholson, Karen Black and Billy Green Bush. BBS Productions, 1970.

Forbidden Planet. Dir. Fred M. Wilcox. Perf. Walter Pidgeon, Anne Francis and Leslie Nielsen. Metro-Goldwyn-Mayer, 1956.

Fried Green Tomatoes. Dir. Jon Avnet. Perf. Kathy Bates, Jessica Tandy and Mary Stuart Masterson. Act III Communications, 1991.

Gamlet (Hamlet). Dir. Grigori Kozintsev. Perf. Innokenti Smoktunovsky, Mikhail Nazvanov and Elza Radzina. Lenfilm Studio, 1964.

Garber, Marjorie. *Shakespeare After All.* New York: Anchor Books, 2004.

Gettysburgh. Dir. Ronald F. Maxwell. Perf. Tom Berenger, Martin Sheen and Stephen Lange. TriStar Television, 1993.

Giddings, R., and E. Sheen, eds. *The Classic Novel: From Page to Screen.* Manchester: Manchester University Press, 2000.

The Godfather. Dir. Francis Ford Coppola. Perf. Marlon Brando, Al Pacino and James Caan. Paramount Pictures, 1972.

The Godfather: Part II. Dir. Francis Ford Coppola. Perf. Al Pacino, Robert De Niro and Robert Duvall. Paramount Pictures, 1974.

The Godfather: Part III. Dir. Francis Ford Coppola. Perf. Al Pacino, Diane Keaton and Andy Garcia. Paramount Pictures, 1990.

The Gold Rush. Dir. Charles Chaplin. Perf. Charles Chaplin, Mack Swain and Tom Murray. Charles Chaplin Productions, 1925.

Gorky Park. Dir. Michael Apted. Perf. William Hurt, Lee Marvin and Brian Dennehy. Eagle Associates, 1983.

Griggs, Yvonne. "On the Road: Reclaiming Korol Lir." *Literature Film Quarterly* 37.2 (2009): 97–108.

Gronsky, Daniel. "Shakespeare in Translation: Foreign Film Versions of Shakespeare's Plays." *Film International* 2.5 (2004): 44–51.

Grossberger, Lewis. "Shakespeare Goes Hollywood." *Vogue* February 1991: 214–220.

Guest, Kristen. "The Subject of Money: Late-Victorian Melodrama's Crisis of Masculinity." *Victorian Studies* 49.4 (2007): 635–657.

Guneratne, Anthony R. "'Thou Dost Usurp Authority': Beerbohm Tree, Reinhardt, Olivier, Welles, and the Politics of Adapting Shakespeare." *A Concise Companion to Shakespeare on Screen.* Ed. Diana E. Henderson. Malden, MA: Blackwell, 2006. 31–53.

Guntner, J. Lawrence. "Hamlet, Macbeth and King Lear on Film." *The Cambridge Companion to Shakespeare on Film.* Ed. Russell Jackson. 2d ed. Cambridge: Cambridge University Press, 2007. 120–140.

Haddad, Miranda Johnson. "A Time for Titus: An Interview with Julie Taymor." *Shakespeare Bulletin* 18.4 (Fall 2000): 34–36.

Hamlet. Dir. Laurence Olivier. Perf. Laurence Olivier, Jean Simmons and John Laurie. Two Cities Films, 1948.

Hamlet. Dir. Tony Richardson. Perf. Nicol Williamson, Judy Parfitt and Anthony Hopkins. Woodfall Film Productions, 1969.

Hamlet. Dir. Franco Zeffirelli. Perf. Mel Gibson, Glenn Close and Alan Bates. Icon Entertainment International, 1990.

Hamlet. Dir. Kenneth Branagh. Perf. Kenneth Branagh, Julie Christie and Derek Jacobi. Castle Rock Entertainment, 1996.

Hamlet. Dir. Michael Almereyda. Perf. Ethan Hawke, Kyle MacLachlan and Diane Venora. double A Films, 2000.

Hamlet 2. Dir. Andrew Fleming. Perf. Steve Coogan, Elisabeth Shue and Catherine Keener. Focus Features, 2008.

Hannibal. Dir. Ridley Scott. Perf. Anthony Hopkins, Julianne Moore and Gary Oldman. Metro-Goldwyn-Mayer, 2001.

Hapgood, Robert. "Kurosawa's Shakespeare Films: Throne of Blood, the Bad Sleep Well, and Ran." *Shakespeare and the Moving Image: The Plays on Film and Television.* Eds. Anthony Davies and Stanley Wells. Cambridge: Cambridge University Press, 1994. 234–249.

Henderson, Diana. *Collaborations with the Past: Reshaping Shakespeare across Time and Media.* Ithaca: Cornell University Press, 2006.

Henry V. Dir. Kenneth Branagh. Perf. Kenneth Branagh, Derek Jacobi and Simon Shepherd. Renaissance Films, 1989.

Hertenstein, Mike. "No Place Like Home: Stromboli." 2006. *Flickerings@Cornerstone-Festival.* 20 February 2011. http://www.flickerings.com/2006/rossellini/stromboli.htm.

Holland, Peter. "Two-Dimensional Shakespeare: 'King Lear' on Film." *Shakespeare and the Moving Image.* Eds. Anthony Davies and Stanley Wells. Cambridge: Cambridge University Press, 1994. 50–68.

Howard, Tony. "Shakespeare's Cinematic Offshoots." *The Cambridge Companion to Shakespeare on Film.* Ed. Russell Jackson. Cambridge: Cambridge University Press, 2000. 295–313.

Howard's End. Dir. James Ivory. Perf. Anthony Hopkins, Emma Thompson and Vanessa Redgrave. Merchant Ivory Productions, 1992.

Howe, Desson. "Bard by Godard: 'Lear' Not Near." n.d. washingtonpostwww. 21 February 2011. http://pqasb.pqarchiver.com/washingtonpost/access/73613848.html?FMT=ABS&FMTS=ABS:FT&date=Jun+17%2C+1988&author=Desson+Howe&pub=The+Washington+Post+%28pre-1997+Fulltext%29&edition=&startpage=n.41&desc=Bard+by+Godard%3A+%60Lear%27+Not+Near.

Hutcheon, Linda. *A Theory of Adaptation.* New York: Routledge, 2006.

In the Name of the Father. Dir. Jim Sheridan. Perf. Daniel Day-Lewis, et al. Hell's Kitchen Films, 1993.

Isenberg, Noah. "Screen Saver." 2009. bookforumwww. 20 February 2011. http://www.bookforum.com/inprint/016_04/4698.

Jackson, Russell. "Filming As You Like It: A Playful Comedy Becomes a Problem." 12 March 2005. *Societe Francaise Shakespeare.* 20 February 2011. http://www.societefrancaiseshakespeare.org/document.php?id=656.

Joe. Dir. John G. Avildsen. Perf. Peter Boyle, Dennis Patrick and Susan Sarandon. Cannon Films, 1970.
Joe MacBeth. Dir. Ken Hughes. Perf. Paul Douglas, Ruth Roman and Bonar Colleano. Columbia Pictures Corporation, 1955.
Jorgens, Jack. *Shakespeare on Film.* Laham, MD: University Press of America, 1977.
Jubal. Dir. Delmer Daves. Perf. Glenn Ford, Ernest Borgnine and Rod Steiger. Columbia Pictures Corporation, 1956.
Jurassic Park. Dir. Steven Spielberg. Perf. Sam Neill, Laura Dern and Jeff Goldblum. Universal, 1993.
Kagemusha. Dir. Akira Kurosawa. Perf. Tatsuya Nakadai, Tsutomu Yamazaki and Kenichi Hagiwara. Kurosawa Production Co., 1980.
Kamilla, Elliot. *Rethinking the Novel/Film Debate.* Cambridge: Cambridge University Press, 2003.
Kauffmann, Stanley. "Stanley Kauffmann on Films." *The New Republic* 7 April 1973: 24–33.
Kehr, Dave. "New DVDs: The Godfather: The Coppola Restoration." 23 September 2008. *New York Times.* 21 February 2011. http://movies.nytimes.com/2008/09/23/movies/23dvds.html?scp=1&sq=kehr%20godfather&st=cse.
Kennedy, Dennis. *Looking at Shakespeare: A Visual History of Twentieth-Century Performance,* 2d ed. Cambridge: Cambridge University Press, 2001.
Keyishan, Harry. "Shakespeare and the Movie Genre: The Case of Hamlet." *The Cambridge Companion to Shakespeare on Film.* Ed. Russell Jackson. 2d ed. Cambridge: Cambridge University Press, 2007. 72–86.
A King in New York. Dir. Charles Chaplin. Perf. Charles Chaplin, Maxine Audley and Jerry Desmonde. Charles Chaplin Productions, 1957.
King Lear. Dir. Jean-Luc Godard. Perf. Woody Allen, Freddy Buache and Leos Carax. The Cannon Group, 1987.
King Lear. Dir. Peter Brook. Perf. Paul Scofield, Irene Worth and Cyril Cusack. Filmways, 1971.
King, Stephen. *Danse Macabre.* New York: Everest House, 1981.
Kiss Me, Kate. Dir. George Sidney. Perf. Kathryn Grayson, Howard Keel and Ann Miller. Metro-Goldwyn-Mayer, 1953.
Korol Lir (King Lear). Dir. Grigori Kozintsev. Perf. Juri Jarvet, Elza Radzina and Galina Volchek. Lenfilm Studio, 1970.
Kott, Jan. *Shakespeare: Our Contemporary.* London: Methuen, 1965.
Kozenyuk, *Alexander Nevsky Monument.* 2002. V.G. Nevsky Prospekt, St. Petersburg.
Kumonosu djô (Throne of Blood). Dir. Akira Kurosawa. Perf. Toshiro Mifune, Minoru Chiaki and Isuzu Yamada. Toho Company, 1957.
The Lady from Shanghai. Dir. Orson Welles. Perf. Rita Hayworth, Orson Welles and Everett Sloane. Mercury Productions, 1947.
Lan, Yong Li. "The Very Painting of Your Fear: Roman Polanski's Macbeth and Akira Kurosawa's *Kumonosu djô.*" *Shakespeare Jahrbuch* 133 (1997): 109–117.
Lanier, Douglas. "Drowning the Book: Prospero's Books and the Textual Shakespeare." *Shakespeare on Film.* Ed. Robert Shaughnessy. London: Palgrave, 1998. 173–195.
Leitch, Thomas. *Film Adaptation and its Discontents: From Gone with the Wind to The Passion of the Christ.* Baltimore: Johns Hopkins University Press, 2007.
Lethal Weapon 2. Dir. Richard Donner. Perf. Mel Gibson, Danny Glover and Joe Pesci. Silver Pictures, 1989.
Levy, Emanuel. "Romeo and Juliet (1938)." 2011. *Emanuel Levy Cinema 24/7.* 20 February 2011. http://www.emanuellevy.com/review/romeo-and-juliet-1938-7/.
Licence to Kill. Dir. John Glen. Perf. Timothy Dalton, Robert Davi and Carey Lowell. Eon Productions, 1989.

The Life and Death of King Richard III. Dirs. Andre Calmettes and James Keane. Perf. Robert Gemp, Frederick Warde and Albert Gardner. Le Film d'Art, 1912.

Limelight. Dir. Charles Chaplin. Perf. Charles Chaplin, Claire Bloom and Nigel Bruce. Celebrated Productions, 1952.

The Lion King. Dirs. Roger Allers and Rob Minkoff. Perf. Matthew Broderick, Jeremy Irons and James Earl Jones. Walt Disney Pictures, 1994.

Little Big Man. Dir. Arthur Penn. Perf. Dustin Hoffman, Faye Dunaway and Chief Dan George. Cinema Center Films, 1970.

Looking for Richard. Dir. Al Pacino. Perf. Al Pacino, Alec Baldwin and Kevin Spacey. Twentieth Century–Fox, 1996.

The Lost World: Jurassic Park. Dir. Steven Spielberg. Perf. Jeff Goldblum, Julianne Moore and Pete Postlethwaite. Universal Pictures, 1997.

Love's Labour's Lost. Dir. Kenneth Branagh. Perf. Alessandro Nivola, Alicia Silverstone and Natascha McElhone. Pathe Pictures International, 2000.

Macbeth. Dir. Orson Welles. Perf. Orson Welles, Jeanette Nolan and Dan O'Herlihy. Mercury Productions, 1948.

Magnolia. Dir. Paul Thomas Anderson. Perf. Tom Cruise, Jason Robards and Julianne Moore. Ghoulardi Film Company, 1999.

Maher, Mary Z. "The Un-Hamlet." Western Conference on Literature, Film and the Humanities. University of Arizona, 3 January 1992.

The Man Who Shot Liberty Valance. Dir. John Ford. Perf. John Wayne, James Stewart and Vera Miles. Paramount Pictures, 1962.

Manheim, Michael. "The English History Play on Screen." *Shakespeare and the Moving Image: The Plays on Film and Television.* Eds. Anthony Davies and Stanley Wells. Cambridge: Cambridge University Press, 1994. 121–145.

Margolies, David. "King Lear: Kozintsev's Social Translation." *Shifting the Scene: Shakespeare in European Culture.* Eds. Ladina Bezzola Lambert and Balz Engler. Cranbury, NJ: Associated University Presses, 2004. 230–238.

The Mark of Zorro. Dir. Fred Niblo. Perf. Douglas Fairbanks, Marguerite De La Motte and Noah Beery. Douglas Fairbanks Pictures, 1920.

MASH. Dir. Robert Altman. Perf. Donald Sutherland, Elliott Gould and Tom Skerritt. Aspen Productions, 1970.

The Matrix. Dirs. Andy Wachowski and Lana Wachowski. Perf. Keanu Reeves, Laurence Fishburne and Carrie-Anne Moss. Warner Bros. Pictures, 1999.

Maunula, Vili. "Ran: Gods as Audience, Audience as Gods." 12 September 2009. *Akira Kurosawa: News, Information and Discussion.* 20 February 2011. http://akirakurosawa.info/forums/topic/ran-gods-as-audience-audience-as-gods.

McCombe, John P. "'Suiting the Action to the Word': The 1908 Clarendon Tempest and the Evolution of a Narrative Silent Shakespeare." *Literature Film Quarterly* 33.2 (2005): 142–155.

McFarlane, B. *Novel into Film: An Introduction to the Theory of Adaptation.* Oxford: Clarendon Press, 1996.

McKernan, Luke. *Silent Shakespeare: Such Stuff as Dreams Are Made on...* Press Kit. Harrington Park, NJ: Milestone Film & Video, 1999.

Melone, Altobello. *Ritratto di gentiluomo (Portrait of Cesare Borgia).* Galleria dell'Accademia Carrara, Bergamo, Italy.

Melo-Thaiss, Janet. "An Earthly Lament: Akira Kurosawa's *Kumonosu djô* and *Ran.*" Unpublished essay. York University, 2005.

Il Mercante di Venezia (The Merchant of Venice). Dir. Gerolamo Lo Savio. Perf. Ermete Novelli, Francesca Bertini and Olga Giannini Novelli. Filme d'Arte Italiana, 1910.

Mickey's Circus. Dir. Albert Herman. Perf. Mickey Rooney. Larry Darmour Productions, 1927.

A Midsummer Night's Dream. Dir. Charles Kent. Perf. Walter Ackerman, Charles Chapman and Dolores Costello. Vitagraph Company of America, 1909.
A Midsummer Night's Dream. Dirs. Max Reinhardt and William Dieterle. Perf. James Cagney, Dick Powell and Ian Hunter. Warner Bros. Pictures, 1935.
A Midwinter's Tale. Dir. Kenneth Branagh. Perf. Michael Maloney, Richard Briers and Hetta Charnley. Midwinter Films, 1996.
Modern Times. Dir. Charles Chaplin. Perf. Charles Chaplin, Paulette Goddard and Henry Bergman. Charles Chaplin Productions, 1936.
Morris, Pam. "A Glossary of Key Terms." *The Bakhtin Reader: Selected Writings of Bakhtin, Medvedev, Voloshinov.* Ed. Pam Morris. New York: St. Martin's Press, 1994. 245–252.
Much Ado About Nothing. Dir. Kenneth Branagh. Perf. Kenneth Branagh, Emma Thompson and Keanu Reeves. Renaissance Films, 1993.
Murphy's War. Dir. Peter Yates. Perf. Peter O'Toole, Sian Phillips and Phillippe Noiret. Helmdale, 1971.
My Darling Clementine. Dir. John Ford. Perf. Henry Fonda, Linda Darnell and Victor Mature. Twentieth Century–Fox Film Corporation, 1947.
National Centre for Post-Traumatic Stress Disorder. "PTSD and Older Veterans." n.d. *PsychCentral.* 23 April 2011. http://psychcentral.com/lib/2006/ptsd-and-older-veterans/.
The Natural. Dir. Barry Levinson. Perf. Robert Redford, Robert Duvall and Glenn Close. TriStar Pictures, 1984.
Nelmes, Jill. *An Introduction to Film Studies,* 2d ed. New York: Routledge, 2003.
North by Northwest. Dir. Hitchcock. Perf. Cary Grant, Eva Marie Saint and James Mason. Metro-Goldwyn-Mayer, 1959.
Octopussy. Dir. John Glen. Perf. Roger Moore, Maude Adams and Louis Jourdan. United Artists, 1983.
Olympia 1. Teil—Fest der Völker. Dir. Leni Riefenstahl. Perf. David Albritton, Arvo Askola and Sulo Barlund. Tobis Filmkunst, 1938.
Olympia 2. Teil—Fest der Schönheit. Dir. Leni Riefenstahl. Perf. Sheigo Arai, Jack Beresford and Ralf Berzsenyi. Tobis Filmkunst, 1938.
"100 Greatest Movies of the 1960s." 30 January 2005. DigitalDreamDoorwww. 21 February 2011. http://www.digitaldreamdoor.com/pages/movie-pages/movie_60s.html.
Otello. Dir. Franco Zefirrelli. Perf. Placido Domingo, Katia Ricciarelli and Justino Diaz. Cannon Productions, 1986.
Othello. Dir. Dimitri Buchowetzki. Perf. Emil Jannings, Werner Krauss and Ica von Lenkeffy. Worner-Filmgesellschaft, 1923.
Othello. Dir. Orson Welles. Perf. Orson Welles, Liam MacLiammoir and Robert Coote. Mercury Productions, 1952.
Pearlman, E. "Macbeth on Film: Politics." *Shakespeare and the Moving Image: The Plays on Film and Television.* Eds. Anthony Davies and Stanley Wells. Cambridge: Cambridge University Press, 1994. 250–260.
Perils of Nyoka. Dir. William Witney. Perf. Kay Aldridge, Clayton Moore and Lorna Gray. Republic Pictures, 1942.
The Petrified Forest. Dir. Archie Mayo. Perf. Leslie Howard, Humphrey Bogart and Bette Davis. Warner Bros. Pictures, 1936.
Pilkington, Ace G. "Zefferilli's Shakespeare." *Shakespeare and the Moving Image: The Plays on Film and Television.* Eds. Anthony Davies and Stanley Wells. Cambridge: Cambridge University Press, 1994. 163–179.
Pirates of the Caribbean: The Curse of the Black Pearl. Dir. Gore Verbinsky. Perf. Johnny Depp, et al. Disney, 2003.
Portrait of Lucrezia Borgia. Musee des Beaux-Arts, Nimes, France.

Prospero's Books. Dir. Peter Greenaway. Perf. John Gielgud, Michael Clark and Michel Blanc. Palace Pictures, 1991.
The Public Enemy. Dir. William Wellman. Perf. James Cagney, Jean Harlow and Edward Woods. Warner Bros. Pictures, 1931.
Ran. Dir. Akira Kurosawa. Perf. Tatsuya Nakadai, Akira Terao and Jinpachi Nezu. Nippon Herald Films, 1985.
The Rapture. Dir. Michael Tolkin. Perf. Mimi Rogers, David Duchovny and Darwyn Carson. New Line Cinema, 1991.
Re Lear (King Lear). Dir. Gerolamo Lo Savio. Perf. Ermete Novelli, Francesca Bertini and Olga Giannini Novelli. Filme d'Arte Italiana, 1910.
Rebellato, Dan. *1956 And All That: The Making of Modern British Drama.* London: Routledge, 1999.
Redfern, Nick. "Shakespeare and National Identity." 21 January 2010. *Research into Film.* 20 February 2011. http://nickredfern.wordpress.com/2010/01/21/shakespeare-and-national-identity/.
The Remains of the Day. Dir. James Ivory. Perf. Anthony Hopkins, Emma Thompson and John Haycraft. Merchant Ivory Productions, 1993.
Richard III. Dir. Frank R. Benson. Perf. James Berry, Alfred Brydone and Kathleen Yorku. Co-operative Cinematograph, 1910.
Richard III. Dir. Laurence Olivier. Perf. Laurence Olivier, Cedric Hardwicke and Nicholas Hannen. London Film Productions, 1955.
Richard III. Dir. Richard Loncraine. Perf. Ian McKellen, Annette Bening and Jim Broadbent. Mayfair Entertainment International, 1996.
Robin Hood. Dir. Alan Dwan. Perf. Douglas Fairbanks, Wallace Beery and Sam De Grasse. Douglas Fairbanks Pictures, 1922.
Romeo and Juliet. Dir. George Cukor. Perf. Norma Shearer, Leslie Howard and John Barrymore. Metro-Goldwyn-Mayer, 1936.
Romeo and Juliet. Dir. Franco Zeffirelli. Perf. Leonard Whiting, Elizabeth Hussey and John McEnery. BHE Films, 1968.
Romeo + Juliet. Dir. Baz Luhrmann. Perf. Leonardo DiCaprio, Claire Danes and John Leguizamo. Bazmark Films, 1996.
Rosencrantz and Guildenstern Are Dead. Dir. Tom Stoppard. Perf. Gary Oldman, Tim Roth and Richard Dreyfuss. Brandenberg, 1990.
Rosenstone, Robert A. *History on Film: Film on History,* 2d ed. Harlow: Pearson, 2012.
Rothwell, Kenneth. *A History of Shakespeare on Screen,* 2d ed. Cambridge: Cambridge University Press, 2004.
_____. "Representing 'King Lear' on Screen: From Metatheatre to 'Metacinema.'" *Shakespeare and the Moving Image: The Plays on Film and Television.* Eds. Anthony Davies and Stanley Wells. Cambridge: Cambridge University Press, 1994. 211–233.
_____, and Annabelle Henkin Melzer. *Shakespeare on Screen: an International Filmography and Videography.* London: Mansell, 1990.
Rudova, Larissa. *Understanding Boris Pasternak.* Columbia: University of South Carolina Press, 1997.
The Scarlet Pimpernel. Dir. Harold Young. Perf. Leslie Howard, Merle Oberon and Raymond Massey. London Film Productions, 1934.
Schindler's List. Dir. Steven Spielberg. Perf. Liam Neeson, Ralph Fiennes and Ben Kingsley. Universal Pictures, 1993.
Schmidt, Howard. "Diachronic Design in Olivier's Henry V." PCA/ACA, New Orleans, 2009.
Sense and Sensibility. Dir. Ang Lee. Perf. Emma Thompson, Kate Winslet and James Fleet. Columbia Pictures Corporation, 1995.

Shakespeare in Love. Dir. John Madden. Perf. Gwyneth Paltrow, Joseph Fiennes and Geoffrey Rush. Miramax Films, 1998.

Shakespeare, William. *Henry V. Shakespeare: The Complete Works.* Ed. G.B. Harrison. New York: Harcourt Brace Jovanovich, 1968. 735–772.

_____. *Henry VI, Part III. Shakespeare: The Complete Works.* Ed. G.B. Harrison. New York: Harcourt Brace Jovanovich, 1968. 184–220.

_____. *King Lear. Shakespeare: The Complete Works.* Ed. G.B. Harrison. New York: Harcourt Brace Jovanovich, 1968. 1136–1183.

_____. *Macbeth. Shakespeare: The Complete Works.* Ed. G.B. Harrison. New York: Harcourt Brace Jovanovich, 1968. 1184–1218.

_____. *The Merchant of Venice. Shakespeare: The Complete Works.* Ed. G.B. Harrison. New York: Harcourt Brace Jovanovich, 1968.

_____. *Othello. Shakespeare: The Complete Works.* Ed. G.B. Harrison. New York: Harcourt Brace Jovanovich, 1968. 1056–1099.

_____. *Richard II. Shakespeare: The Complete Works.* Ed. G.B. Harrison. New York: Harcourt Brace Jovanovich, 1968. 435–467.

_____. *Romeo and Juliet. Shakespeare: The Complete Works.* Ed. G.B. Harrison. New York: Harcourt Brace Jovanovich, 1968. 474–510.

_____. *The Taming of the Shrew. Shakespeare: The Complete Works.* Ed. G.B. Harrison. New York: Harcourt Brace Jovanovich, 1968. 331–364.

_____. *The Tempest. Shakespeare: The Complete Works.* Ed. G.B. Harrison. New York: Harcourt Brace Jovanovich, 1968. 1475–1501.

_____. *The Tragedy of Hamlet: Prince of Denmark. Shakespeare: The Complete Works.* Ed. G.B. Harrison. New York: Harcourt Brace Jovanovich, 1968. 880–934.

_____. *Twelfth Night or What You Will. Shakespeare: The Complete Works.* Ed. G.B. Harrison. New York: Harcourt Brace Jovanovich, 1968.

Shaughnessy, Robert. Introduction. *Shakespeare on Film.* Ed. Robert Shaughnessy. London: Palgrave, 1998. 1–17.

_____. "Stage, Screen, and Nation: Hamlet and the Space of History." *A Concise Companion to Shakespeare on Screen.* Ed. Diana E. Henderson. Malden, MA: Blackwell, 2006. 54–76.

Shelokhonov, Steve. "Biography for Grigori Kozintsev." n.d. IMDBwww. 21 February 2011. http://www.imdb.com/name/nm0468882/bio.

She's the Man. Dir. Andy Fickman. Perf. Amanda Bynes, Laura Ramsey and Channing Tatum. Dreamworks SKG, 2006.

The Silence of the Lambs. Dir. Jonathan Demme. Perf. Jodie Foster, Anthony Hopkins and Scott Glenn. Orion Pictures Corporation, 1991.

Sinfield, Alan. "Introduction: Reproductions, Interventions." *Political Shakespeare: Essays in Cultural Materialism.* Ed. Jonathan Dollimore and Alan Sinfield. 2d ed. Manchester: Manchester University Press, 1994. 154–157.

_____. "Royal Shakespeare: Theatre and the Making of Ideology." *Political Shakespeare: Essays in Cultural Materialism.* Ed. Jonathan Dollimore and Alan Sinfield. 2d ed. Manchester: Manchester University Press, 1994. 182–205.

Sippl, Diane. "Tomorrow is my Birthday: Placing Apocalypse in Millenial Cinema." *CineAction* 53 (2000): 2–21.

The Sound of Music. Dir. Robert Wise. Perf. Julie Andrews, Christopher Plummer and Eleanor Parker. Robert Wise Productions, 1965.

Star Wars: Episode VI—Return of the Jedi. Dir. Richard Marquand. Perf. Mark Hamill, Harrison Ford and Carrie Fisher. Lucasfilm, 1983.

Star Wars: Episode V—The Empire Strikes Back. Dir. Irvin Kershner. Perf. Mark Hamill, Harrison Ford and Carrie Fisher. Lucasfilm, 1980.

Steinbrunner, Chris, and Burt Goldblatt. *Cinema of the Fantastic.* New York: Galahad Books, 1972.

Sterritt, David. "The Bad Sleep Well." n.d. *Turner Classic Movies*. 20 February 2011. http://www.tcm.com/thismonth/article.jsp?cid=290050&mainArticleId=290029.
Stone, Alan A. "For God and Country." February 2005. *Boston Review*. 20 February 2011. http://bostonreview.net/BR30.1/stone.php.
Stoppard, Tom. *Rosencrantz and Guildenstern Are Dead*. London: Grove Press, 1967.
Stromboli. Dir. Roberto Rossellini. Perf. Ingrid Bergman, Mario Vitale and Renzo Cesana. Berit Films, 1950.
The Taming of the Shrew. Dir. Sam Taylor. Perf. Mary Pickford, Douglas Fairbanks and Edwin Maxwell. Elton Corporation, 1929.
The Taming of the Shrew. Dir. Franco Zeffirelli. Perf. Elizabeth Taylor, Richard Burton and Cyril Cusak. F.A.I., 1967.
Taubman, William. *Khrushchev: The Man and His Era*. New York: W.W. Norton, Inc., 2003.
Tempest. Dir. Paul Mazursky. Perf. John Cassavetes, Gena Rowlands and Susan Sarandon. Columbia Pictures Corporation, 1982.
The Tempest. Dir. Percy Stow. Clarendon, 1908.
10 Things I Hate About You. Dir. Gil Junger. Perf. Heath Ledger, Julia Stiles and Joseph Gordon-Levitt. Touchstone Pictures, 1999.
Terminator 2: Judgement Day. Dir. James Cameron. Perf. Arnold Schwarzenegger, Linda Hamilton and Edward Furlong. Lightstorm Entertainment, 1991.
Theatre of Blood. Dir. Douglas Hickox. Perf. Vincent Price, Diana Rigg and Ian Hendry. Cineman Productions, 1973.
Thelma and Louise. Dir. Ridley Scott. Perf. Susan Sarandon, Geena Davis and Harvey Keitel. Pathe Entertainment, 1991.
The Thief of Bagdad. Dir. Raoul Walsh. Perf. Douglas Fairbanks, Julanne Johnston and Snitz Edwards. Douglas Fairbanks Pictures, 1924.
The Third Man. Dir. Carol Reed. Perf. Orson Welles, Joseph Cotten and Alida Valli. London Film Productions, 1949.
Thor. Dir. Kenneth Branagh. Perf. Chris Hemsworth, Anthony Hopkins and Natalie Portman. Paramount Pictures, 2011.
The Three Musketeers. Dir. Fred Niblo. Perf. Douglas Fairbanks, Leon Bary and George Siegmann. Douglas Fairbanks Pictures, 1921.
Titanic. Dir. James Cameron. Perf. Leonard DiCaprio, Kate Winslet and Billy Zane. Lightstorm Entertainment, 1997.
Titus. Dir. Julie Taymor. Perf. Anthony Hopkins, Jessica Lange and Osheen Jones. Clear Blue Sky Productions, 1999.
To Be or Not to Be. Dir. Ernst Lubitsch. Perf. Carole Lombard, Jack Benny and Robert Stack. Romaine Film Corporation, 1942.
Top Gun. Dir. Tony Scott. Perf. Tom Cruise, Kelly McGillis and Val Kilmer. Paramount Pictures, 1986.
The Tragedy of Macbeth. Dir. Roman Polanski. Perf. Jon Finch, Francesca Annis and Martin Shaw. Playboy Productions, 1971.
Triumph des Willens. Dir. Leni Riefenstahl. Perf. Adolph Hitler, Hermann Goring and Max Amann. Leni Riefenstahl-Produktion, 1935.
Twelfth Night. Dir. Charles Kent. Perf. Julia Swayne Gordon, Charles Kent and Florence Turner. Vitagraph Company of America, 1910.
Unforgiven. Dir. Clint Eastwood. Perf. Clint Eastwood, Gene Hackman and Morgan Freeman. Malpaso Productions, 1992.
Vanneman, Alan. "Shakespeare Improved! Cole Porter teaches the Old Bard New Tricks in Kiss Me, Kate." *Bright Lights Film Journal* 42 (November 2003). 20 February 2011. http://www.brightlightsfilm.com/42/kissmekate.php.htm.

WarGames. Dir. John Badham. Perf. Matthew Broderick, Ally Sheedy and John Wood. Metro-Goldwyn-Mayer, 1983.
Warui yatsu hodo yoku nemuru (The Bad Sleep Well). Dir. Akira Kurosawa. Perf. Toshiro Mifune, Masayaki Mori and Kyoko Kagawa. Toho Company, 1960.
Weiss, Barbara. *The Hell of the English: Bankruptcy and the Victorian Novel.* Lanham, MD: Associated University Presses, 1986.
Weiss, Tanja. *Shakespeare on the Screen: Kenneth Branagh's Adaptations of Henry V, Much Ado About Nothing, and Hamlet.* Frankfurt am Main: Peter Lang GmbH, 2000.
West Side Story. Dirs. Jerome Robbins and Robert Wise. Perf. Natalie Wood, George Chakiris and Richard Beymer. The Mirisch Corporation, 1961.
White, Hayden. *Tropics of Discourse: Essays in Cultural Criticism.* Baltimore: Johns Hopkins University Press, 1978.
White, Robert. Interview. Peter Babiak. July 1996.
Who's Afraid of Virginia Woolf? Dir. Mike Nichols. Perf. Richard Burton, Elizabeth Taylor and George Segal. Warner Bros. Pictures, 1966.
Wood, Robin. "Hawke Ascending." *CineAction* 55 (2001): 2–13.
_____. *Hollywood from Vietnam to Reagan ... and Beyond.* New York: Columbia University Press, 2003.
Woodstock. Dir. Michael Wadleigh. Perf. Joan Baez, Richie Havens and Joe Cocker. Wadleigh-Maurice, 1970.

Index

Abbate, Alessandro 163, 164
The Accused (film 1988) 143
Adaptation Revisited (book) 5
Alexander Nevsky (film 1938) 58, 90
Alien 3 (film 1992) 152, 156
Almereyda, Michael 8, 22, 151, 153, 154, 157, 162–164, 165, 168, 178
Anderegg, Michael 10
Anderson, Paul Thomas 151, 159, 165
Apocalyptic Shakespeare (book) 166
As You Like It (film 1936) 21, 51–53, 54, 55, 56, 58, 104, 170
As You Like It (film 2006) 150

The Bad Sleep Well see *Warui yatsu hodo yoku nemuru* (film 1960)
Baker, Stanley 102
Bakhtin, Mikhail 104
Ball, Robert Hamilton 30, 31, 33
Barry, Ann-Marie 64
Barrymore, John 50, 51, 170
Bates, Alan 111
Batman (film 1989) 136–138
Beckett, Samuel 15, 115
Beckinsale, Kate 142
Benny, Jack 13, 14
Benson, Frank 30, 33–34, 38, 168–169
Bergner, Elizabeth 52–53, 54, 55, 170
The Big Chill (film 1983) 111, 131
Bloom, Claire 102
Bluestone, G. 5
Boogie Nights (film 1997) 151
Borgia, Cesare 109
Borgia, Lucrezia 109
Branagh, Kenneth 2, 16, 17, 24, 96, 99, 100, 102, 112, 124, 133, 136–150, 151, 153, 154, 168, 176, 177
Braveheart (film 1995) 146
Breaking Away (film 1979) 15
Brezhnev, Leonid 93, 97
Briers, Richard 144
Brook, Peter 22, 24, 94–95, 115–119, 123, 175
Brown, Constance 64

Brown, Joe E. 47, 48, 170
Buchanan, Judith 17, 25, 26, 34, 35, 47, 125–126, 131, 140, 145, 147, 165
Buchowetzki, Dimitri 35–37, 169
Buhler, Stephen 46, 47, 56, 57, 62, 76, 79, 80, 93–94, 100, 115, 116, 119, 120, 121, 122, 147, 148, 151, 167
Bullit (film 1968) 14
A Bunch of Amateurs (film 2008) 13, 19, 20
Burton, Richard 103, 104, 114, 174
Burton, Tim 136–138
Buruma, Ian 72–73

Cagney, James 47, 48, 170
Cahir, Linda Costanzo 8, 9, 10
Cameron, John Hugh 121
Canby, Vincent 130–131
Cannon, Damian 125
Cardwell, Sarah 5, 6, 9, 10, 103
Cartmell, Deborah 6, 9
Chaplin, Charles 12, 39, 102
Chimes at Midnight (film 1965) 8, 21, 57, 59, 65–67, 79, 100, 102, 114, 162, 171, 172
Christie, Julie 146–147
Cimino, Michael 152
Cinema of the Fantastic (book) 125
Cinemascope 93, 95
The Clarendon Tempest (film 1908) 26; see also *The Tempest*
Close, Glenn 111, 112
Collaborations with the Past: Reshaping Shakespeare Across Time and Media (book) 9, 134, 166
Colley, Nigel 85
Collick, John 11, 25, 63, 69–70, 73, 76, 77, 78, 81
Concise Companion to Shakespeare On Screen, A (book) 166
Coppola, Francis Ford 8, 73, 127–130, 135, 168, 176–177
Croteau, Melissa 132
Crowl, Samuel 25, 38, 69, 83, 100, 133, 136, 141, 142, 144, 145, 147, 153, 161, 162, 164, 167
Cruise, Tom 151

199

Cukor, George 49–51, 52, 53, 104, 109, 170
Cumming, Alan 161
Cymbeline (play) 167
Czinner, Paul 51–53, 54, 56, 58, 104, 170

Dances with Wolves (film 1990) 146
Danse Macabre (book) 126
Davies, Anthony 64, 70–71, 115–116, 118, 124
Dawson, Anthony 73
Dead Again (film 1991) 142
Dench, Judi 141
Devine, Andy 50–51
Dieterle, William 47–49, 50, 52, 53, 54, 104, 170
Dietrich, Marlene 39
DigitialDream-Door.com 101
Dillon, Melinda 151
Dirks, Tim 127
Doctor Zhivago (film 1965) 93, 126, 146–147
Dolan, Frances E. 42, 43
Dollimore, Jonathan 6, 7, 9, 10, 166
Donaldson, Peter 61
Donner, Richard 136–138
The Dresser (film 1982) 13, 15, 19

Eastwood, Clint 127, 152
Ebert, Roger 13, 82–83, 102–103, 108, 149–150
Eisenstein, Sergei 58, 90
Elliott, Kamilla 10
The English Patient (film, 1996) 146

Fairbanks, Douglas 39–47, 54, 169
Faithfull, Marianne 120
Farooqi, Nooruddin 18
Fatal Attraction (film 1987) 111
Fickman, Andy 134–135, 167
Film d'Arte Italiana 30
Filming Shakespeare's Plays (book) 64, 70, 115, 166
Finch, R.D. 75
Fincher, David 152, 156
Five Easy Pieces (film 1970) 126–127, 133
Forbes, Ralph 54
Forbidden Planet (film 1956) 7, 21, 125–126
Ford, John 12
Forrest, Edwin 100
Foster, Jodie 143
Fried Green Tomatoes (film 1991) 143

Gamlet (film 1964) 20, 84–93, 97, 147, 173
Garber, Marjorie 40, 96, 108, 110, 128, 130
Garrick, David 100
Gettysburg (film 1993) 146
Gibson, Mel 111, 112
Gielgud, John 102
Glen, John 136–138
Godard, Jean-Luc 8, 133, 135, 176, 177
The Godfather (film 1972) 21, 127–129, 168, 176
The Godfather: Part II (film 1974) 21, 127, 129–130, 168, 176–177
The Godfather: Part III (film 1990) 21, 130, 177
Goldberg, Whoopi 134

Goldblatt, Burt 125
Gorky Park (film 1983) 87
Grant, Cary 112
Grayson, Kathryn 14
Greenaway, Peter 16, 17, 67–68
Griggs, Yvonne 84
Gronsky, Daniel 85
Grossberger, Lewis 99, 108
Guest, Kristen 31
Guneratne, Anthony R. 47
Guntner, J. Lawrence 62, 146–147

Hall, Peter 147
Hamlet (film 1948) 20, 57, 61–62, 63, 65, 112, 114, 171
Hamlet (film 1969) 21, 119–120, 175
Hamlet (film 1990) 15, 21, 102, 110–112, 174–175
Hamlet (film 1996) 2, 21, 96, 100, 146–150, 153, 154, 177
Hamlet (film 2000) 8, 21, 22, 157, 162–164, 178
Hamlet (play) 7, 15, 16, 18, 23, 73, 74–76, 83, 85, 91, 98, 111, 123, 132, 133–134, 177
Hamlet 2 (film 2008) 13, 18–19, 20
Hanh, Thich Nhat 163, 164
Hapgood, Robert 71, 73, 77
Harris, Richard 127
Harwood, Ronald 14
The Hell of the English: Bankruptcy and the Victorian Novel (book) 31
Henderson, Diana 9, 10, 11, 134, 166–167, 168
Hendry, Ian 12
2 Henry IV (play) 65, 66
Henry V (film 1944) 20, 53, 57–59, 61, 63, 67, 79, 100, 140–141, 170–171
Henry V (film 1989) 2, 21, 100, 124, 136–141, 142, 143, 146, 147, 150, 153, 154, 176, 177
Henry V (play) 136, 137–141
3 Henry VI (play) 34, 64
Hertenstein, Mike 63
History of Shakespeare on Screen, A (book) 100, 151
Hitchcock, Alfred 112
Hitler, Adolf 164
Holland, Peter 7, 8, 10, 79, 93, 94, 117
Hollywood from Vietnam to Reagan (book) 96
Holm, Ian 111
Hopkins, Anthony 162
Hordern, Michael 12
Howard, Leslie 50, 51, 53, 54, 170
Howard, Ron 152
Howard, Tony 130
Howard's End (film 1992) 142
Howe, Desson 133
Hussey, Olivia 110, 142
Hutcheon, Linda 10, 11, 12, 13, 20, 22, 126, 167

In the Name of the Father (film 1993) 142
Irving, Henry 100
Irving, Laurence 47
Isenberg, Noah 50

Index

Jackson, Russell 51–52, 56, 58, 59
Jacobi, Derek 19, 140, 147
Joe (film 1970) 126–127
Joe Macbeth (film 1955) 124
Johnson-Haddad, Miranda 160–161
Jorgens, Jack 7, 8, 9, 10, 11, 104
Jory, Victor 47, 48, 170
Jubal (film 1956) 124

Kaufmann, Stanley 99, 108
Kean, Edmund 100
Keane, James 37
Keel, Howard 14
Kehr, Dave 127
Kenilworth (book) 167
Kennedy, Dennis 115
Kent, Charles 28, 29, 30, 33, 37, 38, 168, 169
Keyishian, Harry 146
Khrushchev, Nikita 85, 93, 97
Khrushchev: The Man and His Era (book) 93
King, Stephen 126
A King in New York (film 1957) 12
King Lear (film 1971) 21, 22, 94–95, 115–119, 175
King Lear (film 1987) 8, 21, 133, 177
King Lear (play) 7, 23, 83, 85, 94–95, 98, 115, 130, 132, 173, 176, 177
Kiss Me, Kate (film 1953) 13–14, 19
Korol Lir (film 1970) 21, 84, 93–97, 173–174
Kott, Jan 15, 22, 24, 114, 115, 116, 119, 120, 121, 123, 175, 176
Kozintsev, Grigori 23, 69, 84–98, 100, 112, 147, 167, 173–174
Krauss, Werner 35
Kubrick, Stanley 80, 172
Kumonosu djô (film 1957) 7, 20, 69, 70–73, 74, 82, 83, 97–98, 156, 171–172
Kurosawa, Akira 7, 23, 70, 84, 85, 97–98, 100, 156, 167, 168, 171–173

Lan, Yong Li 121–122
Lanier, Douglas 16, 17, 67–68
Lawrence of Arabia (film 1962) 147
Lean, David 52, 93, 147, 154
Leitch, Thomas 8, 9, 10
Lenin, Vladimir 90, 149
Leonard, Robert Sean 142, 144
Leone, Sergio 159
Lethal Weapon 2 (film 1989) 136–138
Levy, Emanuel 50
License to Kill (film 1989) 136–138
Limelight (film 1952) 102
The Lion King (film 1994) 7, 21, 133–134, 176
Literature into Film (book) 8
Little Big Man (film 1970) 126–127
Lombard, Carole 13, 14
Loncraine, Richard 151, 153, 154–157, 161, 164, 165, 168, 178
Looking for Richard (film 1996) 13, 17, 18, 20
Lo Savio, Gerolamo 30–31, 32, 37–38, 168, 169
Love's Labours Lost (film 2000) 149, 153

Lubitsch, Ernst 13, 14
Luhrmann, Baz 99, 100, 103, 108, 113, 151, 153, 154, 157–159, 161, 164–165, 168, 178
Luzzatti, Luiggi 32

Macbeth (film 1948) 8, 20, 57, 59–61, 63, 67, 170–171
Macbeth (film 1971) 21, 22, 69, 96, 121–123, 124, 176
Macbeth (play) 7, 83, 124, 129–130, 168, 172, 176–177
Macready, William Charles 100
Macy, William H. 151
Madden, John 18
Magnolia (film 1999) 151–152, 159–160, 165
Maher, Mary Z. 112
Mailer, Norman 133
The Man Who Shot Liberty Valance (film 1962) 12, 51
Manheim, Michael 58–59, 64
Margolies, David 94
MASH (film 1970) 126–127
Maunula, Vili 77
Mazelle, Kym 100
Mazursky, Paul 7, 130–132, 135, 176, 177
McComb, John P. 26
McEnery, John 111
McFarlane, B. 5
McKellen, Ian 155
McKernan, Luke 30
Melo-Thaiss, Janet 76, 81
Melone, Altobello 109
Mendelssohn, Felix 49
Menzies, William Cameron 47
Il Mercante di Venezia (film 1910) 21, 30, 31–33, 37–38, 168
A Midsummer Night's Dream (film 1909) 21, 28–30, 33, 37, 38, 168
A Midsummer Night's Dream (film 1935) 20, 47–49, 50, 53, 54, 58, 104, 170
A Midwinter's Tale (film 1996) 13, 17–18, 20
Moore, Julianne 151
Moranis, Rick 132, 135, 167, 176
Morley, Robert 12
Morricone, Ennio 159
Mrs. Dalloway (book) 167
Much Ado About Nothing (film 1993) 2, 21, 99, 100, 141–146, 147, 150, 151, 153, 154, 177
Much Ado About Nothing (play) 100
Murphy's War (film 1971) 14
My Darling Clementine (film 1946) 12

The Natural (film 1984) 111
Nichols, Mike 103
Nicholson, Jack 127
Noble, Adrian 141
North by Northwest (film 1959) 112
Novelli, Ermete 30

Oldman, Gary 16
Olivier, Laurence 23, 38, 52, 53, 54, 56, 57–59,

61–62, 63, 67–68, 69, 83, 84, 99, 100, 102, 103, 112, 113, 114, 140–141, 142, 147, 151, 154, 155, 167, 170–171
Olympia (film 1938) 64
Otello (film 1986) 99
Othello (film 1923) 20, 35–37, 169
Othello (film 1952) 8, 20, 57, 62–63, 64, 65, 67, 100, 171
Othello (play) 124, 167
O'Toole, Peter 127

Pacino, Al 17, 18
A Passage to India (film 1984) 147
Pasternak, Boris 84–85, 86, 97
Pearlman, E. 72, 121
Perestroika 90
Pickford, Mary 39–47, 169
Pilkington, Ace 99, 108, 110
Pirandello, Luigi 15
Polanski, Roman 22, 25, 69, 96, 121–123, 124, 176
Politburo 88, 89, 90, 93, 97, 173
Political Shakespeare (book) 6, 166
Powell, Dick 48
Price, Vincent 12
Prospero's Books (film 1991) 13, 16–17, 19–20, 67–68

Rafaelson, Bob 133
Ran (film 1985) 7, 21, 69, 76–83, 84, 98, 172–173
The Rapture (film 1991) 152
Rathbone, Basil 50, 54, 170
Re Lear (film 1910) 21, 30–31, 32, 37–38, 168
Rebellato, Dan 120
Redfern, Nick 12
Reed, Carol 171
Reinhardt, Max 47–49, 50, 52, 53, 54, 58, 104, 170
The Remains of the Day (film 1993) 142
Richard II (play) 128, 129, 130, 168, 176
Richard III (film 1910) 21, 30, 33–35, 37, 38, 168–169,
Richard III (film 1912) 37
Richard III (film 1955) 20, 57, 63–65, 67, 102, 171
Richard III (film 1996) 21, 154–157, 178
Richard III (play) 128
Richardson, Ralph 65, 67, 102
Richardson, Tony 24, 119–120, 123, 175
Riefenstahl, Leni 64, 165
Robards, Jason 151
Rogers, Mimi 152
Romeo and Juliet (film 1936) 20, 49–51, 53, 54–55, 104, 109, 170
Romeo and Juliet (film 1968) 10, 21, 99, 101, 102–103, 108–110, 141, 142–143, 154, 174–175
Romeo + Juliet (film 1996) 21, 99, 100, 103, 108, 157–159, 178
Romeo and Juliet (play) 124
Rooney, Mickey 48, 170

Rosencrantz and Guildenstern Are Dead (film 1990) 13, 15–16, 19–20
Rosencrantz and Guildenstern Are Dead (play) 15, 22, 132
Rosenstone, Robert 39
Rossellini, Roberto 63, 171
Roth, Tim 15, 16
Rothwell, Kenneth 100, 116, 151, 153
Rudova, Larissa 85

Schindler's List (film 1993) 146
Schmidt, Howard 59
Scofield, Paul 111, 112
Scott, Ridley 152
Scott, Sir Walter 167
The Seagull (play) 91
Sense and Sensibility (film 1995) 146
Seppuku 74
Shakespeare After All (book) 96
Shakespeare and the Moving Image (book) 166
Shakespeare at the Cineplex (book) 25, 38, 69, 136, 141, 153, 161, 164, 166
Shakespeare, Cinema and Society (book) 11, 25, 69, 73, 166
Shakespeare in Love (film 1998) 13, 18, 20
Shakespeare in the Cinema: Ocular Proof (book) 166
Shakespeare on Film (book) 25, 34, 47, 84, 104, 125–126, 140, 165, 166
Shakespeare on Silent Film: An Excellent Dumb Discourse (book) 35
Shakespeare on the Screen: Kenneth Branagh's Adaptations of Henry V, Much Ado About Nothing, and Hamlet (book) 147
Shakespeare: Our Contemporary (book) 22, 24, 114, 115
Shaughnessy, Robert 84, 120
Shearer, Norma 50, 170
Shelokhonov, Steve 85
Shephard, Sam 163
She's the Man (film 2006) 21, 134–135, 176
Sidney, George 13, 14
The Silence of the Lambs (film 1991) 143
Sinfield, Alan 6, 7, 9, 10, 147, 166
Sippl, Diane 151–152, 153, 159–160
Sonnino, Sidney 32
The Sound of Music (film 1965) 126
Stalin, Joseph 85, 86, 90, 93, 149
Steavenson-Payne, Kate 156
Steinbrunner, Chris 125
Sternberg, Josef von 39
Sterritt, David 73
Stone, Alan 58
Stoppard, Tom 15, 17, 18, 22, 67–68, 132
Stow, Percy 26, 29, 30, 37, 168, 169
Strange Brew (film 1983) 21, 132–133, 177
Stromboli (film 1950) 63, 171
Strunk, William 50–51

The Taming of the Shrew (film 1929) 21, 40–47, 48, 53, 54, 104, 169–170

The Taming of the Shrew (film 1967) 21, 101, 102, 103–108, 109, 114, 141, 142, 145, 154, 174–175
The Taming of the Shrew (play) 10, 13, 44–45, 134, 167
Taubman, William 93
Taylor, Elizabeth 103, 104, 107, 114, 174
Taylor, Sam 40–47, 50, 51, 53, 104, 169
Taymor, Julie 22, 151, 153, 154, 157, 159–162, 165, 168, 178
The Tempest (film 1908) 21, 26–28, 29, 30, 37, 38, 168
Tempest (film 1982) 7, 21, 130–132, 177
The Tempest (play) 7, 16, 125, 126
10 Things I Hate About You (film 1999) 9, 10, 21, 134, 167, 176
Thalberg, Irving 50
Theatre of Blood (film 1972) 12
Thelma and Louise (film 1991) 143
A Theory of Adaptation (book) 10
The Third Man (film 1949) 171
Thomas, Dave 132, 135, 167, 176
Thompson, Emma 142, 144
Thor (film 2011) 150
Throne of Blood see *Kumonosu djô* (film 1957)
Titanic (film 1997) 146
Titus (film 1999) 21, 22, 159–162, 178
Titus Andronicus (play) 160
To Be or Not to Be (film 1942) 13, 19
Tolkin, Michael 152
Triumph des Willens (film 1935) 64, 165
Tropics of Discourse (book) 27–28
Trotsky, Leon 90
Twelfth Night (film 1910) 21, 33, 38, 168
Twelfth Night (play) 134–135

Understanding Boris Pasternak (book) 85
Unforgiven (film 1992) 152

Vanneman, Alan 14
Venora, Diane 159
Verdi, Giuseppe 99

Walton, William 52
Ward, Mackenzie 54
Warner, Jack 47
Warui yatsu hodo yoku nemuru (film 1960) 7, 21, 69, 73–76, 82, 83, 98, 171–172
Washington, Denzel 144
Weaver, Sigourney 152–153
Weiss, Barbara 31
Weiss, Tanja 147, 148
Welles, Orson 8, 23, 38, 52, 54, 56, 57, 59–61, 62–63, 64, 65–68, 69, 79, 83, 84, 99, 100, 102, 103, 113, 114, 141, 142, 147, 151, 154, 162, 167, 170–171, 172
West Side Story (film 1961) 124
Whelehan, Imelda 6, 9
White, Hayden 27–28
White, Robert 141
Whiting, Leonard 110, 142
Who's Afraid of Virginia Woolf? (film 1966) 103
Wilcox, Fred M. 7, 125
Williamson, Nicol 120
Winslet, Kate 146
Wolfit, Donald 14, 100
Wood, Robin 84, 96, 153, 157, 163, 164
Woodstock (film 1970) 126–127
Woolf, Virginia 167

Yarvet, Yuri 93
Yates, Peter 14

Zeffirelli, Franco 23, 69, 99–113, 114, 135, 141–143, 145–146, 154, 174–175

www.ingramcontent.com/pod-product-compliance
Ingram Content Group UK Ltd.
Pitfield, Milton Keynes, MK11 3LW, UK
UKHW042006140426
5217IPUK00015B/1006